Praise for *Killing Yourself to Live*

"One of America's top cultural critics."

—*Entertainment Weekly*

"As entertaining as it is unpredictable, as madcap as it is occasionally maddening. [Klosterman] is funny, sad, tormented, insightful, ludicrous, and occasionally precious in a way that is all his own. And his observations on American culture, pop and otherwise, are often trenchant and thought-provoking."

—Joe Heim, *The Washington Post*

"An affecting meditation on classic rock, mortality, and girls."
—William Georgiades, *New York Post*

"Klosterman is like the new Hunter S. Thompson. Only it's as if Hunter were obsessed with KISS instead of Nixon."

—Kyle Smith, *People*

"He's killing his artform, in hopes of reviving it."
—Noel Murray, *The Onion A.V. Club*

"Full of sharp observations and dry wit as well as clever musings on society and personal failings."

—Eric Fidler, *The Miami Herald*

"Reading Klosterman is like hanging out with your favorite drinking buddy in college and riffing all night on your pop culture obsessions."

—Will Crain, *San Francisco Chronicle*

"An amusing gazetteer of modern America."
—Mark Rozzo, *Los Angeles Times*

"Riveting and poignant, both side-splitting and stirring. . . . Nobody understands identification through pop culture like Chuck Klosterman. . . . *Killing Yourself to Live* is terribly funny, astute, canny and yet incredibly sensitive. I read it. Then read it again. Chuck Klosterman is a fucking genius."

—*NOW Magazine* (Toronto)

Also by Chuck Klosterman

Killing Yourself to Live ›››››››››

85% OF A TRUE STORY

CHUCK KLOSTERMAN

SCRIBNER
New York   London   Toronto   Sydney

SCRIBNER
1230 Avenue of the Americas
New York, NY 10020

The excerpt from *Chuck Klosterman IV*, "Bending Spoons with Britney Spears,"
first appeared in the November 2003 issue of *Esquire*.

First Scribner trade paperback edition 2006

SCRIBNER and design are trademarks of Macmillan Library Reference USA, Inc.,
used under license by Simon & Schuster, the publisher of this work.

For information about special discounts for bulk purchases,
please contact Simon & Schuster Special Sales:
1-800-456-6798 or business@simonandschuster.com

DESIGNED BY ERICH HOBBING

Text set in Bodoni

Manufactured in the United States of America

7   9   10   8   6

Library of Congress Control Number: 2005042498

ISBN-13: 978-0-7432-6445-7
ISBN-10: 0-7432-6445-2
ISBN-13: 978-0-7432-6446-4 (Pbk)
ISBN-10: 0-7432-6446-0 (Pbk)

This is a story about love, death, driving, narcissism, America, the ill-advised glamorization of recreational drug use, not having sex, eating breadsticks at Olive Garden, talking to strangers, feeling nostalgic for the extremely recent past, movies you've never seen, KISS, Radiohead, Rod Stewart, and—to a lesser extent—prehistoric elephants of the Midwestern plains. If these are not things that interest you, do not read this book.

The journalism in this book is, to the best of my abilities, completely accurate. The stuff about my personal life is merely the way I remember it, as I do not tape-record every conversation I have on a day-to-day basis. There is also some minor manipulation of time, and one sequence near the end of the book actually happened in New Zealand.

Some names have been changed, as well as a few minor details that could cause potential discomfort to people whose names have been changed.

I tell you what's really ridiculous—going into a bookstore and there's all these books about yourself. In a way, it feels like you're already dead.

—Thom Yorke

Killing Yourself
to Live ›››››››››

THE DAY BEFORE THE FIRST DAY

New York ➤ Dead Horses ➤ Looking for Nothing

I am not qualified to live here.

I don't know what qualifications are necessary to live in any certain place at any given time, but I know I don't have them.

Ohio. I was qualified to live in Ohio. I like high school football. I enjoy Chinese buffet restaurants. I think the Pretenders' first record is okay. Living in Ohio was not outside my wheelhouse. But this place they call New York . . . this place that Lou Reed incessantly described to no one in particular . . . this place is more complicated. Everything is a grift, and everyone is a potential grifter. Before moving to Manhattan, I had only been here twice. Two days before I finally packed up my shit and left Akron, I had a phone conversation with the man who would be my immediate supervisor at *Spin* magazine, and I expressed my relocation insecurities. He tried to explain what my life here would be like; at the time, the only details I could remember about my two trips to New York were that (a) the bars didn't close until 4 A.M., and (b) there seemed to be an inordinate number of attractive women skulking about the street. "Don't let that fool you," my editor said as he (theoretically) stroked his Clapton-like beard. "I grew up in Minnesota, and I initially thought all the women in New York were beautiful, too. But here's the thing—a lot of them are just cute girls from the Midwest who get expensive haircuts and spend too much time at the gym." This confused me, because that seems to be the definition of what a beautiful woman is. However, I have slowly come to understand my bearded editor's pretzel logic: Sexuality is 15 percent real and 85 percent illusion. The first time I was here, it was February. I kept seeing thin women waiting for taxicabs, and they were all wearing black turtlenecks, black mittens, black scarves, and black stocking caps . . . but no jackets. None of them wore jackets. It was 28 degrees. That attire (particularly within the context of such climatic conditions) can make any woman electrifying. Most of them were holding cigarettes, too. That always helps. I don't care what C. Everett Koop thinks. Smoking is usually a good decision.

Spin magazine is on the third floor of an office building on Lexington Avenue, a street often referred to as "Lex" by cast members of *Law & Order*. It is always the spring of 1996 in the offices of *Spin*; it will be the spring of 1996 forever. Just about everybody who works there looks like either (a) a member of the band Pavement, or (b) a girl who once dated a member of the band Pavement. The first time I walked into the office, three guys were talking about J Mascis for no apparent reason, and one of them was describing his guitar noodling as "trenchant." They had just returned from lunch. It was 3:30 P.M. I was the fifth-oldest person in the entire editorial department; I was 29.

I'm working on an untitled death project, and you are reading said project. Today, I will leave the offices of *Spin* and go to the Chelsea Hotel. Once I arrive there, I will ask people about the 1978 murder of Nancy Spungen, a woman whose ultra-annoying shriek was immortalized in the 1986 film *Sid & Nancy*. The "Sid" in that equation was (of course) Sid Vicious, the fabulously moronic bass player for the Sex Pistols and the alleged murderer of Nancy. Gene Siskel and Roger Ebert reviewed *Sid & Nancy* on their TV show *At the Movies* the week the film was released, and it was the first time I ever heard of the Sex Pistols. At the time, the Sex Pistols didn't interest me at all; I liked Van Halen. In 1987, a kid in my school told me I should listen to the Sex Pistols because they had an album called *Flogging a Dead Horse*, which was the kind of phrase I would have found noteworthy as a sophomore in high school. However, I didn't follow his advice; I liked Tesla. In 1989, I bought *Never Mind the Bollocks* on cassette because it was on sale, and it reminded me of Guns N' Roses. Johnny Rotten had an antiabortion song called "Bodies," yet he still aspired to be the Antichrist. This struck me as commonsense conservatism.

The chorus of the song "Pretty Vacant" is playing inside my skull as I saunter through the *Spin* offices, but it sounds as if the vocals are being sung by Gavin Rossdale. I pass the interns in sundresses, and the reformed riot grrrls making flight reservations, and at least three people who wish they were outside, smoking cigarettes. It's 2:59 P.M., and it's time for me to start finding some death.

My voyage into darkness has officially started: I am in the lobby, down the stairs, out the street exit, and into the stupefying heat. New York summers are hotter than summers in Atlanta. Now, I realize the *temperature* is higher in Atlanta and Atlanta has more *humidity*, and things like *temperature* and *humidity* are extensions of *science*, and science is never *wrong*. But Manhattan is a hipster kiln, and that makes all the difference; heat is 15 percent real and 85 percent perception. The ground is hot, the brick buildings are hot, the sky is low, people are pissed off, and everything smells like sweat and vomit and liquefied garbage. It's a full-on horror show, and I have learned to despise July. People at *Spin* ridicule me for wearing khaki shorts to work, always insisting that I look like a tourist.

I don't care. We're all tourists, sort of. Life is tourism, sort of. As far as I'm concerned, the dinosaurs still hold the lease on this godforsaken rock.

It takes me 45 seconds to get a cab on Lex, and now I'm moving west, haltingly. I've been to Chelsea, but I don't really know where it starts and where it ends; I realize I'm there only if (a) someone tells me so, or (b) I find myself in a Thai restaurant and suddenly notice that everyone working there is a pre-op transvestite. This traffic sucks, but we're getting there; with each progressive block, things look cheaper and older, like B-roll footage from *Sesame Street*. Ten minutes ago, I was drinking Mountain Dew in *Spin*'s self-conscious 1996; now I'm driving through an accidental incarnation of 1976. It's the summer of 2003. I've traveled down three vertical floors, across four horizontal blocks, and through five spheres of reality.

Perhaps you are wondering why I am starting this project at the Chelsea and not the Dakota, the hotel where John Lennon was assassinated in 1980; part of me is wondering that, too. Lennon's killing is undoubtedly the most famous murder in rock history, and it's something I actually know about: I know how many Beatles tapes Mark David Chapman had in his jacket when he shot Lennon in the chest (14), and I know the score of that evening's *NFL Monday Night Football* game, when Howard Cosell announced the assassination on-air (Miami 16, New England 13—in overtime). I know that Chapman slowly came to believe that he actually *was* John Lennon (going so far as to marry a woman of Japanese descent who was four years his senior), and I remember my dad dismissing the murder at supper the following evening, bemoaning the fact that a musician's death somehow warranted more publicity than the unexpected death of Pope John Paul I. As an eight-year-old, I was confused by Lennon's death, mostly because I could not understand why everyone was so enamored with a rock band's rhythm guitarist; for some reason, I was under the misguided impression that Paul McCartney was the only member of the Beatles who sang. I felt no sadness about the event. As I get older, the murder seems crazier and crazier but not necessarily more tragic; I don't think I have ever been moved by the death of a public figure. I do think about what it would have been like if John Lennon had lived, and sometimes I worry that he would have made a terrible MTV *Unplugged* in 1992. But Lennon is not someone I need to concern myself with today; today, I am totally punk rock. My boss is requiring me to think like a punk. I am tempted to spit on a stranger in protest of the lagging British economy.

My boss at *Spin* (a striking blonde woman named Sia Michel) strongly suggested that I go to the Chelsea Hotel because "our readers" love punk rock. This fact is hard to refute; I am probably the only employee in the history of *Spin* magazine who thinks punk rock—in almost every context, and with maybe one exception[1]—is patently ridiculous. Still, the death of Spungen intrigues me; Sid and Nancy's relationship forever illustrates the worst part of being in love with anyone, which is that people in love can't be reasoned with.

Sid Vicious was not the original bassist for the Pistols; he joined the band after they fired original member Glen Matlock. The only thing everyone seems to know about Vicious is that he could not play bass *at all*. Ironically (or perhaps predictably), Sid's inability to play his instrument is the single most crucial element in the history of punk; he is the example everyone uses (consciously or unconsciously) when advocating the import of any musical entity that is not necessarily musical. The fact that he could not do something correctly—yet still do it significantly—is all that anyone needs to know about punk rock.

1. The Clash, 1977 to 1982.

That notion *is* punk rock, completely defined in one sentence. It's like that scene in *The Breakfast Club*, where nerd caricature Anthony Michael Hall explains why he considered suicide after failing to make a fully functioning elephant lamp in shop class, prompting Judd Nelson to call him an idiot. "So I'm a fucking idiot because I can't make a lamp?" Hall's character asks. "No," says Nelson. "You're a *genius* because you can't make a lamp." Sid Vicious was a musical genius because he couldn't play music, which is probably an unreasonable foundation to build one's life on. Which only grew worse when he met a terrible person and decided his love for her was so intense that she needed to die.

Spungen was from Philadelphia, a city whose sports fans throw D batteries at Santa Claus and cheer when opposing wide receivers are temporarily paralyzed. Since Nancy was not a celebrity in the traditional sense (she had no talent, per se, though neither did Sid), Chloe Webb's portrayal of her in the aforementioned *Sid & Nancy* is the image most modern people have of her. As such, she is generally remembered as the most annoying human of the late 20th century. She was (at best) a drug-addled groupie. But what matters about her interaction with Vicious is the way they destroyed each other in such an obvious—and social—manner. And what I mean by "social" is that everyone who knew them had to exist inside the walls of their destruction; as far as I can tell, every single one of Sid's friends despised Nancy Spungen. This, of course, is common. Everybody has had the experience of loathing a friend's girlfriend. My second year in college, I had a goofy little roommate everyone loved; sadly, he had a girlfriend that everyone hated. Her own friends hated her. Even my roommate seemed to hate her, because all they ever did was fight and attempt to hit each other with half-empty cans of Dr Pepper. She had no redeeming qualities; there was nothing about her that was physically, intellectually, or ideologically attractive. We all implored my roommate to break up with her. It was a bizarre situation because he would agree with us 99 percent of the time; we would say she was fat and whiny and uninspiring, and he would concede all three points. Sid Vicious was the same way; he once described Spungen as "the kind of girl who licked out toilets." But Sid wouldn't break up with Nancy, and my roommate didn't break up with his potato-sack sweetheart for almost three years. There is something sickeningly attractive about being in a bad relationship; you start feeding off the unhappiness. It becomes darkly interesting. Supposedly, Sid (as a 16-year-old) once told his mother, "Mum, I don't know what people see in sex. I don't get anything out of it." That sentiment explains everything. If you find sex unsatisfying, you need something to take its place. You need a problem. Nancy was a good problem for Sid. Heroin was also a good problem for Sid. The only problem is that good problems are still problems, and Mr. Vicious was just not designed for problem solving. His genius scheme was to move himself and Nancy into Room 100 of the Chelsea in August of '78, where they could stay high for the rest of their lives. This kind of (but not really) worked for two months, until he (almost certainly) stabbed Nancy, who was wearing only a bra and panties, and watched her bleed to death underneath the bathroom sink. Vicious purposefully OD'd on smack before the case ever went to trial, so I suppose we'll never really know what happened in that room, though he did tell the police, "I did it because I'm a dirty dog." This is not a very convincing alibi. He may as well have said, "I got 99 problems, but a bitch ain't one."

When I finally walk into the Chelsea, I can't decide if I'm impressed or underwhelmed; I can't tell if this place is nicer or crappier than I anticipated (I guess I had no preconceived notion). There are two men behind the reception desk: an

older man with a beard and a younger man who might be His-
panic. I ask the bearded man if anyone is staying in Room
100, and—if it's unoccupied—if I can see what it looks like.

"There is no Room 100," he tells me. "They converted it
into an apartment 18 years ago. But I know why you're asking."

For the next five minutes, these two gentlemen and I have a
conversation about Sid Vicious, mostly focused on how he was
an idiot. However, there are certainly lots of people who dis-
agree with us: Patrons constantly come to this hotel with the
hope of staying in the same flat where an unlikable, oppor-
tunistic woman named Nancy was murdered for no valid reason. The staff is not thrilled by this tradition ("We hate it when
people ask about this," says the younger employee. "Be sure you
write that down: *We hate it when people ask us about this*."). I
ask the bearded gentleman what kind of person aspires to stay
in a hotel room that was once a crime scene.

"It tends to be younger people—the kind of people with col-
ored hair. But we did have one guy come all the way from
Japan, only to discover that Room 100 doesn't even exist anymore. The thing is, Johnny Rotten was a musician; Sid Vicious
was a loser. So maybe his fans want to be losers, too."

While we are having this discussion, an unabashedly annoyed
man interjects himself into the dialogue; this man is named Stanley Bard, and he has been the manager of the Chelsea Hotel for
more than 40 years. He does not want me talking to the hotel
staff and asks me into his first-floor office. Bard is balding and
swarthy and serious, and he sternly tells me I should not include
the Chelsea Hotel in this article.

"I understand what you think you are trying to do, but I do
not want the Chelsea Hotel associated with this story," says
Bard, his arms crossed as he sits behind a cluttered wooden
desk. "Sid Vicious didn't die here. It was just his girlfriend, and

she was of no consequence. The kind of person who wants to stay in Room 100 is just a cultic follower. These are people who have nothing to do. If you want to understand what someone fascinated by Sid Vicious is looking for, go find *those* people. You will see that they are not serious-minded people. You will see that they are not trying to understand anything about death. They are looking for nothing."

At this point, he politely tells me to leave the Chelsea Hotel. And after we shake hands, that is what I do.

THE NIGHT BEFORE THE FIRST DAY

Confusion ➤ Construction ➤ Exposition

Fuck, man. This shit is complicated.

I have no idea how people travel.

I have no idea what to pack. How many pairs of pants does one need for a three- (or possibly four-) week trip? I bet it's fewer than I suspect. Do I need more than one pair of shoes? It doesn't seem like I would, but I predict that I will. Maybe three pairs? This is a nightmare. Should I bring some hats? One hat, perhaps. And a sweatshirt. Granted, it's going to be August, but I can still imagine a scenario in which a sweatshirt could pay sweeping dividends. But will such a scenario actually emerge? Am I already missing the point? I could never be one of those people who climb mountains recreationally; I'd be one of those clowns who dies halfway down Everest because I'd bring extra powdered cocoa instead of extra rope.

Perhaps I should explain why I am packing.

Let me begin by saying this: Death is part of life. Generally, it's the shortest part of life, usually occurring near the end. However, this is not necessarily true for rock stars; sometimes rock stars don't start living *until* they die.

I want to understand why that is.

Two months ago, my striking blonde editor sent me an e-mail.

She asked me if I had an interest in pursuing an "epic story." This, obviously, is a strange request; the word *epic* is not often used in the offices of *Spin*, except in the context of measuring coworkers' public meltdowns and/or describing people's drinking problems. My e-mail response to her query was, "Of course." However, neither of us had any idea what this story would be, and—judging from the description—I feared it might involve the construction of a full-size replica of a first-century Viking ship.

Over the next two weeks, I would periodically walk into my editor's office and we'd discuss what this epic story could be; my editor would sit behind her desk, and I would pace about the room while making stupidly extravagant hand gestures, not unlike a young Benito Mussolini. It's difficult to be epic on command, especially when you have no idea what constitutes epochal behavior. For some reason, my editor was pretty confident it would involve a shitload of driving. Though we did not know where I was supposed to go or what I was supposed to do, it seemed crucial that I spend a long time getting there; this would constitute the "epicness." Ultimately, she decided I should drive to every marginally interesting rock 'n' roll landmark in the continental United States and "experience" what it was like to be there. This trip would take, by our estimate, just under 400 years. That certainly seemed adequately epic, and I honestly didn't have anything better to do.

Over the next few days, I began mapping a tentative odyssey. This task presented a previously unforeseen problem: What deserves to be classified as "marginally interesting"? I kept finding two answers to that question: pretty much everything, and absolutely nothing. Is ZZ Top's hometown barbershop interesting? Is Madonna's childhood bedroom interesting? Is any private residence where Jerry Garcia bought heroin interesting? Who knows such things? There seemed to be a lot of moral relativism within my potential wanderings. However, I did conclude that a handful of locations will *always* be interesting—I always find any location where somebody died compelling. This is probably because I think about death all the time; it is, I think, the most interesting thing absolutely everybody does. That's especially true with celebrities. Unless you're Shannon Hoon, dying is the only thing that guarantees a rock star will have a legacy that stretches beyond temporary relevance. Somewhere, at some point, somehow, somebody decided that death equals credibility. And I want to figure out why that is. I want to find out why the greatest career move any musician can make is to stop breathing. I want to find out why plane crashes and drug overdoses and shotgun suicides turn longhaired guitar players into messianic prophets. I want to walk the blood-soaked streets of rock 'n' roll and chat with the survivors who writhe in the gutters. This notion became my quest. Instead of going to the places where everything happened, I would go to the places where everything stopped. I would get my death on.

"Now, to do this," I told my striking blonde editor, "I will need a rental car."

Death rides a pale horse, but I shall ride a silver Ford Taurus. It's currently parked outside my apartment. The moment I turn the key, I decide to rechristen this vehicle the "Ford Tauntaun," just in case I drive into an August blizzard and I need to stuff a freezing Luke Skywalker into the cozy engine block. Though I don't know it yet, I will eventually drive this beast 6,557 miles, guided by a mind-expanding Global Positioning System that speaks to me in a strong yet soothing female voice, vaguely reminiscent of Meredith Baxter-Birney during her later years on *Family Ties*. If you are unaware of how a GPS operates (and until I rented this Tauntaun, I had no idea, either), imagine a machine that should only exist in Tokyo in the year 2085. It's a box on the dashboard that has an ever-changing digital map, and it literally speaks to me and gives perfect advice; it tells me when I need to exit the freeway, and how far I am from places like Missoula, Montana, and how to locate the nearest Red Lobster. This mechanized siren will lead us down the eastern seaboard, across the Deep South, up the corn-covered spinal cord of the Midwest, and through the burning foothills of Montana—finally coming to rest on the cusp of the Pacific Ocean, underneath a bridge Kurt Cobain never slept under. In the course of this voyage, I will stand where 119 people have fallen, almost all of whom were unwilling victims of rock's glistening scythe. And this will teach me something I already knew.

But that's the future. Right now, I'm trapped in the present, standing in my bedroom, holding a hooded sweatshirt in my hands, staring at its viperlike drawstrings, silently questioning its value. Sometimes I wish I lived in 2085, the year we'll all start wearing matching jumpsuits and consuming vitamin-fortified sludge. Of course, my attire is only a secondary concern, all things considered; I'm far more worried about (a) which CDs to pack, and (b) how much pot to bring. The former issue is especially pressing; I just bought an iPod, but I don't know how to hook it up to the car stereo. I will have to fight this war conventionally. And this is critical, because—as far as I can tell—the only pleasurable element of this entire trip will be sitting behind the wheel of my rental car and having my skull crushed by deafening music. I moved to Manhattan in the spring of 2002 and haven't owned a car since my arrival; by and large, that makes me happy, as I am one of the worst drivers in America. I don't miss driving at all, and I'm probably the worst candidate imaginable for a cross-country road trip. However, I do miss Car Rock, and I miss it profoundly. I love the way music inside a car makes you feel invisible; if you play the stereo at maximum volume, it's almost like other people can't see into your vehicle. It tints your windows, somehow.

It will take three hours to decide which compact discs to put in the backseat of my Tauntaun. This is the kind of quandary that keeps people like me from sleeping; I never worry about nuclear war or the economy or if we need to establish a Palestinian state, but I spend a lot of time worrying about whether I need to purchase all the less-than-stellar Rolling Stones albums from the 1980s for cataloging purposes (particularly *Undercover,* which includes the semi-underrated "Undercover of the Night"[1]). I have 2,233 CDs. Approximately 30 percent of these were given to me for free by record labels; that number represents less than 1 percent of how many promotional discs I've actually received. Another 30 percent of those 2,233 have been played less than five times, including one (*The Best of Peter, Paul and Mary*) I've never even listened to once—it's still wrapped in cellophane (I store it next to a used copy of Hüsker Dü's *Zen Arcade* in the hope that they will slowly fuse into a Pixies' B-side collection). I would say that I've owned at least 500 of these albums twice (once on cassette and once on compact disc) and that I've owned a few of them three times (for example, I bought all 26 KISS releases on tape, and then I bought them all on disc, and then I bought them on disc *again* when they were remastered in 1999, which really just means somebody went back into the studio and made them louder). I have never owned anything on vinyl, except for *The Yes Album* and *Electric Warrior,* both of which were sent to me free from Rhino Records (despite the fact that I do not own a record player). The first CD I ever purchased was *Stairway to Heaven / Highway to Hell,* a charity album featuring hair-metal bands

---

1. The song's video, incidentally, includes the image of Mick Jagger being executed by Central American forces. In my memory, Mick is actually shot by Keith Richards, but maybe I'm just getting this video confused with the opening scene of *Miller's Crossing.*

performing cover songs by icons who died from substance abuse (the Scorpions cover "I Can't Explain" by the Who, Cinderella remakes Janis Joplin's "Move Over," etc.). That purchase was made in October of 1989. The last CD I bought was *Diary* by Sunny Day Real Estate, which I picked up two days ago. The only CD I ever stole (for real) was *The Best of the Doors*, a double album I drunkenly stuck in my pants during a keg party in 1991 (and when I say "for real," I mean "unless you count ripping off the Columbia House music club"). I have 14 discs[2] by the Smashing Pumpkins, and I only like two of them. I have everything Britney Spears has ever released to the public; this is because I think I will "need them" someday, although I have no theory about what might prompt such a necessity. I have more CDs than 99 percent of America, but fewer CDs than 40 percent of my friends; if an acquaintance has more CDs than me, I feel intimidated and emasculated. I think about my CDs a lot. I find it oddly reassuring to look at them when I'm intoxicated. Right now, my eyes are scanning their alphabetized titles, and I'm wondering how many will make the cut for my drive across America. This decision will dictate everything. Space will be limited, so I can only select those albums that will be undeniably essential.

I elect to bring 600.

2. This is counting the *The Aeroplane Flies High* box set, obviously.

THE FIRST DAY

Diane ➤ Hippies ➤ Ithaca ➤ The Hand of Doom

Let me begin with a confession: I'm lying. Not to you or to the world, but to my striking blonde editor at *Spin*; she thinks I'm driving straight from New York to West Warwick, Rhode Island, to "investigate" the Great White club tragedy. I am actually driving to Ithaca, New York, with a woman, solely because this woman asked me to take her there and I immediately said yes.

Traveling to Ithaca might seem harmless, but it's actually a metaphor. In fact, there may be a day in the near future when you find yourself in a conversation about this book, and someone will ask you what the story is *really* about, beyond the rudimentary narrative of a cross-country death trip based on a magazine article. And it's very likely you will say, "Well, the larger thesis is somewhat underdeveloped, but there is this point early in the story where he takes a woman to Ithaca for no real reason, and it initially seems innocuous, but—as you keep reading—you sort of see how this behavior is a self-perpetuating problem that keeps reappearing over and over again." In all probability, you will also complain about the author's reliance on self-indulgent, postmodern self-awareness, which will prompt the person you're conversing with to criticize the influence of Dave Eggers on the memoir-writing genre. Then your cell phone will ring, and you will agree to meet someone for brunch.

But ANYWAY, the woman I am taking to Ithaca is named Diane. She works with me at *Spin*, although not directly. As of right now, I am in love with her, and that love is the biggest problem in my life. It's the only problem in my life, really. And by this time tomorrow, I will have given Diane an ultimatum about our future together, which is ironic because I will do this in response to an ultimatum given to me by a different woman who lives in Minnesota (a woman who has yet to be introduced into the story). So—ultimately—that will be the crux of this book: I will be driving across the country with two ultimatums hanging in the balance, delivered to (and from) two different women who have never met each other. And the larger irony will be that neither of these women will be the central female character in the narrative; that will actually be a *third* woman, but she will never tangibly appear anywhere in this entire book.

> **fore·shad·ow** *(vt.)*: To represent something to come; to indicate or suggest beforehand: PRESAGE.

So ANYWAY, Diane is enchanting, and she is sleeping on the right side of the bed right now, unaware that I am typing about my love for her.

For the first 15 hours of our secret excursion, there has been little talk of death between Diane and myself. It's mostly just driving, eating hot pork sandwiches in diners, reading *The New York Times* aloud, skipping stones across shallow rivers, playful banter over issues that aren't actually issues, and better-than-average physical collisions on a feather bed in the Rose Inn, an establishment named "one of America's 10 finest hotels" by Uncle Ben's rice. I'm unsure why Uncle Ben feels socially obligated to advocate hotels, but I can't deny his good taste: This place is unnecessarily luxurious, and I think it makes Diane uncomfortable; staying in a room that seems like a honeymoon suite makes it hard for her to pretend that we're not actually dating, although she is certainly still trying. This is something she does constantly, despite the fact that (a) we spend all our time together, (b) we sporadically see each other naked, and (c) I pay for pretty much everything, pretty much all the time. But as I said, I will explain all this later. The bottom line is that we are having a wonderful time together, and I really wish she was coming along on this trip. However, after our night in Ithaca, we will need to drive to Lake Ontario because Diane is going camping with a bunch of hippies she met at a food co-op during college. She does this once a year. Diane is something of an urban hippie. She actually listens to electronica, the last musical subculture in which hippies still thrive (they all take drugs and listen to terrible, overlong music while talking about ridiculous ideas like "community" and "sharing the love"). Diane wants to overthrow the government and blow up Nike factories, but I blame those interests on her parents. She's quite clever, and she looks like the woman described by Dolly Parton in the song "Jolene": ivory skin, emerald eyes, and an avalanche of auburn hair. Diane's hair is astounding: It's thick and red and relentless (sort of like Axl Rose in the "Welcome to the Jungle" video, only natural). She is the anti-Medusa. If push came to shove, I would probably help her blow up a Nike factory if it meant I could spend 20 minutes playing with her Jew-fro.

You would be fascinated by the myriad components of Diane's life, were I so inclined to explain them; it's an unfathomable collection of events, all things considered. And when I say "all things," I truly mean the entire spectrum of existence: her ex-boyfriend, her father, Bowling Green University, the role of women in the media, Judaism, her ex-boyfriend, hydroelectric fossil fuel alternatives, an ill-fated stint in the Peace Corps, Kraftwerk, Pedro Martinez, the Internet, a grizzly bear who attacked her car four years ago, Alfred Hitchcock's 1938 film *The Lady Vanishes*, competitive speed chess, the principles that once governed the Soviet Union, and her ex-boyfriend. However, all that stuff is *her* life; that stuff has nothing to do with me, really, and it would be wrong for me to comment on anything that doesn't affect me directly (in fact, it's probably wrong for me to even comment on the things that *do* affect me directly, since she's obviously a real person who probably did not expect to end up in a book when she first kissed me, although—by this point—I have to assume any woman who kisses me halfway expects I'll eventually write about her in some capacity, since I always do). But here are the bare bones of what you need to know in order to understand this story: Diane ended a long-term relationship and was very sad, and I found her sadness electrically attractive. I tend to equate *sadness* with *intelligence*. I met Diane when I was deeply, deeply obsessed with being in New York, and she seemed to embody New York with the very fabric of her existence. We talked and talked and e-mailed and e-mailed and drank and drank and drank, and she told me not to fall in love with her, and I fell in love with her in something like 19 days. That was seven months ago. However, things have never really changed since the first time we got drunk together; this has never become a conventional relationship. In fact, one could argue that this hasn't been a relationship *at all*: I can count the number of times we've slept together on one hand. She has never been my girlfriend, and I have never been her boyfriend. Everyone *thinks* we're a couple because we go to films together, and we have coffee every afternoon, and I once walked over to her apartment during a raging blizzard to help her hang a clock. I make no attempt to hide that

I am in love with her, and I don't think there's anyone who knows either of us who isn't totally aware of that fact.

So—clearly—there are problems here.

But it gets worse.

It gets worse because Diane's inability to love me makes me love her more. Without a doubt, not loving me is the most alluring thing Diane (or any woman) can do. Nothing makes me love Diane as much as her constant rejection of my heartfelt advances. This is compounded by Diane's own insecurities; the fact that she can reject me time after time after time is what she finds most endearing. She knows I will never give up. She could hate me and I would love her anyway.

So—clearly—this is not a healthy interaction.

But it gets worse.

It gets worse because Diane did something two months ago that is unforgivable (I'm not going to elaborate on this, but feel free to fabricate any scenario you're comfortable with). Now, in the weeks that have passed since this event, I have told her countless times that I forgive her for what she did. But I have been lying, both to her and to myself. So even though I *feel* like I love her, part of my brain resents her with an unspeakable ferocity. That resentment has changed the way I feel about everything. Now, whenever I feel love, I unconsciously feel grains of rage. And it is becoming harder and harder for me to differentiate between those two emotions.

So—clearly—I am not psychologically flawless.

But it gets worse.

It gets worse because I am now sitting across from Diane at a steak house in upstate New York, and she is eating a salad, and she has the cutest smile I have ever seen. And it gets worse because she's telling me her thoughts on *The Merchant of Venice*. I have never read *The Merchant of Venice*, and I'll never read it, and I don't even care what the fuck it's about. But

I love sitting across from this adorable person and listening to her talk about ostensibly intelligent bullshit, and I know that we are going to go back to our hotel room in 40 minutes, and I know that I am going to get to cradle her little body for the next seven hours. But this is still a problem. It's a problem because— as she chews her salad and smiles away—she is looking into me. And I can just tell that no matter how hard she looks, she will never know that I am not telling her about Lenore. And Lenore is probably someone she would want to know about.

THE SECOND DAY

The Conversation ➤ Self-Reflexive Insanity ➤
The Honesty Room ➤ How to Win at Yahtzee

Diane is in the shower. I am imagining what it looks like when she shampoos her hair, because that is something I have never actually seen. I am lying in bed, motionless, satiated, and wondering if I have Cotard's syndrome.

French military surgeon Jules Cotard lived only 49 years (1840–1889), but he will be forever remembered for discovering one of nature's most sincerely fucked-up mental illnesses: Cotard's syndrome is a mental disorder where the victim concludes that he or she is dead. Sometimes the symptoms are more specific: Patients believe that they are missing certain internal organs, or that there is no blood in their veins, or that they have lost their soul. However, the ultimate manifestation of Cotard's syndrome (classified medically as a nihilistic delusional disorder) is the victim's unshakable conviction that he does not exist. It is not that these people fear they are dying; it's that they are certain they are already dead.

Sometimes the victims of Cotard's syndrome think they can smell their own flesh rotting. I must concede that this has never happened to me. I probably don't have full-on Cotard's, but there are moments when I feel like I'm dead. This is especially true when I'm in airports. Anytime I'm in a foreign place with lots of strangers who all share an identical (yet completely unrelated) purpose, I start to think I'm in purgatory. For as long as I can remember, I've had a theory that life on earth *is* purgatory, because life on earth seems to have all the purgatorial qualities that were once described to me by nuns. It's almost like we're all Bruce Willis in *The Sixth Sense*, but nobody on "earth" has figured this out yet, even though it will suddenly seem obvious when we get to the end. Sometimes I think that the amount of time you live on earth is just an inverse reflection of how good you were in a previous existence; for example, infants who die from SIDS were actually great people when they were alive "for real," so they get to go to heaven after a mere five weeks in purgatory. Meanwhile, anyone Willard Scott ever congratulated for turning 102 was obviously a terrible individual who had many, many previous sins to pay for and had to spend a century in his or her unknown purgatory (even though the person seemed perfectly wholesome in this particular world). This hypothesis becomes especially clear inside any airport. It's like a warehouse full of dead people rushing from gate to gate to gate, all of whom are unaware that—if they are lucky—they will have the good fortune to board a 727 that crashes into a mountain. Then they'll be out of purgatory.

Those other people don't know they're dead, though. They think they're alive, wordlessly walking through the airport and chomping down three-dollar Cinnabon cinnamon rolls. I might be the only one who's aware of this, which means I am quite possibly a prophet. It also means I quite possibly have Cotard's syndrome. It's always 50-50.

Now, this next part is kind of important.

Diane and I are in the Tauntaun, and the sky is overcast (but just barely). It's mid-afternoon, and I suspect we will make it to

Lake Ontario by 7:30. After refueling outside of Syracuse, Diane begs me to let her drive, even though she no longer possesses a driver's license. I give her the keys. She pulls onto the interstate, and I say this:

"Diane, I want to be clear about something," I begin, "and I want this to be the last time we have this conversation."

Diane keeps driving, but she raises her eyebrows.

"I can't handle this anymore," I say. "I have been very clear about my feelings toward you. I have run out of ways to say I love you. So this is it. You have three weeks."

"I have three weeks to do what?"

"You have three weeks to decide if you want to be with me. And if your answer is that you do not want to be with me, I don't want to hang out with you, ever."

Silence.

"Chuck, I can't guarantee that I will be able to answer that question."

"You have to."

"This is unfair."

"I don't care."

Silence.

"If you think you love me so much, how would you be able to just cut off all contact with me?" Diane says. "That makes me question your sincerity."

"You know how these things work," I say. "This is how these things work."

Silence.

"That is so fucked-up," she says. "I can't decide whether or not I love you just because *you say* I have to."

"Well, maybe you can't. And if you can't decide, that's fine. But I will take 'I don't know' as a *no*, because it always means the same thing, anyway."

"But if I haven't been able to make that decision in six

months," she asks, "why do you think I'll be able to make it in three weeks?"

"Because you don't have any other alternative. This is it. And even if you make no decision, that will count as a decision. So, in a way, there's really no pressure. I'll get back in three weeks, and you can just tell me how you naturally feel, and that will dictate everything else."

Diane tries to pout but reflexively coughs. She sighs.

"Okay," she finally says. Maybe 20 seconds pass. "So this is your ultimatum?"

"This is my ultimatum," I respond. "My ultimatum has been made."

"That's fucked-up," says Diane. "You're fucked-up. But . . . okay. I'll make this fucked-up decision to satisfy the statute of limitations on your fucked-up ultimatum."

"Thank you," I say. "You know this is for the best."

I look away. A sign by the highway says we are 11 miles from Syracuse. I can remember this clearly, because that's exactly when I started thinking about Lenore again. It's also when I started to think that everything in my life would improve if we crashed into a caribou.

Don't ever cheat on someone. I'm serious. It's not worth it. And I'm not saying this because cheating is morally wrong, because some people have a very specific version of morality that doesn't necessarily classify actions as right or wrong. The reason you should never cheat on someone is because you won't enjoy it. No matter which person you're with, you'll always be thinking of the other one. You will never be in the romantic present tense; your mind will solely exist in the past and the future. Let's say you sleep with your mistress on Friday and your wife on Saturday: To an epicurean, this is the dream lifestyle. This is sexual utopia. But it never works out that way. When you're having sex with your mistress on Friday, you will find yourself thinking about your wife. You will be thinking about how this act would destroy her, and how humiliated she would feel if she knew the truth. But then on Saturday, when you're back in the arms of your trusting wife, your mind will immediately drift toward decadence. At the height of your physical passion, you will think back to how exciting things were 24 hours ago, when you were with a new, strange body. Except that it *wasn't* exciting to be with someone else; it's only exciting in your memory (at the time, it just made you wracked with guilt). So now you're having sex with someone who loves you, but your mind isn't even in the same room. And suddenly it's Sunday; you have now had sex with two people on two consecutive nights, and you didn't appreciate either episode. Algebraically, $a + b = c$ and $a + c = b$. The only thing infidelity does is remind you of the people you're *not* having sex with, which is something you can just as easily think about when you're completely alone.

Now—granted—Diane is not b, and Lenore is not c. Diane is not actually my girlfriend, and Lenore lives 2,000 miles to the west. But there is a reason talking about being in love with Diane makes me think of Lenore, and it's the same reason I was thinking about Diane a few weeks ago when I kissed Lenore good-bye and told her I'd see her in a month.

The density of my relationship with Lenore cannot be over-stated.

If Diane is like the woman from the song "Jolene," Lenore is like a combination of the girl described in "Chantilly Lace" (minus the ponytail) and the individual depicted in Mötley Crüe's "Looks That Kill" (although not technically bullet-proof). I met her at a party in Fargo, North Dakota; actually, I didn't meet her. I saw her. About 15 of us were watching the documentary *Unzipped*, and she arrived late and spent 10 minutes trying to open a bottle of wine. We never spoke. Three days later, I sent an e-mail to my friend Sarah Jackson. All the message said was, "I don't know who that blonde girl was, but she is superfoxy x 1,000." Sarah forwarded this message to Lenore, which (of course) was precisely my plan; anytime you tell a woman something positive about one of her female friends, the friend will be informed of this statement within 48 hours. I had no real aspirations of dating Lenore when I did this, because that seemed absolutely impossible. We were not, as they say, in the same league (she was in the NBA and I had a 10-day contract with the Quad City Thunder). But this is something all men do: Men always want to make sure that attractive women are informed of the fact that they are, in fact, attractive. I have no idea why this happens, but it happens all the time. I guess it's the hope that—somewhere on earth and against all odds—there is a beautiful woman who has managed to live her entire life without anyone mentioning that she has a desirable physical appearance, and this singular comment will be so flattering that no other courtship will be necessary. I knew a guy in college who only dated freshmen; when I asked him why, he said, "Because I exclusively hit on very hot women, and I don't want to meet anyone who has been told she is beautiful more than 20 or 30 times in the course of her lifetime. By the time any semi-attractive woman has completed one-third of her junior year, she's been told she's beautiful 4 million times by 3 million guys, 2 million of whom were drunk when they said it." I believe this fellow majored in statistics and is now divorced.

But ANYWAY, Sarah Jackson started dragging Lenore into the vinyl bar booth that I essentially lived in, and we started hard-core, bone-crushing, kamikaze flirting. This was 1996, when the world was without problems. Every Tuesday night, we would banter and drink and attempt to create national catchphrases, most notably the memorable axiom "Don't get nervous," an expression that generally meant "Our life is not going to get any better than this." Sometimes we would dance to Steely Dan's "Bodhisattva," but we'd do so in a manner that resembled awkward attacks from bipedal grizzly bears. One night we were bear-dancing in front of the jukebox (the bar had no sanctioned dance floor), and I pulled her into an alcove that led to the basement. It was a little five-by-five-foot foyer with green walls and a nonworking pay phone, lit by one lightbulb and separate from the rest of the tavern. I decided that this alcove was the Honesty Room, where duplicity could not exist.

"I want to kiss you," I said.

"I know you do," she said. "But why are telling me this now? And why are you telling me here?"

"Because we're in the Honesty Room," I said. "In the Honesty Room, there are no secrets."

"How many people have you slept with?" she asked.

"Three," I said. This was true.

"That," said Lenore, "is the perfect number."

Two weeks later, Lenore removed her turtleneck while we were making out in the front seat of her Chrysler LeBaron. Nothing in my life has ever been the same. It was like touching the obelisk and realizing I could use tapir bones as a weapon.

How did I get into this situation with Diane, you ask? I don't even know anymore. I probably never knew. It seems like it happened a long, long time ago, but it's actually been less than a year. One day I watched her play Frisbee, one day I noticed she was cute, one day we had a conversation about how much it might cost to go to the Bronx Zoo, and one day I was structuring my entire life around spending time with her. A critical moment in our courtship occurred after we saw a documentary about Henry Kissinger that accused the former secretary of state of war crimes. There is a scene in this film where Christopher Hitchens explains why Richard Nixon appreciated a Jewish intellectual like Kissinger, despite the fact that Nixon generally despised both Jews and intellectuals. What Nixon loved (according to Hitchens) was that Kissinger always knew what to do without being told; this struck me as one of the most insightful definitions of true intelligence I'd ever heard. When I told this to Diane during our postfilm debriefing at some boringly expensive bar in Greenwich Village, she was aghast. "This movie is supposed to help you understand why Henry Kissinger should be in prison for politically motivated murder," she said. "It is not supposed to make you think he's somehow more *interesting*." It immediately dawned on me that we were never going to agree on anything as long as we lived. Our worldviews were so diametrically opposed that we would never share any experience in totality; even if we saw the same film at the same time in the same place, there would be no common ground whatsoever.

I found this profoundly desirable.

As we pull into her lake cabin at dusk, part of me considers staying with her, an offer she has made three times in the last hour. However, the scene at the cabin is even worse than I anticipated: There are already a dozen neo-hippies on-site, and everybody has a dog or a baby or a beard. At least half of the people at this party are sleeping in tents. The cabin itself might have electricity, but it also might not; it definitely doesn't having a working toilet. It appears that these people are going to subsist on hippie provisions (tofu, watermelon, American Spirit cigarettes, etc.), that they all know each other intimately, and that I can't imagine having a conversation that wouldn't make me want to jam C-4 plastic explosive into my eardrums in the hope of blowing up my brain. Diane, on the other hand, appears ecstatic. She is hugging old friends and telling them how great they look. The only thing that's making her uncomfortable is my presence; the last five times Diane saw these people, she was with her ex-boyfriend. Now there is no boyfriend; now there is some guy who thinks Henry Kissinger is interesting. The hippies insist that I spend the night and roast marshmallows and (I assume) talk about why the Boards of Canada album *Music Has the Right to Children* is underrated. "We have an extra tent," they say. "All you have to do is set it up." Diane looks at me with hopeful eyes, but that might just be because she already knows I will turn them down.

The sun begins to set. Diane and I hug each other and look at Lake Ontario for 10 minutes while drinking warm Labatts from the Tauntaun's trunk, and then she tells me I should get going. Which I do, although I feel vaguely guilty about leaving. I drive back to the east, into the darkness. It's an easy drive; I listen to the Drive-By Truckers' *Southern Rock Opera* and David Bowie's *Hunky Dory,* and then a talk-radio show that's inexplicably focused on what's been happening at the Denver Broncos training camp (we should all expect big things from Clinton Portis, it seems). Three hours later, Diane calls me on my cell phone; I'm in Room No. 5 of the Red Carpet Inn in Mohawk, New York, which is where I'm typing this very sentence at this very moment. She sounds okay, but not so okay that she didn't need to call. It's only a five-minute conversation, mostly about how Diane wants to fall asleep. Meanwhile, my motel has walls so thin that I can hear a family of three playing Yahtzee in the next room. I can hear every detail of the game. I can hear the dice shaking in the tumbler, and I suddenly want to hear *Exile on Main St.* The walls are so thin that I can actually keep score of the Yahtzee game in my head; the mom should have kept her "fives" instead of filling in her "chance" space so early in the game. You can always pick up "chance" at the end.

THE THIRD DAY

Fire ➤ Metal ➤ Drugs ➤ Despair ➤ Q

SPRINGFIELD, MASSACHUSETTS, the road signs say. I am one exit away from the Basketball Hall of Fame, and I suddenly feel obligated to check it out; I won't stay long, but I want to call my friends in Minnesota and tell them I'm looking at Bobby Knight's sweater. Springfield is a poorly organized town, but I eventually find the Hall of Fame (the building is spherical, so that kinda helps). Like all museums, it's a rip-off. I care about basketball with an intensity I feel toward little else in my life, but I still find scant satisfaction from looking at Artis Gilmore's ABA jersey through a plate of Plexiglas.

In theory, the Basketball Hall of Fame should simply serve as a pleasant distraction from the road and an opportunity to buy a T-shirt. I certainly didn't think it would factor into this story. But something depressing happens while I'm here. The bottom floor of the Hall of Fame is a full-length basketball court with a regulation wooden floor, and there are iron hoops and leather spheroids everywhere. Any museum patron can take an elevator down to court level and shoot free throws and three-pointers and skyhooks; you can even try to shoot into a peach basket, just like the students of Dr. James Naismith in December 1891. I cannot resist an opportunity to squeeze off a

33

few mid-range jump shots, even though I had not touched a rock in two years; the cacophony of 100 balls bouncing semi-simultaneously reminded me of going to basketball camp in seventh grade. But as I launch my leather rock alongside three black kids and a teenage Asian girl, something slowly dawns on me: I'm fucking terrible. Most of my shots are off by at least nine inches, and a few of them are humiliating public air balls. This 16-year-old Asian girl could shut me down and hold me scoreless. I find myself thinking about when I was 16 years old, and how I used to play basketball on my farm for four hours a day, and how I used to be able to stand at the top of the key and go 17 of 20 while wearing Levi's 501s and listening to Bon Jovi's *New Jersey* on a $40 boom box. It feels so exhausting to be so bad at something I loved so much.

It was a mistake to come here. I'm better off remembering things alone.

It takes most of the day to get to West Warwick, Rhode Island, but the sun is still relatively high when I roll into town. It's hot, and I'm staring at colorless dirt. For some reason, I assumed the plot of land where 100 people burned to death during a rock concert would look like a parking lot. I assumed that the whole area would be leveled and obliterated, and there would be no sign whatsoever of what happened on February 20, 2003, the night pyrotechnics from the blues-metal sauropods in Great White turned a club called the Station into a torture chamber. Small towns usually make sure their places of doom disappear. But that's not the case here: In West Warwick, what used to be a tavern is now an ad hoc cemetery—which is the same role taverns play in most small towns, but not as obviously as this.

The population of West Warwick is just under 30,000. It does not look the way I always imagined Rhode Island; it seems more like South Dakota. There's not really a "downtown," per se, and the intersections don't make right angles; if not for the sun and the Tauntaun's GPS, I wouldn't have a clue which direction I was facing. However, I find the Station location in under 10 minutes, almost by accident. It's surrounded by lush trees and soulless garages. The ground is not white, yet it has no definable color. Is there a shade between brown and gray? That's all I see when I look at this earth.

When I pull into what used to be the Station's parking lot, I turn off my engine next to a red F-150 Ford pickup with two dudes sitting in the cab. They get out before me and walk through a perimeter of primitive crosses that surround the ruins of the club; once inside, they sit on two folding chairs next to a pair of marble gravestones. I follow. The two guys are James F____ and his cousin Glenn B____. The two gravestones are for James's uncle Tommy and Tommy's best friend Jay. Tommy died while sitting at the bar (James aligned the gravestones where the beer taps used to be). The narrative they tell me is even worse than I would have anticipated: After Tommy died in the fire, James's grandfather—Tommy's father—died from a stroke one week later, exactly seven days and five minutes after his son was burned alive.

I realize this story must sound horribly sad, but it doesn't seem that way when they tell it: James F____ and Glenn B____ are both as happy as any two people I've ever met. James is like a honey-gorged bear, and he reminds me of that guy who starred in *The Tao of Steve*; he's wearing a tie-dyed shirt and a knee brace, and he starts talking to me before I start talking to him. It turns out he comes to this cemetery every single day.

"I will remember the night this place burned down forever," James tells me. "I was in a titty bar in Florida—I was living in Largo at the time. I looked up at the ceiling of the bar, and I noticed it was covered with black Styrofoam, just like this place always was. And I suddenly knew something was wrong.

I could just feel it. And then my mom called me, and she told me what happened. Right after that, I moved up here to help out my grandma. She obviously has been through a lot, what with losing her son and then her husband a week later. The doctor said my grandfather's stroke was completely stress-related, which doesn't surprise me. I mean, he stroked out a week after the fire, almost to the very minute. That was fucking spooky."

James is 34; his dead uncle, Tommy, was just four years older, so they were actually more like brothers. The year before, James had come up to West Warwick to see an AC/DC tribute band with Tommy, a longtime regular at the Station. Somewhat ironically (or I suppose just tragically), his uncle didn't even want to see Great White the night they played in Rhode Island: He referred to them as "Not-So-Great White" and only went because someone gave him free tickets.

James, Glenn, and two anonymous lesbians built all of the Station's crosses in one night a few months after the accident. The crosses are oak, and the wood came from the Station's surviving floorboards. Originally, the crosses were all blank; that was so survivors could come to the site, pick their own personal crucifix, and decorate it however they saw fit. There are only about five clean crosses remaining, but this is partially because some people have been inadvertently memorialized multiple times.

As we talk, I find myself shocked by how jovial James is. "I hide it pretty well," he tells me. "And between you and me, I just did a line. Do you wanna go do some blow?"

So now I'm on the passenger side of this dude's Ford F-150 pickup, and we're inhaling cheap cocaine at 5:45 in the afternoon, maybe 40 feet away from where 100 rock fans were incinerated. But before I go any further on this subject, I want to be completely clear about something: *I am not writing about cocaine in order to seem cool.* I am not a cocaine person; I am a marijuana person. This is a critical, critical distinction. At *Spin*, for example, there are two diverse camps: the "Pot/Creedence" Contingent, and the "Coke/Interpol" Contingent. The Pot/Creedence people go to unpopular bars at 6:15 P.M., drink Miller High Life until 9:00, smoke pot at 9:20, and then spend two hours discussing why the Creedence Clearwater Revival song "Ramble Tamble" illustrates a larger truth about Vietnam, despite the fact that the lyrics of "Ramble Tamble" are not about war. This discussion ends around 11:20, at which time the Coke/Interpol Contingent finally leave their apartments and immediately begin snorting cocaine in the bathrooms of semi-gay dance clubs; 90 minutes later, they will try to meet members of the semi-shitty Brooklyn band Interpol in the hope that the well-dressed bozos in that band will be able to locate better cocaine and more luxurious bathrooms. The upside to joining the Pot Contingent is that you get to be intellectual and hungry and completely alienated from everyone you might want to sleep with; the upside to joining the Coke Contingent is that you feel awesome and danceable and alone, pretty much all the time.

Predictably, I am part of the former contingent, and I will never transfer my loyalties. I can't be a cocaine person; the culture that comes with cocaine is simply too preposterous. Until I moved to New York, I had never even *seen* coke, and I figured if I'd made it 30 years without cocaine, I probably shouldn't go looking for it. But then I went to a birthday party at this place called the Slipper Room. The Slipper Room is a bar for people who want to be faux-decadent and mock-ironic at the same time; for example, the Slipper Room has topless dancers performing onstage, but it's not supposed to be sexual. It's *funny*, you see, because these dancers are gothic suicide girls who are caricaturing the misogynistic depravity of strip joints like Scores and Déjà Vu. Of course, the girls in the Slipper Room are doing precisely what normal strippers do at Scores and Déjà Vu, and men still tend to stare at the girls' tits while swallowing over-priced cocktails. I'm not sure where the irony is, except that the women at the Slipper Room dance to the Cult instead of Faster Pussycat. But ANYWAY, I went to a birthday party there, and a guy wearing sunglasses (indoors, at 10:00 P.M.) asked me if I wanted to do some blow, and I said, "Of course." Because I can never say no to drugs, even if I don't know what they'll do to me. So now I'm following this dude around the bar, trying to seem natural, trying to pretend like I understand how you're supposed to snort cocaine in public. We go down to the base-ment, but all the bathrooms are occupied. We go back upstairs, and—somehow—we find a bathroom backstage; this is appar-ently where the goth-girl strippers change clothes. We walk into the room, and the first thing I see are two very angry women, both of whom are naked from the waist down. The shorter one screeches, "Get the fuck out, you fucking faggots." This strikes me as a bad sign. But then the guy in the sunglasses simply says, "I have coke," and everything changes. Suddenly, these bottomless women are our closest friends. And it dawns on me that I'm about to do cocaine—for the first time in my life—with two half-naked strippers. I am David Lee Roth, touring with Sabbath in 1978. I am Bret Easton Ellis, two weeks after *American Psycho* was unsuccessfully crucified by *The Wash-ington Post*. I am Bruce Wayne, making curious social decisions inside Gotham City's hottest discotheque. But I'm also com-pletely terrified, because I might also be Len Bias. "I'm going to die exactly like Len Bias," I thought. "I'm gonna snort this shit, and my heart is going to explode. I will be the exception that proves the rule. My mom is going to get a phone call tomorrow morning and some cop is going to tell her I overdosed on cocaine in a public bathroom. She is going to go to Mass every morning for the next year, and she will cry every single time. Moreover,

I'll never play a minute of power forward for the Celtics. This is so wrong."

I then dipped my apartment key into a tiny plastic bag, withdrew a nice little nipple of white powder, and sucked it through my right nostril. Seconds later, I had two wholly new thoughts: (a) *This is actually no big deal*, and (b) *I feel perfect*.

There's no question in my mind that the dangers of cocaine have been wildly exaggerated by the antidrug lobby. Oh, I'm sure it's not *good* for you, but you can certainly enjoy it recreationally, assuming you have disposable income and you hate yourself. Unlike pot or mushrooms or liquid Vicodin, it doesn't shift reality; it just makes reality louder, brighter, and more interested in the availability of fashionable footwear. It makes you feel like you're walking down the street—minding your own business—and the smartest, most attractive person you've ever met suddenly jumps out from behind a bush and gives you a compliment. This sensation lasts between 16 and 21 minutes, after which you become singularly obsessed with finding more cocaine. That desire forces you to enter "cocaine culture" (at least for one night). Cocaine culture contains the worst of everything: the worst conversations, the worst friendships, and the worst kind of unspeakable joy. But the instant you've received a powdery compliment from this imaginary stranger, entering cocaine culture becomes the goal of your entire evening. People who want cocaine will lie about anything; people will surrender integrity they never had to begin with. To get free cocaine, women will have sex with men they normally wouldn't dance with. Cocaine makes you more popular, but also less likable; cocaine makes you feel guilty in advance. When you snort cocaine, you consciously allow yourself to become foolish in the hope of seeming cool, and that's the worst choice any smart person can make. This is why I am not a Cocaine Person, and this is why I will (probably) never become a Cocaine Person.

That said, I am currently snorting cocaine in a Ford pickup at 5:45 P.M. with a man I met 20 minutes ago. And I am doing this because—somehow—it seems reasonable.

James's truck is facing away from the Station, but I can see the 101 crosses in the door mirror; technically, those objects should be closer than they appear. It doesn't feel that way. It feels like they're somewhere across the Atlantic Ocean. The thought of people writhing in pain and burning alive is freaking me out. My teeth feel hollow. Battery acid is sliding down the back of my throat, and I kind of love it. Like the amateur coke fiend that I am, I spill a bunch of his drugs on the floor of the vehicle; he insists he doesn't care, but I know he's lying. Suddenly, I feel incredibly close to this person. I tell him that I feel guilty getting high while sitting next to a tragedy; he tells me not to worry. It turns out that this kind of behavior is not uncommon: These grounds have fostered a community of both spirituality and decadence. Almost every night, a collection of mourners comes to the Station cemetery to get high and talk about how they keep living in the wake of all this sadness. We get out of the truck and walk back to the burial grounds, and I start to understand death.

"Nothing in West Warwick is the same," James says as he paints his uncle's gravestone. "It changed everyone's personality. Everybody immediately started to be friendlier. For weeks after that show, if you wore a concert T-shirt into a gas station, everybody acted real nice to you. If they knew you were a rocker or a head, they immediately treated you better. It's that sense of community. It's kind of like the drug culture."

I ask him what he means by that.

"Well, okay—the fact that you did cocaine with me immediately makes me trust you. I mean, I just met you, but I would give you a ride anywhere in the whole goddamn state of Rhode

Island if you asked me, because I know you're a good guy. I have something on you, and you have something on me. It's like that here. The people who hang out here at night—it's definitely a community of people dealing with the same shit. I call it 'the fellowship.'"

While James is explaining this to me, a kid with a soul patch pulls into the Station parking lot and hauls an upright bass out of his vehicle. This is not an electric bass; this is one of those seven-foot acoustic monsters the Stray Cats used to play when people still thought rockabilly was charming. He faces the grave markers, whips out a bow, and begins to play Henry Eccles's Sonata in G Minor. This is pretty fucking weird and pretty bizarrely cinematic. Either I have arrived at the Station at the perfect journalistic moment, or West Warwick is America's new *Twin Peaks*.

"Oh, I used to play at this club all the time," the kid says stoically when I wander over and get his attention. "I was in a band called Hawkins Rise, and I played upright bass through an amp. It was rock stuff. We were sort of like Zeppelin or the Who." He begins playing again, not seeming to realize I want to interview him. When I stop him a second time, he tells me that his name is Jeff Richardson and that he is a 23-year-old jazz fanatic, and that when his aunt called him on the morning of February 22 to tell him that the Station had burned down, he initially thought she was talking about a local TV station. A few hours later, he would realize that he knew five people who died there and that he was at least vaguely familiar with many of the other 95.

"I recognized a lot of the faces when they were on the news. The same people came here every night," Richardson says. "When a band like Great White or Warrant would come to town, all those same people would come out. There was never any pretentiousness at this club. This was the one club where

you wouldn't have to worry about some drunk guy yelling
about how much your band sucked. The people who came here
were never like that."

To me, that's what makes the Great White tragedy even sad-
der than it logically was: One can safely assume that *none* of the
100 people who died at the Station that night were trying to be
cool by watching Great White play 20-year-old songs. This was
not a bunch of hipsters trying to be seen by other hipsters; these
were blue-collar people, all trying to unironically experience
music that honestly meant something to them when they were
teenagers. So many of the rock concerts I've attended have been
filled with people who were there only *to be there,* who just
wanted to be seen by other people who were there only *to be
there*. They want to be able to say, "I saw the Vines at the
Mercury Lounge before they released *Highly Evolved,* and
they already sucked." They want to say, "I saw the Strokes right
before they started to get serious, and it was amazing." They
want to say, "I saw Jane's Addiction on the *Nothing's Shocking*
tour, and I thought I was seeing the new Zeppelin. It was amazing. But then I saw them again, and they sucked." Half the people who attend concerts only go so that they can tell other
people that (a) certain shows were amazing, and (b) other
shows sucked. But that couldn't have been the case at the Station. I remember everyone gossiping about the Station fire the
day after it happened; people would concede that it was tragic,
but no one could discuss it without a fraction of a smirk. People
were sending e-mail one-liners about the fire while the cops were
still counting the bodies. Somehow, it was acceptable to conde-
scendingly chuckle at the death of the overtly uncool people in
Rhode Island, sort of how you can immediately make a joke
about a massive earthquake as long as it happens in some distant place like Iran or China. I honestly believe that people of
my generation despise authenticity, mostly because they're all

so envious of it. It's almost like they *want* to be burned alive, because that would prove they had grit.

Tonight, I will go back to the Station graveyard at 11:00 P.M., and lots of working-class survivors will pull up in Camaro IROCs and Chevy Cavaliers, and they'll sit in the vortex of the crosses and smoke menthol cigarettes and marijuana, and they will talk about what happened that night. I will be told that the fire started during the first song ("Desert Moon," off *Hooked*). I will be told that the Station's ceiling was only 10 feet high and covered in synthetic foam, and when the foam ignited, it (supposedly) released cyanide into the air. I will be told it took exactly 58 seconds before the whole building became a singular fireball. I will be told that one of the kids who died had just turned 21 and was "a great fucking golfer." I will be told that a few firefighters at the scene compared it to seeing napalm dropped on villages in Vietnam, because that was the only other time they had ever seen skin dripping off bone.

I will also be told (by just about everyone in the entire town) that Great White vocalist Jack Russell is a coward and a hypocrite, and that they will never forgive him. Around 1:00 A.M., James will read me a poem he wrote about how much he despises Russell, and—after he finishes—he will stare off into the night sky and say, "I would really like to hit him in the face." But he won't sound intimidating or vengeful when he says this; he will just sound sad. And it will strike me that this guy is an omnipresently sweet person with a heart like a mastodon, and I would completely trust him to drive me anywhere in the whole goddamn state of Rhode Island, even if he had never offered me free drugs.

At 1:30 A.M., West Warwick is actually a bit scary. It's not scary like East St. Louis (or even scary like East Cleveland), but it has "rural scariness": There seems to be a preponder-

43

ance of mooks driving around in pickups, blasting Limp Bizkit albums, and sipping Big Gulps half full of Southern Comfort. I get some food at an all-night Arby's, and the kids trailing me in the drive-through are yelling obscenities in my general direction; I head straight back to the Springfield Suites on the outskirts of town to cower with my chicken-fillet sandwich. As I eat, I check my e-mail. There is a message from Quincy, who's responding to a message I sent two days earlier. When I am in Minnesota, I will see Quincy for the first time in two years.

It will be really, really great to see Quincy.

Former Dallas Cowboy quarterback Roger Staubach is my hero; this is because whoever is your hero when you're nine remains your hero forever. I met Quincy when I was 23. She will be my favorite person forever, and my explanation as to why that is the case would be pretty much the same as my logic for why I still lionize a football player who retired when I was in second grade. If I were to list the 25 greatest moments in my life, Q would be involved in 16 of them. If I listed the 25 worst moments, she would be involved in at least 21. Intellectually, I will always be aware of this ratio. But every year I don't die, those 16 wonderful moments become more and more lucid, and the 21 bad ones morph into one big fight that almost seems charming. If Diane is Dolly Parton's Jolene and Lenore is a fusion of the Big Bopper's libido with Nikki Sixx's scariest wet dream, Quincy is akin to the girl in Ben Folds Five's "Kate," multiplied by the woman described in Sloan's "Underwhelmed," divided by the person Evan Dando sings about in the Lemonheads' slacked-up, Raymond Carver–esque ballad "My Drug Buddy." And I realize those are obscure fucking references, but some people demand obscurity.

Q says she can't wait to see me. I respond to her by typing the words *jazz wolf*. This is a hilarious inside joke we share, which I won't explain here because I am certain it's entirely unfunny.

Everything that ever happened between us is both hilarious and unfunny. One winter day, Quincy said she thought she was pregnant. She told me this in her car; the Spin Doctors were on the radio. Obviously, this is unfunny. She made me buy a pregnancy-test kit at a Hornbacher's grocery store (I'm not sure why that task was my responsibility, exactly) and we went back to my apartment. She wordlessly went into the bathroom. I stood in my living room and listened to *Synchronicity* by the Police, and I thought about how the rest of my life was suddenly set in concrete. I would live in Fargo for the next 50 years, unless I somehow got a job at the *Minneapolis Star-Tribune*. I would be married before I was 25. I would be the first of my college friends to become a father, which they would all find disturbing, as everyone who knows me knows that I despise children. But I would grow to love this child, perhaps even more profoundly than the way I loved Quincy, and I hoped Quincy and I wouldn't end up getting a divorce, because our divorce would probably devastate that little person's life. We would buy a house, and I would have to mow its lawn. I'd probably mow the lawn catty-corner, because that usually looks better. In the spring, I'd clean wet leaves from the eaves trough, but maybe that would be satisfying, somehow. Maybe I would find a Zen relationship within those wet leaves. If I had to live this life, I could make it work, you know?

Two minutes later, Quincy told me she was not pregnant.

She walked out of my bathroom and dropped to her knees. We exchanged high fives, which in retrospect seems like a peculiar response. We then decided to get as stoned as humanly possible and videotape ourselves talking about nonsense, which was the one thing we loved to do more than anything else (including, curiously, the thing that led me to buy her a pregnancy test). Our bong had an American flag on it because Quincy liked to champion representative democracy; we always filled it with ice cubes because I liked to champion the properties of ice. After 20 minutes of arguing over the comedic merit of the phrase *powder monkey*, Quincy slowly determined that our cigarette lighter was broken. It was February, and we were in North Dakota. The idea of driving to a convenience store to buy a new lighter seemed absolutely impossible.

"Why don't you ask one of your neighbors?" Quincy said. "Maybe they have an extra lighter."

"You are a genius," I replied. "I will save the day for all involved. But what should I say we need a lighter for?"

"Say anything," said Q.

I walked out into the hallway and confidently pounded on the door of a man who lived two doors down. Like all modern people, I had no relationship with anyone in my building. The man who opened the door was roughly 33 years old. He was wearing a wife-beater and watching *Cheers*. For some reason, I felt this man could not be trusted.

"Hey there," I said. "You don't know me, but I live on this floor—we're neighbors, as you may or may not know—and I will be entertaining some guests this evening, and many of these people are cigarette smokers, so I was wondering if you had a cigarette lighter I could borrow."

This came out less fluently than I had anticipated.

"Oh. Hmm. Well, that seems reasonable," he said. "But if these people smoke, won't they bring their own lighters?"

This was a good point.

"What do you mean?"

"Well, it just seems like smokers who carry around cigarettes usually carry around cigarette lighters, too," he said. "Or at least some matches."

"Well, yes. Usually, that's true," I replied. "But I also own many candles."

This made even less sense, but he gave me a lighter and told me I didn't even need to return it. I triumphantly returned to my apartment and relayed the details of this exchange to the Q.

"So let me see if I grasp our scenario," Quincy said. "You essentially lied to this guy, just as I instructed. But the particular lie you selected was that you are having a huge party in this tiny apartment on a Thursday night, and the party will be populated with shortsighted cigarette smokers, and he is not invited. And just in case he isn't already freaked out by this, you also mentioned that this tiny, crowded apartment will be filled with burning candles."

"This is all true," I said, "but the ends justify the means. You cannot deny that we now have a working cigarette lighter. Within these strangely specific conditions, everything is perfect. We are perfect."

"Maybe so," she replied.

I think about that night a lot; I think about how weird it is that I can recall borrowing a cigarette lighter more vividly than I can recall how my entire existence almost changed completely. After I moved to Akron, I used to get drunk and think to myself, "Jesus Christ, if Q had been pregnant, I'd remember that night for the rest of my life."

Which I did anyway.

It will be more than a little awesome to see Quincy.

THE FOURTH DAY

Crazy ➤ In ➤ Love

There is a new song on Top 40 radio right now that's so good I want to kill myself. I'm not sure why exceptionally good hip-hop singles make me want to commit suicide, but they often do. I don't know what the title of this song is, but it's that religious woman with the perfect stomach from Destiny's Child and Jay-Z doing a duet featuring a horn riff from the '70s that I've never heard before (but that sounds completely familiar), and the chorus is something along the lines of, "Your love is driving me crazy right now / I'm kind of hoping you'll page me right now." It's also possible that Jay-Z compares himself to Golden State Warriors guard Nick Van Exel during the last verse, but I can't be positive.

ANYWAY, by the time you read this sentence, the song I am referring to will be ten thousand years old. You will have heard it approximately 15,000 times, and you might hate it, and I might hate it, too. But right now—*today*—I am living for this song. As far as I am concerned, there is nothing that matters as much as hearing it on the radio; I am interested in nothing beyond Beyoncé Knowles's voice. All I do is scan the FM dial for hours at a time, trying to find it. And you know what? I've never heard the entire song once. I never catch the beginning. But I've heard the end about 25 times, and it makes me want to drive my Tauntaun into the mouth of an active volcano.

If I knew I was going to die at a specific moment in the future, it would be nice to be able to control what song I was listening to; this is why I always bring my iPod on airplanes. When I read Elizabeth Wurtzel's *Prozac Nation* in 1995, I remember being impressed that she intended to play "Strawberry Fields Forever" if she ultimately slit her wrists in the bathtub, opting for the Beatles instead of her own personal Jesus, Bruce Springsteen. I guess this was so that no one would blame her suicide on "Thunder Road," which is similar to what happened to Judas Priest in 1985. Years after reading *Prozac Nation*, I actually met Wurtzel (for maybe five minutes) in the offices of *Spin* magazine, and I told her that I had always liked that particular passage from her book. She told me she had no recollection of writing such a sentiment but conceded that it sounded like something she would have written. It was an awkward conversation; in the span of those five minutes, I think I said 14 words, while Wurtzel unleashed somewhere in the vicinity of 82,000 complete sentences. She is a conversational avalanche. I found myself both repulsed and attracted, which probably happens to her a lot. She had nice hips. After the conversation, I walked over to the desk of Lucy Chance, a 111-pound editorial assistant who can drink more than any white-collar woman I've ever met.

"Hey," I said. "I just met Elizabeth Wurtzel."

"Oh, really," Lucy said. "I'm sorry."

"Why are you sorry?"

"I just think it's unfortunate that you had to meet such a horrible, horrible person."

"Is she *horrible*?" I asked. Very often, I have no idea if the people I meet are horrible. Lucy often has to point these people out to me.

"Well, did she *seem* horrible?"

"I don't know," I said. "Maybe. She certainly did a lot of talking."

"She is a terrible, terrible writer," said Lucy.

"Oh, I don't know if I agree with you," I said. "Do you remember that part of *Prozac Nation* where she talked about playing the Beatles when she was thinking about killing herself? And how that whole idea sort of addresses the concept of art as a way to understand death, not unlike the manner in which art is often used as a prism for understanding life? That's brilliant, I think. I think maybe Elizabeth Wurtzel is brilliant."

"That's dubious," said Lucy.

"Why do you say that?"

"Because people who sincerely want to kill themselves don't worry about which Beatles song they'd play while their bathtub fills up with blood. Those kind of people probably don't even like the Beatles."

"Lucy, there is nothing to indicate that suicidal people don't like the Beatles."

"Well, true," Lucy said. "There's no data on this sort of thing. But it's not like people who want to die spend their afternoons rifling through their record collections."

"Oh yes they would!" I insisted. "If I was committing suicide, I would *totally* worry about what Beatles song I would play. That's *all* I would worry about. I'd probably pick 'Tomorrow Never Knows,' but I'm not sure if it's long enough. I'm not sure if I could bleed to death in two minutes and 56 seconds."

"Dubious," she replied.

Considering that (a) I have not killed myself, and (b) I do not even have access to a bathtub, it is difficult for me to contradict the nay-saying of Lucy Chance. In fact, the more I think about it, the more I'm prone to agree with her, because just two hours after recalling this very conversation, I thought I was about to die *for real*: While trailing a petroleum truck on the Jersey Turnpike, a rock suddenly kicked up from under one of its rear wheels and collided with the Tauntaun's windshield, instantly smashing the glass into a massive spider web. Looking back, I now realize that this was not a life-or-death situation. But within the fraction of a moment when something like that happens, your heart stops. It feels like the prelude to an execution. It's like having the wind knocked out of your lungs. The *crack* of my windshield sounded like the hammer of my brother's .357 Magnum, and the splintering of the safety glass made me squeeze the steering wheel like an orangutan strangling a kitten. And those were wholly natural reactions; those were unconscious physical responses to the sudden realization that I was about to perish, even though I wasn't. And when this event happened— this unforeseen moment when I honestly thought I was about to die and I was caught inside that singular second when my soul prepared to leap out of my chest—I did not care what was playing on the radio *at all*. That was the least of my worries. In fact, it was half a minute before I had the wherewithal to notice what song was still pouring out of my speakers, just like the fantasy blood from Elizabeth Wurtzel's fantasy suicide.

And I'd like to say that the song I heard was that new Beyoncé Knowles single, because that would be really, really symbolic.

But it wasn't.

It was Cheap Trick's "Surrender."

I'm spending a rainy evening in Washington, D.C., a town where the leaders of the free world can often be seen jogging. It's strange—I could not resist stopping at the Basketball Hall of Fame yesterday afternoon, but I have no interest whatsoever in looking at any of the tourist attractions in (arguably) America's most beautiful, most important city. I guess I don't understand what such things are supposed to teach us. For example: While driving to an Outback Steakhouse for supper, I saw the Washington Monument out of the passenger's window. The Washington Monument is big, and I suppose it could also be classified as impressive or noble or something along those lines; *symmetrically presidential* might be the ideal term. But what is this 550-foot masonry structure supposed to tell me? What is it supposed to make me understand? Am I supposed to specifically think about George Washington? Because I didn't. Am I supposed to be reminded that I am in the nation's capital? Because I already knew that. Am I supposed to feel patriotic? Because I don't understand how an inanimate object has any relationship to how I feel about living in this country. I'll never understand why people need to *see* things just so they can say they saw them. My best friend, Mr. Pancake, always wants me to visit him in Arizona so that he can show me the Grand Canyon, but I know I'll never go. I mean, I'd love to see Mr. Pancake, but I have no desire to see the physical manifestation of erosion. The Grand Canyon is just an attractive accident; it has no inherent meaning. I'd be far more impressed if a collection of civil engineers used dynamite and laser beams to construct a perfect replication of the Grand Canyon on a one-to-one scale; that would show mankind's potential to master nature. That would speak to man's desire to overcome 5 million years of adversity. But what does the Washington Monument speak to? Man's potential to master concrete? Man's desire to overcome gravity? I really don't get it. It's just . . . tall.

Tonight is a Sunday, but I still grab a few drinks with a friend who lives on Capitol Hill. This friend is also from North Dakota, but now he works for the Republican Party. He takes me to a tavern which (I'm told) is a GOP bar; apparently, this is a city with Republican bars and Democrat bars. Those establishments are filled with idealistic, underpaid interns who are killing themselves in the hope of networking with anyone who could put them in a position to network with someone else. It seems like a thrilling, confusing, horrific way to live. In New York, people are unhappy on purpose, because unhappiness makes them seem more complex; in Washington, D.C., it just sort of works out that way.

My conservative North Dakotan acquaintance is among the most ambitious people I've ever met. He travels the world, he seems to have little problem meeting women who aspire to give him blowjobs, and he's made himself independently wealthy. He is a workaholic, and that is a conscious decision. And midway through our second beer, he admits the one thing I've always known about him—that he is utterly and hopelessly depressed. "I want my life to be different," he tells me, and his voice sounds as lonely as Morrissey's on *Bona Drag*. "I want adventure. I want something to look forward to."

"That's what we all want," I say in response. But here's the problem: My friend is telling the truth, and I'm lying.

THE FIFTH DAY

Breakdown ➤ Downtown ➤ Dear Catastrophe Waitress

I started watching a made-for-TV movie on the Lifetime network, but I had to stop after 10 minutes. This happened late last night. I could immediately sense that it was part of a particular genre of film I can't handle; it was one of those "Nobody Believes Me" movies. This idiom includes films like Harrison Ford's *Frantic* and Kurt Russell's *Breakdown*: They are narratives in which something terrible happens to the main character (such as having his wife kidnapped), but everyone the character tries to notify assumes he's insane. Whenever I watch a movie like this, I get nervous. I always feel like I'm about to vomit.

Though my physical response to this type of movie is strange, it's not exactly rare. Lots of people have specific cinema phobias that stop them from enjoying certain movies. Lucy Chance, for example, can't watch movies that depict TV game shows. This is an especially unique foible, because Lucy enjoys watching *real* game shows; she only dislikes fictionalized interpretations of such programs. As a consequence, she refuses to see films like *Magnolia* (whose plot includes a game show called *What Do Kids Know?*), *Quiz Show* (about the seminal TV game *Twenty-one*), and *Confessions of a Dangerous Mind* (which includes fake footage of *The Dating Game*, *The Newlywed Game*, and

The Gong Show). I'm not sure what this says about her personality. I have another friend who hates any movie in which a character unexpectedly rides a horse; as a result, he hates *The Last Boy Scout* (where Damon Wayans rides a horse onto a football field), *The Song Remains the Same* (where Robert Plant travels by steed on a Viking challenge), and even *Raiders of the Lost Ark* (where Indiana Jones steals an equine to chase down the Nazi caravan). Oddly, this fellow has absolutely no problem with movies that involve "predictable" horse riding, such as *Young Guns* and *Seabiscuit*. I don't know what that symbolizes, either. However, I fully understand why I become so emotionally shackled by the "Nobody Believes Me" oeuvre of filmmaking: I empathize too much with the protagonist. This is how I feel all the time. Whenever I try to be ironic, people think I'm serious—but every time I'm actually right about something, everyone assumes I'm crazy. Nobody ever believes me when I'm telling the truth. If I ever get married, I'll live in constant fear that my wife will fall into the hands of sadistic kidnappers. I just know I'd be profoundly fucked if that ever happened. The authorities would never buy my story.

I'm lost. I know where I am, but I'm still lost.

As previously noted, my car is specially equipped with a device that is supposed to stop this from happening. But this is still happening. I tried to get on the interstate, but I (somehow) ended up in the heart of Washington, D.C. Is it possible a GPS doesn't work within the perimeter of our nation's capital? Could it be that satellites purposefully give incorrect information to operating systems within the District of Columbia, as such information could be used by lazy terrorists who intend to blow up the White House without the assistance of conventional road maps? It seems like my GPS is giving me bad advice on purpose. Go to hell, Meredith Baxter-Birney.

On the upside, I'm getting a chance to see D.C.'s downtown sector. I'm listening to the soundtrack of *Girl, Interrupted*, a mainstream art film in which Angelina Jolie makes Winona Ryder seem rational. It's an ideal backdrop for my present downtown location, because Petula Clark's song "Downtown" is outlining the myriad advantages to urban living. They are as follows:

1. Incessant noise and an accelerated pace of life decrease anxiety.
2. Neon lights are attractive.
3. It's hard to lose.
4. The lighting is generally better.
5. Movie theaters are plentiful.
6. Many establishments have liberal 24-hour policies.
7. Bossa nova music provides a danceable, reassuring backdrop.
8. There are people like you who already reside here, and you may find them.
9. These people will understand you.
10. Things will be great, for sure.

In autumn of 1995, Quincy had a very short haircut, much like Winona's hair in this particular film. There is a scene in *Girl, Interrupted* where Ryder sits on the floor and plays "Downtown" on an acoustic guitar, and—the moment I saw it— it completely reminded me of the Saturday morning I walked down into Q's basement bedroom while she was sitting on the carpet playing "Maggie May" on her acoustic guitar, real sad-like, and sporting that same severe haircut. It was the morning after we had drunkenly had sex for the first time, four hours after attending a screening of *Leaving Las Vegas*. That sexual encounter was something that was never supposed to have happened between us, and she was certain it was going to ruin both our lives. I remember feeling extremely guilty because I was so not-so-secretly ecstatic that it had finally happened. But when I saw her playing the guitar, I could tell that we were about to have a bone-wrenching discussion about what had happened the night before, and she was going to tell me things I did not want to hear, and that the only reason she slept with me is because she thought it would make me happy, somehow. And even though our relationship lasted for a year beyond that morning, and even though lots of things happened and lots of things changed, it is hard for me to reconcile that she probably hated herself on that overcast Saturday, and I'll always wonder if the remorse she felt while she strummed her guitar never really went away. So, when I finally saw that aforementioned scene from *Girl, Interrupted*—and when I saw this image of Winona playing a guitar that looked exactly like my memory of Quincy playing a guitar—that overcast Saturday morning was immediately what I thought about. It was like getting smashed in the throat with a 38-ounce Louisville Slugger. And the irony is that I've always loved the song "Downtown." It's one of my 50 favorite songs of all time; it's either the happiest sad song ever recorded, or it's the saddest happy song ever recorded. But now, every time I hear Petula Clark's voice from December 1964, I think of a scene from 1999's *Girl, Interrupted*, which makes me think of the morning of February 11, 1996, which makes me feel guilty for prompting a woman to perform a heartfelt rendition of a Rod Stewart song from 1971.

Artists who believe they have any control over the interpretation of their work are completely fooling themselves.

Like most humans, I need food. Unlike most humans, I need food *right now*, lest I consume the living flesh of my own left hand. I'm Donner Party hungry. Utilizing the keypad of my

GPS, I punch the words *Olive Garden* into the computer system. I do this for two reasons. For one, the Olive Garden is good; it always makes me happy. But the second reason is because the Olive Garden is "in the news," sort of. There is currently a popular reality-television show called *The Bachelor,* and it just aired a classic TV moment that is (apparently) unspeakably uproarious: A contestant named Amber was having dinner with the aforementioned Bachelor (tire heir Andrew Firestone), and she asked him, "What's your favorite restaurant chain? I like the Olive Garden." This, you see, is funny, because . . . well, I'm not sure why this is funny, to tell you the truth. And I'm not sure anybody else in America knows, either, but it still got mentioned in *Entertainment Weekly*.

This happens all the time: Americans seem to know what's funny, but they don't know why. I suppose some people would say, "This exchange was funny because the Olive Garden sucks," but that insight isn't really *funny,* you know? Why would going to a bad restaurant be *funny*? Still, everyone I know (myself included) seems well aware that this quote is unspeakably amusing, even though there's no explanation as to why. People behave this way all the time; we all sign a social contract that requires us to universally ridicule certain sentiments on principle, even though no such principle exists. When I was in sixth grade, there was a kid in fifth grade whom everyone called Ippy, a nickname that was supposed to be a combination of the words *imp* and *hippy* (the origin of this moniker remains unclear—it was possibly due to an unorthodox haircut). Ippy was precocious and clever and popular, inasmuch as any fifth grader can be popular. He could draw exceptionally and was well known for his pencil sketches of military aircraft.

But then Ippy became a sixth grader. And then—all of a sudden and for no valid reason—everyone decided they hated him.

For the next two years, Ippy was mercilessly attacked on a daily basis. Almost nobody talked to him, unless they were trying to trick him into drinking a can of Mountain Dew that was half filled with piss. I remember two kids stealing his gym shoes and dropping them into the locker room whirlpool. People would throw half-chewed food at the back of his head while he worked on math problems. This was real horror-show, *Welcome to the Dollhouse* shit, and it emerged out of nowhere. He had done nothing to warrant this. Moreover, the torture ended as capriciously as it began: Halfway through his eighth-grade year, Ippy was completely reabsorbed into the junior high coolness coven. Everyone liked him again, although (for reasons unknown) he was no longer called Ippy; now his nickname was "Caveman," which had to do with the fact that he was the only eighth grader who needed to regularly shave.

Looking back, I have to believe those two years were unspeakably traumatizing for good ol' Ippy. I mean, his experience is retrospectively traumatizing *for me,* and I barely participated in the unexplained hazing. The thing that I can't stop wondering about is how everyone universally agreed to hate that kid; I don't wonder *why* they hated him, because that query clearly has no answer. However, I still wonder *how* it happened. How could *everyone* cruelly agree on something that could not be justified by *anyone*? It wasn't the fear of retribution; there were kids in my school so popular that no one would have turned against them no matter who they did—or did not—befriend (in fact, the one kid who never betrayed Ippy— the photogenic, Skoal-chomping quarterback on our junior high football team—suffered no social stigma whatsoever). And it was more than just mob mentality. Something made all of us *believe* Ippy was a pariah. In fact, I can distinctly recall thinking, "I obviously must hate this kid," even though I didn't; I had shared a school bus seat with Ippy for seven years, and I always thought he was cool (in fact, when I was in third grade, I madly envied his Ace Frehley doll). But this is how popular culture works: You allow yourself to be convinced you're sharing a reality that doesn't exist. Every summer, Hollywood movie studios convince millions of people to see blockbuster movies they know they're going to hate. Every day, shows like *Access Hollywood* force 2 million housewives to ask themselves, "Who really cares who Lindsay Lohan is dating?" And you know what the answer to that question is? *Almost no one.* There are very few Americans who honestly care who Lindsay Lohan is dating. But it's still information they need to have. This is because those people care about something else entirely; they're worried about the possibility of everyone else understanding something that they're missing. This is what they're afraid of, and this is how they deduce societal truth. And that's the same fear that made me hate a totally friendly person from 1985 to 1986: It somehow made sense to hate him. This is also why it seems weird not to laugh at a woman on reality TV who likes the Olive Garden. It somehow makes sense to laugh at what isn't funny.

I can't wait for those fucking breadsticks.

This is not exactly a good story, but it's a good "nonstory": This afternoon, I'm rolling south on I-85 when I see an exit sign. The exit sign reads, CHINA GROVE. The sign (of course) makes me wonder if this is the town the Doobie Brothers sang about in the 1973 hit "China Grove." I take the exit and drive down Main Street; China Grove is a community of maybe 3,200 people, and the city's only Italian restaurant—a place called the Italian Grove—has a sign out front advertising the town's best *buffalo wings* (the South is awesome). I'm looking around for . . . well, I don't know what I'm looking around for, to be honest. Perhaps a statue of "Skunk" Baxter. I'm trying to sing "China

Grove" in my head (in the hope of coming up with a few other geographic clues), but I can't remember any of the words except for the part that goes, *"Whoa oh, China Grove!"* I finally stumble across a guitar shop called Coleman's Music, so I park the Tauntaun and step inside to ask for advice. I am greeted by a man behind the counter with a gray ponytail and a Hawaiian shirt that's open to the fifth button; he is conversing with a bald patron and a dude with radically long hair (possibly an employee) who looks like he should *be in* the fucking Doobie Brothers.

The person behind the counter is the owner, Chip Coleman. I ask him my query.

"What I always tell people when they ask me this—and I've been asked that question seven or eight times a week for the past 18 years—is that you have to listen to the rest of the lyrics," Coleman says. "The lyrics mention being 'way down by San Antone,' so it's about a China Grove that's located in Texas. But I tell ya what: That song is *popular*. When a guy from Japan[1] walks into your store and wants to know if the Doobie Brothers wrote about this town, you start to realize how big a band like that really is."

Coleman is one of those charming "rebel types" you sometimes meet in small towns (I knew loads of them in rural North Dakota, and they usually sold fireworks). His father was a minister. He tells me that the whole town hates him because of his long hair, but I can tell he doesn't seriously believe that. As I start to exit the store, the bald guy stops me. "Hey," he says. "Do you wanna meet someone who used to shoot up the Doobie Brothers?" He proceeds to tell me that his next-door neighbor

---

1. I also find it interesting that this is the second time in the span of a week someone has used "traveling from Japan" as the ultimate indication of rock fanaticism.

is a former Marine Corps nurse who used to inject the Doobie Brothers with heroin while they were on tour; he swears she has pictures of this. I consider the idea of interviewing this woman, but (before I can say yes) the bald guy smiles and says good-bye, and he tells me to have a nice trip. My meeting with the Doobie nurse never happens. So maybe he never actually intended to introduce me to this woman; maybe that was all a lie. But these are good Americans. I could live in China Grove. Or at least that's what I think to myself as I drive away, never to return again.

The sun was still halfway up the sky when I left China Grove, but I'm not going much further. I need to get out of this fucking car; my blood is thick and stagnant. My veins feel like they're filled with turkey gravy. Road signs direct me to a hotel that is on the outskirts of a North Carolina town called Concord, and I check in before 6:00 P.M. It's a huge hotel, but virtually no one is staying here. The plump woman at the front desk seems unusually happy to see me, and she asks a bunch of innocuous questions: Where am I from? Where am I going? Did I get caught in the rain? Do I need to use the hotel's fax machine? After a solitary day of driving, you'd think I'd appreciate the conversation, but I don't. I begin lying to this woman for no reason. She now thinks I'm driving to Las Vegas, which impresses her. I have no redeeming social value.

I take the stairs up two flights to my room and put on yellow shorts, yesterday's Weezer T-shirt, and a different pair of Nikes. It is time to run. My acquaintances in New York tend to act shocked when they discover that I am an avid runner, since the rest of my lifestyle skews unhealthy (my cholesterol is 383). But that is why I *must* run: Running keeps me alive. Physically, I almost never enjoy the process of exercise, but I feel mentally tougher when I finish. More important, running lets me eat anything I want, and it allows me to drink every day (if I need to). So I run, and I run fast. I run with focus. In 1989, I could run 400 meters in 53.9 seconds. And the fact that I can so precisely remember this reminds me why I will never, ever be cool.

There is a little gravel path behind the hotel, and I run the path, loping like a pronghorn buck (a.k.a. North America's fleetest ungulate). The earth is crimson and the air is dense; it's like jogging through the Dead Sea. The sky is dark and there is jagged lightning on the horizon. I smell ozone. Within 90 seconds, I'm sweating like Patrick Ewing, but I can feel the muscles in my calves slowly regain their elasticity after hours in the Tauntaun. This North Carolina oxygen is delicious; no wonder those slack motherfuckers in Superchunk always seemed so happy. This might be the greatest running experience I've had in seven to ten years.

The path forks: One trail remains flat, the other goes up a hill. I take the hill. I'm Jerry Rice. I'm Sergei Bubka. I'm Franka Potente. This is perfect. But as my legs pump like grand prix pistons, and as I physically dominate this inanimate mound of red earth, my mind drifts to a slightly darker question: If I died right here, how long would it take for people to find out?

Let's pretend I had a heart attack halfway up this hill (or let's say I conquered the hill and got struck by a rogue bolt of the aforementioned lightning). Certainly, no one would find me tonight; this path is underused and the sky is rapidly fading to black. I suspect someone would find my body tomorrow morning. But I'm wearing running clothes, and I'm carrying no identification, and I'm at least two miles from the hotel; the authorities probably wouldn't figure out who I was until the day *after* tomorrow. Using the information from my rental car, they'd call *Spin* early on Wednesday morning. But nobody ever shows up at the *Spin* offices until 10:30 A.M., so they'd just leave a phone message.

Now, the first person who gets to *Spin* every day is a Bouncing Souls fan named Caryn, but I doubt she would return this call; she'd just tell the managing editor that we received a message from a cop in North Carolina. Our managing editor would call the authorities that afternoon; she'd then inform Sia about what had transpired, and then there would be a meeting in Sia's office. In this meeting, everybody would find out I was dead. I think several people would cry, but definitely not everybody. Work would be dismissed for the afternoon, unless we were closing an issue. Someone would have to call my parents, but probably not Sia; I suspect Sia would be crying *a lot*. Calling my mom would be the managing editor's job. Meanwhile, *Spin* reviews editor Alex Pappademas would take the responsibility of informing my roommates that I was dead, because Alex could get my roommate Michael's cell phone number from our mutual friend Farrin (these relationships grow incredibly complicated when you start to think about them realistically). My Manhattan roommates, Michael and David, would have no idea who to contact, but I suspect Michael would call my editor at Scribner, our ex-coworker David Giffels in Akron, and possibly Sarah Jackson (who now lives in Olympia, Washington), because Michael and Sarah dated three years ago (and I assume he still has her number). Sarah would immediately tell my buddy Ross, and Ross would inherit the obligation of informing just about everyone else who's ever met me. Then again, my sister-in-law in North Dakota knows the father of my college friend Jon Blixt, so perhaps Jon would find out (via his father) the day after my mom was phoned by our managing editor. Jon would then tell two people (Mike Schauer and Mr. Pancake), and the three of them would have to do all the expository work. Jon would actually be terrific at this; he's very efficient. I bet he could make all the necessary calls in less than two hours.

Since she works in the office, Diane would find out about my termination at the initial *Spin* meeting, unless Sia told her privately beforehand. Lenore would be informed by Ross, and I bet she would wear black at my funeral; this is excellent, because Lenore looks amazingly hot in black. Quincy might not find out for weeks, unless Mr. Pancake still has her e-mail address (which I doubt). Q would probably miss my funeral. One of my closest drinking companions from the early '90s was a fellow named Shane Howatt, but I have no idea where he even lives anymore; he might *never* find out I'm dead. In fact, it's entirely possible that *he's* dead and I just don't know about it.

I don't want to die, but I certainly adore the idea of being dead. I know it's pathetic to enjoy the notion of your friends calling each other to discuss your untimely demise, but I love it. Maybe *Spin* would dedicate an issue to me. Maybe they would run a one-page obituary, which would be written by either Alex or senior editor Jon Dolan. Maybe they'd each get to write blurbs about me; this would be fascinating because they both have unique blurbing styles. Jon would likely compare me to some dead genius I've never even heard of (possibly Joseph Mitchell). Alex would quote especially poignant Thin Lizzy lyrics (probably something from the second verse of "The Rocker"). I hope the blurbs are not too somber, though; I hope they stress that I had a great life and that I was already ready to die when I turned 27. No need to be maudlin about this. My death is no tragedy. I've climbed every mountain, really.

Twelve more strides and the hill is mine. This is the run of a lifetime. I'm a driver. I'm a winner. But things aren't going to change, and I can't feel it. I'm not a loser, baby, so no one is gonna kill me. I anticlimactically arrive at the top of my mountain, and then I head back down.

At the moment, nobody in New York knows that I'm dead. And this is because I am not.

➤   ➤   ➤

Hotel showers are flawless. Within the realm of your hotel shower, you are an emperor. A tyrant! Everything is designed solely for you: one little bar of soap, one little bottle of shampoo, and a circular heating lamp stationed above your skull. I can hear the TV while I rinse off my North Carolina sweat; it's a preseason football game between the Green Bay Packers and the Kansas City Chiefs. They're playing the Hall of Fame Game in Canton, Ohio, and nobody cares. Even Al Michaels is unabashedly stating that the game's final outcome is meaningless. There's something interesting about the way Americans completely disregard exhibition sporting events; when you really think about it, *all* sporting events are "exhibitions." Nothing is truly at stake. There are never any profound consequences for the winners or the losers; if the Packers lose, we won't execute Ahman Green or sell Brett Favre into slavery. At their core, the final outcome to *every* football game (including the Super Bowl) is wholly meaningless. So how did we all become convinced that a preseason game is somehow different than the 16 "legitimate" games Green Bay will start playing next month? Who decides what matters and what does not? How do we know the things that we know? There is no truth. There is no culture.

I am unsure why the water in this hotel shower is making me think like a Maoist.

Meanwhile, Mr. Favre throws a meaningless preseason incompletion while I joylessly dry myself and consider where I shall eat supper. Outside, the rain has started to fall. Perhaps I can find a restaurant that will let me sit by a window and stare at the lightning. That would be moving. I see no difference between romance and solitude.

It turns out I only need to drive 45 seconds to find the establishment I desire: There is a Cracker Barrel across the road.

Cracker Barrel is sublime: You can order chicken and dumplings *with a side order of dumplings*. That's advanced. I buy a newspaper and tell the hostess I want to sit by the window, but only families get to do that—you need at least five people to get window seats. Instead, my booth overlooks the Cracker Barrel outlet store, a cluttered shop where travelers buy $22 sweatshirts promoting the state flag of North Carolina. It reminds me of the Chilean flag. I see no difference between commerce and patriotism.

My Cracker Barrel waitress is more beautiful than Elizabeth Taylor in *Cat on a Hot Tin Roof*. Actually, that's not true; my Cracker Barrel waitress is an ectomorphic 19-year-old woman with a semi-tragic haircut and slightly big teeth. However, by the time our four-minute conversation ends, I will be in love with her.

"What brings you through here?" she asks when she delivers the menu.

"I'm writing this story about dead people," I say. "I'm driving around the country visiting the locations of famous rock-star deaths. Like, tomorrow I'm driving to where Duane Allman died."

"Who?"

"Duane Allman. He was a rock star from the '70s."

She registers no response to this description. Maybe she blinked, but I doubt it. So I keep talking.

"He was in the Allman Brothers Band, which is kind of funny, because after he died, there ended up being only *one* Allman brother in the Allman *Brothers* Band. His brother is Gregg Allman. Gregg Allman was married to Cher for like a week in 1975."

"That doesn't matter," she says. "But what will you do when you get to the place where he died?"

"I actually have no idea," I admit. "I'll just . . . I guess I'll just walk around the general vicinity of where his motorcycle accident happened. Did I mention he died in a motorcycle crash? He died in a motorcycle crash. I don't really have a plan, though. I guess I probably should."

"That's an interesting vacation," she says.

"It's a not a vacation," I say. "I'm going to write about it for a magazine."

"Well, what's the point of your article, sugar?" And she really did refer to me as "sugar," which is a totally discombobulating thing to hear from someone born in 1984.

"I don't know if there *is* a point," I say. "I mean, there *will* be a point, I assume, but I don't have one yet. I'm hoping the story will just be this hazy, morbid trip across America. Kind of like a dream. I want to write something that feels like an unsentimental dream."

"Like Kafka," she says. And at the risk of sounding condescending and elitist, this blows my fucking mind.

"Yes," I say. "Yes, exactly. I mean, I could never write anything that good, of course, but . . . yes. Yes. Like Kafka! Exactly. Do you *like* Franz Kafka?"

"Can I ask you a question about dreaming?"

"Yes," I say. "Yes, you can. You can absolutely ask me a question about dreaming. That would be tremendous. Yes, you can. What is your name?"

"Mary Beth," she says. "So here is my question: Have you ever had a dream that seemed to last five years, even though you were only asleep for a few hours? Or did you ever have a dream that seemed to last *100 years*? Or have you ever had a dream where you were married to someone for your entire life? Or a dream where you were lost in the arctic circle for decades and decades and decades?"

"Yes!" I say. "Yes I have. I completely understand where you are coming from."

"Okay, cool. Now—obviously—dreams don't last 100 years. Dreams last like 20 minutes. So that means we are somehow able to understand an accelerated passage of time while we dream. We can just naturally tell—somehow—whether the dream is happening in 'real time,' or if it's happening in 'dream time.' And if it's happening in dream time, what we experience in the span of 20 minutes can *feel* like a span of 20 years. You follow me?"

"Yes. Absolutely. You are absolutely right."

"Okay, cool. But that's not my question." She adjusts her Lisa Loeb–like eyeglasses and places her hand on her hip. "My question is this: Are we only able to understand this because of books and movies and television? Because the difference between real time and dream time seems like something that would be impossible to understand organically."

"Why do you possibly work here?" I ask.

"Take me seriously," she says.

"I am taking you *very* seriously," I say. "I am taking you more seriously than any woman I have ever met in a restaurant."

"Ha," she says, but she does not laugh. "What I'm wondering is if TV taught people how to have longer dreams. Because TV is always flashing forward: If sitcom characters are in the living room, and then a commercial for Tide comes on, and then those same people are suddenly lying in bed when the show returns, we all automatically understand that time has advanced. We just take for granted that the story has moved from daytime to nighttime. This is something we have all come to understand completely, and without even trying. Books do this all the time, too. Like, I'm reading *One Hundred Years of Solitude* right now, and—"

"What in the hell is going on here?"

"—and the unspoken encroachment of time is the crux of that entire book. You couldn't write that book if people didn't understand narrative time travel, because the story could never be told in real time. Nobody can read for 100 straight years. So what I'm wondering is how people dreamt *before* the invention of media. And not just before movies and TV but even before printed novels. I mean, how would a caveman dream? Would his dreams only happen in real time, like in Kiefer Sutherland's *24*? How could the subconscious mind of a caveman calibrate the idea of two things happening 10 years apart?"

"Well, there was always oral tradition," I say, "and even the most rudimentary kind of storytelling demands that the listener imagine the passing of time. I suppose the larger question is how a caveman could tell the difference between his 'actual life' and his dream life, since I would have to assume they'd be identical; they'd probably both involve a lot of mastodon hunting. But regardless, I find your ideas fascinating. You are a fascinating Cracker Barrel waitress."

"Thank you," Mary Beth says. "I like to think about crazy shit sometimes."

"So do I," I say. "That's all I like to think about, to be honest. But why did you tell this dream stuff to *me*? Do you talk to all your customers like this?"

"Oh, God no," she says. "I thought maybe you were smart, because you were reading the newspaper."

"But, but . . . but this is *USA Today*!"

"I know," she says. "But you also looked bored. And you have glasses."

And then Mary Beth walks away. And when she brings me my side order of dumplings, she barely even smiles.

I see no difference between winning and losing.

The rain hits my hotel-room window in inconsistent sheets, almost as if some meteorological hooligan is throwing buckets of water at the side of the building every time a wind machine kicks up. It must be raining everywhere, because a man on TV just told me that the Chiefs beat the Packers 9–0 in the aforementioned Hall of Fame game, but the exhibition was canceled in the second half because of rain. Preseason football may as well be baseball.

I turned off the television seconds ago, so the room is pitch black. My eyes have not yet adjusted. I'm suddenly inside a Dixieland sarcophagus. The sound of the rain is putting me to sleep, but I want to stay awake and listen to it thwack against the glass. I love a rainy night; perhaps not to the extent of Eddie Rabbitt, but still. There was a time when Quincy couldn't sleep unless she heard rain: Every night in her apartment, she would put on her pajamas and slip one of those hokey "thunderstorm" CDs into her stereo, and the fake rain would fall for hours and hours on repeat. Even when it was actually raining, she would play that ridiculous thunderstorm disc. "This is crazy," I would say. "This is like bringing a Walkman into a rock concert. Let's just listen to the rain *for real*." My argument always failed. "It's not the same," she would say. "The rain doesn't sound like rain. It's not rainy enough." It was never rainy enough.

Before I got into bed tonight, I checked my e-mail. There was a sweet message from Diane. I miss her very much and I want to call her. But I'm afraid if I call her, she won't answer. And if she doesn't answer, I'll wonder why, and my unconscious conclusion will be that she must be having sex with someone else. That notion is unjustified, but it's what I always assume whenever a women I love doesn't pick up the phone. I start thinking about Quincy again, and I wonder if she is listening to her rain disc as she lies next to her architect boyfriend. My thoughts are maudlin. I also think about Lenore, who is undoubtedly sleeping by a lake in Minnesota, probably in only a T-shirt. My thoughts are lascivious. I also think about Mary Beth, the

Cracker Barrel waitress who reads Kafka. I bet Mary Beth sleeps in sweatpants. Should I have asked Mary Beth to come over to my hotel for drinks? Did I totally blow it? Maybe I would have seemed like an exotic literary stranger, dashing across the country with my radical ideas about Duane Allman, coolly buying vodka tonics for underage ingenues. In the empty hotel bar, she would have said, "I'll go home as soon as the rain stops." But the rain never stopped. We would have kept drinking. She would be in my room right now, 85 percent naked. I would be lecturing about George Orwell's relationship to Queensrÿche's *Operation: Mindcrime* album, and she would be fascinated, partially because of my insights but mostly because I come from New York and cavalierly read the *USA Today* while waiting for dumplings. "I never do things like this," she would say. "I know you don't," I would respond. My thoughts are unoriginal.

In my mind, I am in three different beds with three different women, and Diane is having unmatchable sex with a faceless stranger who does not exist. In reality, I am alone in the dark, afraid to make a phone call to a woman who is probably asleep.

I can still hear the rain, but I want it to be louder. I want it to keep me awake.

It's never rainy enough.

THE SIXTH DAY

Los Angeles ➤ Ice Age Coming, Ice Age Coming ➤
The Meaning of What Is Interesting

"I don't think I can make it to California."

I am speaking on my cell phone inside the RaceTrac, a colossal truck stop in Massoponax, Virginia; I am sitting in a red vinyl booth in front of a plate covered with lumpy white gravy and chicken-fried chicken. My striking blonde editor is on the line, and I can't help but imagine how all the bearded truckers who currently surround me would be way impressed if they could see what she looks like. Of course, this fantasized envy would suggest that they could (somehow) see through a phone line and into another city, yet they would still (somehow) misinterpret the relationship I have with my editor. This is, of course, illogical; if they had the omnipotence to see two disjointed people simultaneously, one would assume they'd likewise possess the power to understand the context of what these two people were talking about. My imagination has problems with plot mechanics.

"Why can't you go to California?" she asks. "I think you need to get there."

"But it's already been six days, and I've only made it to Virginia," I say. "If I have to drive down to Joshua Tree after I get to Seattle and then back up to Los Angeles to get to LAX, that will take at least three more days. I don't want to live like this." My initial strategy was to end this road trip in Room 8 of the Joshua Tree Inn, the motel where Gram Parsons died in 1973 after replacing his blood with Jack Daniel's, cocaine, barbiturates, morphine, and THC. I intended to replicate that evening, but that's not going to happen. Still, Sia has hope.

"It would be great if you looked into Biggie's death while you were in L.A., though," she says. "And that would be just a few hours from Vegas, so you could also do Tupac." Biggie Smalls (a.k.a. the Notorious B.I.G.) was the New York rapper "assassinated" in 1997, just six months after Tupac Shakur had been "assassinated" after watching a 109-second Tyson fight at the MGM Grand. Those murders marked the height of the rap war between the East Coast and the West Coast, and conspiracy theorists continue to intertwine the two murders. Rock magazines will run retrospective stories about the impact of those two killings for the next five decades, partially because they're culturally significant but primarily because most white rock critics feel extremely ashamed about not being black.

"Sia, I am calling you to *shorten* this trip. I am not calling you to make it longer. And who even knows where the fuck Biggie was killed? Those details have been lost to the sands of time. Nobody remembers that shit."

"It was a drive-by shooting outside the Petersen Automotive Museum," she says. "He was sitting in his car. It was at a party following the Soul Train Music Awards." I had forgotten that Sia was one of the last reporters to interview Biggie before he died. I had also forgotten than Sia is approximately four times smarter than I am.

"Maybe so," I respond. "This is your decision. If you really, really, *really* want me to go to Los Angeles, I'll go to Los Angeles."

"Don't you want to cruise the Sunset Strip?"

"No."

"Why not? Lots of excellent people died there."

"I'm tired."

"Are you drunk?"

"What?"

"Are you drunk?"

"Sia, it's 1:20 in the afternoon."

"Well, whatever, fine, I don't care. If you feel you have enough material by the time you get to Seattle, you can skip California. But I think you'd have an awesome time in Los Angeles."

"Sia, I hate Los Angeles."

"You could write about dead strippers."

"Sia, I hate Los Angeles."

"You could try to get shot by Phil Spector."

"Sia, I hate Los Angeles."

"You could write about Hanoi Rocks drummer Razzle Dingley."

"That's a valid point," I say. "I'll think about it. But I'm going to eat some chicken-fried chicken now."

"Awesome. See you in a month, assuming you don't die in a car accident."

"I suppose."

"Good-bye, Chuck."

Sia always acts surprised when I tell her I hate L.A. She always seems to think I should I love it. It remains unclear how she came to this conclusion: I'm shocked by anyone who doesn't consider Los Angeles to be anything less than a bozo-saturated hellhole. It is pretty much without question the worst city in America. The reason "Walking in L.A." by Missing Persons was the most accidentally prescient single of 1982 was because of its unfathomable (but wholly accurate) specificity: Los Angeles is the only city in the world where the process of *walking on the sidewalk* could somehow be (a) political, and (b) humiliating. It is the only community I've ever visited where absolutely every cliché proved to be completely accurate. The first time I landed in LAX, I went to the rental-car agency, and the only vehicles available were Ford Aerostars and Mustang convertibles. That was all they had in stock: You could get a minivan or you could get a sports car. This is because everyone who flies into Los Angeles is either (a) going to Disneyland, or (b) meeting with Colin Farrell at Sky Bar. It shocks me that the *Los Angeles Times* has a circulation of 1.3 million; I have yet to hear anyone in California ever mention current events in any context whatsoever, unless you count speculation over whose contract has been renewed on *The O.C.* Now—normally—this would not be a problem; I don't care if 85 percent of Los Angeles is stupid. I can deal with the stupid. My problem is that every stupid person in Los Angeles is also (a) unyieldingly narcissistic, and (b) unyieldingly nice. They have somehow managed to combine raging megalomania with genuine friendliness. It's a personality combination that infects your blood like leukemia. After two days in the Malibu sun, you find yourself admiring people you hate. You start to see an integrity to networking. You start to think that writing a screenplay might be more productive than writing a novel, because screenplay writing seems more artistically effective and way, way, way easier. What follows is the opening sequence of a major motion picture I first conceived during a 2003 visit to SoCal; it is a major motion picture I have tentatively titled . . .

EVERY CONVERSATION I'VE EVER HAD EVERY TIME I'VE EVER GONE TO LOS ANGELES FOR ANY REASON WHATSOEVER

ACT 1
SCENE 1

[Scene opens on the outdoor patio of the Standard Hotel at 8300 Sunset Boulevard. It is January or possibly July. **CHUCK** is sitting at a table in the bar, waiting to interview some shitty rock band (probably Audioslave). He is looking poolside at four mildly attractive women, three of whom have fake breasts and two of whom are bulimic. CHUCK is approached by 22-year-old **BLANDLY HANDSOME WAITER** with extremely thick triceps.]

BLANDLY HANDSOME WAITER:

Do you, like, need more Pepsi? Or some, you know, soup?

CHUCK:

This was a Coke.

BLANDLY HANDSOME WAITER:

Oh yeah. You're right! My bad, dude. My bad. That one is all on me, dude. Hey, can I mention something? Don't take this the wrong way, but that's a really great T-shirt you're wearing. Is that the logo for a band, or do you just dig elephants? Not that it matters or anything, because it's totally fucking cool regardless, but I'm really interested in graphic design and I was just curious about some of those fonts, which actually look a lot like a poster I designed in high school that got a lot of attention in certain circles of the graphic design community. Believe it or not, I'm kind of a "font guy." Nobody believes that, but it's true. There are a lot of people

79

out here who think I should have pursued graphic design full-time, as in like a job, and some of my friends still tell me I should just freelance out of my apartment and design stuff for record labels and some of the smaller studios, and I *would* be totally willing to do that if the right opportunity came along, and I actually have a good relationship with several of the people at Warner Bros. and Shady Acres and Columbia Tri-Star, so that might be happening in the future. Who knows, you know? But the fact of the matter is that graphic design is not my passion, and I'm not going to throw my energy into something I'm not passionate about—unless the opportunity is just too good to ignore. But even then, I could never completely commit to being a designer, even though I sort of have a natural knack for composition and font selection. I'm absolutely a visual person.

CHUCK:

That's tremendous.

BLANDLY HANDSOME WAITER:

Man, it's just so great to meet somebody who's obviously not in the industry. I'm always stoked to get fresh impressions from someone who has a clue, and I can already tell *you* know what the fuck is going *on*. When I moved out here, it was such a mind fuck. I came from this bum-fuck town in Texas you've probably never of—it's called Austin, and it's actually the state capital, which most people don't realize, because they assume the capital must be Dallas—and when I finally got to L.A., the first thing I realized is that I didn't know anything. I mean, I was really smart in high school—all the people I grew up with always assumed I'd go to Harvard or Notre Dame or LSU or Yale or wherever—but I wasn't *culturally sophisticated*. You know? And what I mean by that is that I didn't understand all the shit that you need to do in order to make it at this level, or on any major level. Obviously, the level I'm at now is not where I want to be in six months, but—considering how long I've been here, which isn't that long, and considering my experience, which I'm still getting—I'm at a really *great* level. A pretty incredible level. It's maybe one, maybe two levels below the level where I can completely start having input into my own decisions, which is really the only way to control yourself as a talent. And if things keep going as they are—and I really have no reason to assume they won't—I should be at that level in six or nine months. It's hard, though. It's fucking tough. One thing I've really learned is that guys like Ben Affleck and Keanu Reeves aren't just cool-looking guys, which is what most people think. They're incredibly, incredibly smart. You wouldn't believe it. They are so creatively orientated. I was getting fucked-up at the side bar at the Casa Marquis a few months ago, and Affleck was down there with his posse . . . this is before he went to rehab. Anyway, I was kind of hanging out by their table, just sort of chillin' like Bob Dylan, and you would not believe the shit that was coming out of Affleck's mouth. He was talking about how technology was changing film-making, and it was like being at a lecture at USC. I was just like, What the fuck? How the fuck does he even know this shit? And it started to occur to me that this was why he made $7 million for *Boiler Room* and $11.5 million for *Pearl Harbor*. I mean, I know he's widely considered to be a hot guy, but we're *all* hot guys, you know? I mean, he has a *look,* I suppose—kind of that classic, old Hollywood, Tom Cruise-on-steroids look. But I have a *look*. You have a *look,* sort of. We all have a *look*. But that's not enough. Bruce Lee always said he considered the mind to be his greatest weapon, and I totally understand why he would say that.

CHUCK:

[*pause*]

Chuck Klosterman

BLANDLY HANDSOME WAITER:

Great example of what we're talking about: Lots of people assume I'm a model. For all I know, maybe *you* assumed I'm a model, because that's not uncommon. And if you did, don't worry, because I completely take that as a compliment. But the fact of the matter is that I'm not a model. Now, *would I do some modeling* if given the right situation? Probably, and I have almost done so in the past. Because it's easy money, right? Well, yes and no. Yes, it's easy in the sense that you're being paid to wear clothes. But it's harder than that. Good models make it look easy. They just make it look like they're people wearing clothes . . . just dudes being cool and looking at their watch and shit. But what you have to realize—*when you're modeling*—is that there is no way to communicate beyond just standing around or walking. Obviously, I'm an idea person, so I want to project my ideas onto everything I do. I want to attack the world with love, but also with my own style. So if you're somebody like me, or if you're just somebody who is really trying to project an idea that is more than just a great jacket or great pants or whatever, you need to concentrate like a mother-fucker every moment of the photo shoot. You gotta be a full-on laser beam. You can never break focus. Because that's the only way to project your ideas in a non-communicative way. Now, I'm not necessarily saying all models are as message-orientated as myself, but I do believe that some of them probably are, as I have many friends in that industry. But I'm not ready to make that kind of commitment to a career that only vaguely intrigues me, because— for me—it's got to be all or nothing.

CHUCK:

That's a remarkable perspective. This was Coke, by the way.
[CHUCK jams a steak knife into his own heart . . .
twice . . . not unlike singer-songwriter Elliott Smith.
End of scene 1]

KILLING YOURSELF TO LIVE

ACT 1
SCENE 2

[Fantasy sequence ends; narrator, who will not be continuing on to Los Angeles, returns to car and previous cross-country narrative. He's in Georgia now.]

Like Han Solo trapped in a Hoth blizzard, I have to pull my Tauntaun off the road. The weather conditions dictate my immobility; it's pouring so hard I can't see the lines on the highway. If rain is God crying, I think God is drunk and his girlfriend just slept with Zeus. It never rains like this is New York; there are almost never thunderstorms there. In New York, it rains the way it rains on TV. It used to storm like this in Akron, and that was electrifying. Northeast Ohio has the loudest thunder in North America (I suspect that might have to do with the cool air that forms over Lake Erie, but this is merely my own hypothesis). The downpour I'm experiencing right now is the real deal, though: Georgian rain can bring the pain. The silver dollar droplets are beating the crap out of my car. As previously noted, I love listening to rain. I realize this is a pretty cliché thing to love, but I am a cliché person (at least I am when it comes to thinking about the weather).

It occurs to me that pulling onto the shoulder of the highway might be a potentially deadly decision, because truckers never stop driving (regardless of the weather). Some 18-wheel Peterbilt behemoth could plow into me while I sit here listening to water collide with my roof, and I'd never know what hit me. This possibility creates an interesting quandary: I can drive ahead blindly and risk hitting somebody else, or I can sit here and risk being clobbered by something coming up behind me. I decide to remain motionless. I am not proactive. The rain makes me turn up the stereo, and I want to play the new Radio-

head album *Hail to the Thief,* chiefly because it has one song
("Sit Down, Stand Up") in which Thom Yorke repeats the
phrase "the rain drops" 46 consecutive times. Unfortunately,
my copy of *Hail to the Thief* is a burned promo copy sent
directly from Capitol Records, and the laser in the Tauntaun's
CD player refuses to recognize its right to exist. As an alternative, I put in Radiohead's *Kid A,* which forces me to stare into
the falling rain and think about domestic terrorism.

My memories of September 11, 2001, are—I think—entirely
inconsequential. This is partially because I was living in Ohio at
the time but mostly because everybody in the United States has
an anecdote about what they were doing that day, and almost all
of those anecdotes have become boring. The events of 9/11 are
often compared to the events of a nightmare. This is a surprisingly savvy analogy, because hearing someone's memories from
the morning of 9/11 is not unlike having someone preface a conversation with the words, "I had the weirdest dream last night."
When someone wants to talk about a dream, you can never say,
"I don't care." You have to care. You just have to stand there
and listen, because people who talk about their dreams are
actually trying to tell you things about themselves they'd never
admit in normal conversation. It is a way for people to be honest without telling the truth. It's the same situation with people
who need to give you a detailed account of what they were
doing on September 11. You cannot say, "I don't care." You
have to care. You have to listen, because that person is actually
trying to show you that they can talk about life without the
safety of ironic distance. September 11 is one issue every American can be completely earnest and unguarded about.

That being the case, I have nothing to say about what happened to me that morning. However, I do have something to say
about Radiohead's *Kid A.* It's something I actually wanted to
write about in the *Akron Beacon Journal* two weeks after Sep-

tember 11, but everyone I knew advised me that it would probably end my career. In retrospect, that seems like a hyperbolic overreaction—but people have forgotten how reactionary America felt during that period. I probably *would* have lost my job. People have mentally blocked out that one-month window when you simply could not talk about popular culture *at all*, except to say how vapid it was and how we as a society would never be interested in anything frivolous again; this was that brief era when every U.S. citizen suddenly decided they were "political," and all these Ikea shoppers who couldn't remain focused for an entire episode of *Will and Grace* were suddenly commenting on the volatility of Syria. This was that bizarre period when lefty pacifists who had voted for Ralph Nader were suddenly dropping terms like "glass parking lot" into conversations about Afghanistan.

Those circumstances are why I never wrote about how Thom Yorke accidentally predicted the events of September 11 on *Kid A*.

Five hours after the attacks on New York and D.C., I was driving all over Akron, trying to interview average people for a story about the "local reaction" to what had happened (as if—somehow—the citizens of Akron would provide a unique emotional perspective on this tragedy, such as blaming the attacks on Art Modell). *Kid A* was in my car's CD player, and I played it whenever NPR became too depressing, which was always. That night, I remember thinking how all those swoony, shadowy *Kid A* tracks seemed to reflect the attacks on the World Trade Center. But I dismissed that idea immediately. I assumed that this was akin to how—if you're in the midst of breaking up with someone—every pop song on the radio seems to directly address the way you feel at that very moment. It occurred to me that anything I had been playing that afternoon would have undoubtedly felt like a terrorist attack; had I played Michael

Jackson's *Off the Wall*, it would likely have had the same effect.

Except that it wouldn't have.

Maybe it would have on that afternoon, but not beyond supper. Not beyond the moment when I wasn't freaked and my feelings started to normalize. However, the opposite thing happened with *Kid A*. The more I played it, the more this connection became real. And it keeps getting more and more symbolic, and the imagery becomes more and more lucid, no matter how often I listen. There are those who made similar points about Wilco's *Yankee Hotel Foxtrot*, primarily because that album includes songs with titles like "Ashes of American Flags" and "War on War." However, that record also has songs about watching KISS cover bands and raking the leaves. *Kid A* has no gaps in logic, perhaps because its logic is never overt; it almost seems like a musical storyboard for that particular day. I played it compulsively for an entire year. At this point, I am certain *Kid A* is the official soundtrack for September 11, 2001, even though it was released on October 3, 2000.

The first song on *Kid A* paints the Manhattan skyline at 8:00 A.M. on Tuesday morning; the song is titled, "Everything in Its Right Place." People woke up that day *"sucking on a lemon,"* because that's what life normally feels like on the Manhattan subway; the city is a beautiful, sour, sarcastic place. We soon move to song two, which is the title track. It is the sound of woozy, ephemeral normalcy. It is the sound of Jonny Greenwood playing an Ondes Martenot, an instrument best remembered for it's use in the *Star Trek* theme song. You can imagine humans walking to work, riding elevators, getting off the C train and the 3 train, and thinking about a future that will be a lot like the present, only better. The term *Kid A* is Yorke's moniker for the first cloned human, which he (only half jokingly) suspects may already exist. The consciously misguided message is this:

Science is the answer. Technology solves everything because technology is invulnerable. And this is what almost everyone in America thought at around 8:30 A.M. But something happens three and a half minutes into "Kid A." It suddenly doesn't feel right, and you don't exactly know why. This is followed by track three, "The National Anthem."

This is when the first plane slams into the north tower at 470 mph.

"The National Anthem" sounds a bit like a Morphine song. It's a completely different direction from the first two songs on *Kid A*, and it's confusing; it's chaotic. *"What's going on?"* the lyrics ask. *"What's going on?"* It gets crazier and crazier, until the second plane hits the second tower (at 9:03 A.M. in reality and at 3:42 in the song). For a moment, things are somber. But then it gets more anarchic.[1] Which leads into track four, "How to Disappear Completely." This is the point where it feels like the world is possibly ending. People try to convince themselves that they are not there. People keep repeating, *"This isn't happening."* People are *"floating"* (read: falling) to the earth. We are told of strobe lights and blown speakers; there are fireworks and hurricanes. This is a song about being burned alive and jumping out of windows, and this is a song about having to watch those things happen. And it's followed by an instrumental piece without melody ("Treefingers"), because what can you say when skyscrapers collapse? All you can do is stare at them with your hand over your mouth.

Time passes. It's afternoon. *Kid A*'s side two, if you have it on vinyl. Action is replaced by thought. The song is "Optimistic," a word that becomes more meaningful in its absence. It has lyrics about Ground Zero (*"vultures circle the dead"*), and it

---

1. Reader's Note: You may want to consider playing *Kid A* right about now, since I'm not always so good at explaining shit like this.

offers a glimpse into how Al Qaeda members think Americans perceive international diplomacy (*"the big fish eat the little ones, the big fish eat the little ones / Not my problem, give me some"*). Track seven, "In Limbo," is about how the United States has been shaken out of its fantasy, with *"nowhere to hide,"* finding only *"trap doors that open, I spiral down."* Now we're at "Idioteque," where it's *"women and children first."* Survivors slowly conclude, *"I'm alive."* Unlike "How to Disappear," "Idioteque" offers the first moment of acceptance: We concede, *"this is really happening."* We wonder *"who's in a bunker"* across the ocean, trying to murder us for working in a 110-story office building? Yorke says, *"We're not scaremongering,"* yet some of us already are; there is an *"ice age coming, ice age coming."* In "Morning Bell," a shell-shocked nation becomes uncharacteristically compassionate (*"Everyone wants to become a friend"*), but there is no way to deal with loss: On "Motion Picture Soundtrack," Thom sings, *"Red wine and sleeping pills / Help me get back to your arms."* Suddenly, everyone needs Vicodin. Everyone needs to drink more merlot. We fill our void with *cheap sex* and *sad films*, and, *baby*, we think we're *crazy*. But there is no answer to the question of reality, except the faith that there is something greater than this world, which is how *Kid A* ends: *"I will see you in the next life."* And maybe you will, and maybe you won't. It's always 50-50.

Now, please do not misinterpret my thoughts on this album; I am not saying that we should have been warned by it, or that John Ashcroft should have played *Kid A* in spring 2001 and said, "You know, we really need to ramp up airport security." I am also not suggesting that Thom Yorke is some kind of pop Nostradamus; in fact, the opposite is probably true. When composing this album in the wake of Radiohead's *OK Computer*, Yorke had a severe case of writer's block and resorted to scribbling discarded lyrics on scraps of paper, throwing them all into a top hat and withdrawing them at random, one line at a time (Yorke apparently got this idea from a technique David Byrne used when writing the 1980 Talking Heads album *Remain in Light*). Lyrically, there is no conscious structure to *Kid A*'s songs *at all*. Which is, of course, the only way this could have happened. A genius can be a genius by trying to be a genius; a visionary can only have a vision by accident.

If there was ever a band doomed to die by the side of the road, it was the Allman Brothers. And I don't say this because of how they lived or because they deserved to be punished for unnamed sins; I say this because the only thing I know about the Allman Brothers Band is that they seem to die a lot. Still, they did record "Whipping Post," a song title that is ironically yelled at indie-rock concerts almost as often as "Free Bird." This counts for something.

The well-documented coincidence about the Allman deaths is that two members of the band—Duane Allman and the Other Guy—died in motorcycle accidents at the same Macon, Georgia, intersection, almost exactly one year apart (Duane in 1971, and the Other Guy[2] in '72). The crossroads are Forsyth and Zebulon, and they're remarkably difficult to find: The Tauntaun's GPS doesn't even recognize Zebulon Road as an existing street. I have to ask several gas station employees for geographic assistance, and—holy fucking Christ—the people of Macon *love* to give driving directions. They are constantly pointing out landmarks and giving me advice like, "Ya gotta keep to the left after you hit the new Denny's," but this is actually *more* confusing, as I am woefully uninformed as to when specific Denny's franchises in the greater Macon area have opened and/or closed.

Eventually, I find the Forsyth/Zebulon nexus. It does not

2. Who's sometimes referred to as "Berry Oakley."

seem dangerous: It's just a main road with a paved tributary, and the speed limit is posted at 45 mph. The power lines are slung low, kind of like the way Cliff Burton of Metallica used to wear his bass before he died in 1986 (a tour bus fell on him outside of Copenhagen). Across the street, there is a State Farm Insurance branch and an animal clinic. Nothing marks the site of impact. I try to deduce how a motorcycle accident might occur, and I really can't do it beyond imaging a conventional car-bike collision that could have just as easily happened anywhere else in America. I also have a hard time feeling sympathy for the victims, since I always assume anyone riding a motorcycle probably wants to die (and kind of deserves it if they do). I will pay anyone $1 if they can explain to me why absinthe is illegal in this country and motorcycles are not.

It feels callow to write so little about the Allman Brothers and to have almost nothing to say about the deaths of two of the band's members. I keep trying to think of things about the Allmans that might be metaphoric, but I'm failing. In 1976, Gregg Allman testified against a longtime roadie who ended up taking the fall in a well-publicized heroin and pharmaceutical cocaine bust, so I suppose that qualifies him as a narc. But who am I to judge? You can never trust Drug People, and other Drug People should know that.

One detail about the Allmans that's a little symbolic (sort of) is that they were the band Cameron Crowe toured with when he was 15, prompting him to eventually make the film *Almost Famous*. This means that the Allman Brothers were (at least partially) the inspiration for Billy Crudup's band Stillwater (although Crowe also injected a few bits of Zeppelin and Skynyrd and other '70s bands, and the Crudup character is supposed to be the Eagles' Glenn Frey). What's funny is that— ever since I started working as a rock critic at *Spin*—people constantly ask me if my life is similar to the kid in *Almost Famous*. It is not. I've never become friends (or even casual acquaintances) with any band I've ever interviewed. In fact, it would be virtually impossible to write a Cameron Crowe–like profile in this day and age, because modern rock musicians never give unlimited access to anyone working in the media (unless the reporter more or less promises not to write anything interesting, or if the musician is a drugged-up, bankrupt, *Boogie Nights*–obsessed Courtney Love). You usually get two hours in a hotel room, and often less than that. Right now, most rock journalism is just mild criticism with a Q&A attached; nobody learns anything (usually) and nothing new is created (ever). As a result, people who do this for a living tend to have a peculiar self-image; the relative worth of rock criticism is their core existential crisis. It's the semi-Zen quandary you're forced to consider any time the vortex of your vocation is (a) getting free albums, (b) playing these albums in an empty room, (c) thinking about what these albums remind you of, and (d) writing something that vaguely resembles an argument for why said album is relevant or uncool. The former lead singer of Soul Coughing once disregarded the entire career of *Village Voice* rock critic Robert Christgau by saying, "Let's face facts here—what Robert Christgau does is write about his mail." And this is completely true; as a rock critic, you make a living reviewing your mail, and anybody who disagrees with that assertion is kidding themselves. Thus, the deeper question that drives (and/or depresses) rock critics is this: "How *important* is my job?" My uninformed assumption is that Robert Christgau would probably say his job is vitally (or at least marginally) important, and writers who consider themselves disciples of Christgau tend to see criticism almost like science; they worry a lot about taste. These are the critics who honestly believe their personal opinions on Run-D.M.C.'s *Raising Hell* are no more or less true than the molecular structure of sulfur, or the square root of 144, or the atomic weight of lead. These are the people who worry about being *right*. And for most of my life, I have disagreed with those people (or at least thought them foolish). I have traditionally argued that rock criticism is almost always unimportant. But what I've grown to realize is that—whenever people argue over the "importance of rock criticism"—they are not arguing about rock criticism. They are arguing about the definition of the word *important*. That's the entire issue. And for some reason, the pursuit of intellect and the so-called "life of the mind" makes people broaden their classification for what can be reasonably classified as *important*. This is why you will continually hear rock academics say things like, "I never appreciated the Allman Brothers sonically, but I understand why that band was so important to working-class Southerners." This is also why you can walk into any working-class bar in rural Alabama and ask someone if *Eat a Peach* is important, and a half-drunk dude in coveralls will say, "Important? Fuck no. But I love that shit. That's real music, brother." Now, this doesn't mean smart people are actually dumb or dumb people are actually brilliant; it just means that any opinion on the import of rock criticism is just a personal opinion on where the category of "essential things" deserves to begin. Which is honestly a much more compelling question; it's just harder to slip into conversation when you're listening to "Ramblin' Man."

THE SEVENTH DAY

Ice ➤ Snakes ➤ God ➤ Arkansas

We are immersed in football country, my friends. As I drive from town to town, I can look out the driver's side window and see 16-year-old boys throwing around their Wilson pigskins and running pass patterns against imaginary cornerbacks. School won't start for several weeks, but kids in Alabama are already practicing. Right now, I'm driving alongside a field populated by at least 30 players; this must be one of those "unofficial" practice sessions that are organized by the squad's senior captains, because there is no adult supervision and nobody is wearing pads or helmets. Still, you can tell this isn't just teenagers goofing around; these kids are focused. This kind of thing is not uncommon at schools where everyone is maddeningly serious about football, which I have to assume is just about every school in Alabama.

Watching these kids makes me want to suck on ice.

Now, I know there's nothing more tedious than someone who insists on reminiscing about their bygone glory days; it always comes off as pathetic, obnoxious, and/or alienating. Nobody is impressed and nobody cares. But let me tell you this: It is not the storyteller's fault. We can't help ourselves. Anyone who ever played high school football in a small town has been implanted with specific memories that will occasionally make them a boring conversationalist; just the sight (or even just the sound) of undersized kids colliding into one another prompts you to remember bizarre details of how your life used to be. For example, these particular kids are making me think about ice. When I was in high school, we practiced twice a day during the two weeks before school started in late August. We were always dehydrated, so our coach allowed us to suck on ice cubes during one 10-minute break in the middle of practice. Ice became the most delicious substance in the world. I do not miss practicing football in 80-degree weather; the only thing worse was practicing when it was 8 below (which would inevitably be the case in November). Reminiscing about high school football is kind of like reminiscing about Vietnam, minus the slaughter and the Thai stick and the shitty Doors music. I feel no nostalgia for being screamed at by a 45-year-old social studies teacher who still wished he was in high school, nor do I miss the sensation of my bones hurting for three straight months. Football practice was never fun; sometimes things sucked, and sometimes things were boring. You always hoped for boring; boring was always better. But during August, it was both. I recall fat kids vomiting after practice. Everyone would sweat like imprisoned rhinos and the sweat would pool up in your helmet strap, so everybody on the team would get horrific acne on their chins. You would practice for two hours and 30 minutes at 7:30 A.M. and two more hours at 7:00 P.M., and you'd spend the middle of the afternoon sleeping on the couch, watching reruns of *Little House on the Prairie* and eating six bowls of Cap'n Crunch. We listened to *Dr. Feelgood* in the locker room and shared one bottle of White Rain shampoo. Perhaps this experience sounds unremarkable; I assure you, it was not. My high school was fucking insane. The summer before my senior year, our cheerleading squad became obsessed with Tim Burton's *Batman,* and they decided to base many of their cheers around the Prince song "Batdance." When we played our opening game that same season, I remember standing in the huddle on second down and nine, and I could hear our cheer squad chanting about *Br-Br-Br-Bruce Wayne.* I recall trotting to the line of scrimmage, wondering how Bruce Wayne could possibly relate to anything associated with the memory of Jim Thorpe. We ran a wingback reverse pass on that second and nine. I was the primary receiver. I ran a post route. I was wide open, and a five-foot-six-inch sophomore named Troy Vosberg threw a 35-yard laser beam that hit me in the paws. And I dropped it, so I guess that made me the Joker. It sounded like the entire crowd simultaneously sighed. These kids in Alabama have no idea what they're getting into. I would like to offer them some ice.

I don't think I can get any deeper into the South than I am right now. Nine hours and 547 miles ago, I was standing where Duane Allman crashed a motorcycle; now I'm semi-lost in rural Mississippi. And when I say "rural," I mean fucking *rural*: Ten minutes ago, I almost drove into a cow. This strikes me as especially amusing, because—if I *had* driven into a cow—I would only be the second person in my immediate family to have done so. When my sister Teresa was in high school, she accidentally plowed into a cow with our father's Chevy. Teresa hit that beef at 40 mph, and the old sleepy-eyed heifer went down like Frazier getting tagged by Foreman. Those were good times.

But ANYWAY, I am not car-hunting for cows, as that would be unsporting. I am hunting for the site of the Lynyrd Skynyrd plane crash, which is supposed to be just west of Magnolia. It took forever to get to this town, and a few of the roads were unpaved. My first plan of action was to find a hotel, but there is no hotel in Magnolia. There is, however, a preponderance of signs promoting the consumption of butterfly shrimp, so I eat supper and then start driving around aimlessly, looking for anyone who might know where Skynyrd's jet crashed into the wilderness back in 1977, subsequently killing singer Ronnie Van Zant, guitarist Steve Gaines, and Gaines's sister Cassie (who served as a back-up singer).

My initial plan is to ask someone at the local bar, but there doesn't seem to be one. All I find are churches. Near the outskirts of town, I spy a gas station. The crimson-haired woman working behind the counter looks a little beautiful and a little pissed off, and she doesn't know where the crash site is. However, there is a man in the store buying a 12-pack of Bud Light, and he can help me. "My old lady can probably tell you for certain," he says. "She's waiting in my pickup."

We walk out to his extended-cab 4x4 Ford, and his "old lady" (who looks about 25) informs me to take the interstate south until I see a sign for West 568, and then I should follow that road for 10 miles until I see some chicken coops. I do this, but there's one problem: There are a lot of goddamn chicken coops in rural Mississippi.

It's getting dark and I am almost ready to give up. By chance, I see a sign by a gravel driveway that promotes "motefarms.com." This is the first time I have ever seen a farm with its own website, so I suspect this is more than just a chicken ranch. And I am right about this assumption, because—when I pull into the yard—I am immediately greeted by a shirtless fellow on a Kodiak four-wheeler.

The fellow is John Daniel Mote, the 21-year-old son of the farm's owner. He is a remarkably handsome dude; he looks and talks like a young John Schneider. "This is the right place," he says. "Follow me." He takes off on his four-wheeler, and I pursue; we amble down a dirt road behind the chicken coops. I can hear the underbrush rubbing against the bottom of the

Tauntaun, and it sounds like the drum fills on Bob Seger's "Hollywood Nights."

He finally leads me to a landmark that his father constructed years ago: It's dominated by an archway that has FREE BIRD printed across the top. There is a Confederate flag, of course, and a statue of an eagle. Mote—who punctuates every one of his sentences with the phrase "Please don't quote me in your magazine"—informs me that if I were to walk through the Free Bird arch and 50 yards into the trees, I would find a tiny creek and some random airplane debris. I start to walk in that direction. He immediately stops me. "You don't want to go in there," he says. I ask him why. "Snakes. Cottonmouths. Very poisonous. Not a good idea." And then young John Daniel Mote drives away on his four-wheeler, and I am alone with the bones of Lynyrd Skynyrd.

By now, the sky is as dark as Johnny Cash's closet. I am surrounded by fireflies. There is heat lightning to the east. Three hours ago, I had passed a Mississippi Wal-Mart, and its electronic sign posted the temperature at 98 degrees; it's maybe (maybe!) eight degrees cooler at the moment. It feels like I'm trapped in the penultimate scene from *Raiders of the Lost Ark*, when Indiana Jones and Marion are tied to a stake while the Nazis try to open the Ark of the Covenant. Or maybe I'm just thinking of that movie because Mote mentioned the snakes.

Still, part of me really wants to see where this plane went down. I feel like an idiot for having driven 547 miles, only to be stopped five first downs from pay dirt. I hop into the car and drive the Tauntaun up to the mouth of the arch, shining the high beams into the blackness. I leave the driver's side door open so that I can hear the stereo; it's playing "Round and Round" by Ratt. The headlights don't help much; the trees swallow everything. I start to walk into the chasm. However, I don't make it the full 50 yards. I don't even make it 50 feet. I can't see anything, and the cicadas are so loud that they drown out the Ratt. It looks like the ground is alive, but this is my imagination. I will not find the spot where Ronnie Van Zant was driven into the earth. I turn around, and the cottonmouth snakes gimme three steps toward the door.

According to my cell phone, it's 11:44 P.M. (and I have no reason to be skeptical of my cell phone). I am in McComb, Mississippi, a town maybe 10 miles from Magnolia; I couldn't stay *in* Magnolia because (as stated earlier) that community does not appear to have a hotel. Here in McComb, I'm in a Comfort Inn. It's relatively comfortable, so there will be no need to get into a semantic argument with the woman at the front desk. I'm standing next to the window, trying to exhale my marijuana smoke through the window screen. I feel like a man on the run, almost as if I am being chased by another man. The man chasing me wears only black. He is the Man in the Black Hat. We have a symbiotic relationship, this man and myself. He is my archenemy. We were once close friends, but circumstance has turned us against each other; eventually, we will go to war. I scan the shadows for the Man in the Black Hat, but I know he will not be seen; he is far too wily. I study the darkness only out of respect.

(READER'S NOTE: This pot must have been much more expensive than I remember.)

You would not believe what is on television right now. It's pretty outstanding. I am watching the Victory Television Network (VTN), a channel devoted to helping Christians in the Arkansas area "connect" with one another. This is somewhat confusing, because their assumed "connection" equates only to watching certain TV shows at the exact same time, and TVs are not exactly the Internet. This strikes me as a very low standard for what constitutes a "connection." For example, I would hate to consider myself "connected" to everyone in America who happens to watch *The Real World/Road Rules Challenge*. However, it is not my role to question the logic that drives VTN's promotional slogans; I'm just here to enjoy its quality programming while stoned. The movie showing tonight is mesmerizing. And I am not saying this to be ironic or sarcastic or snarky or condescending; I'm saying this because I just realized something important about born-again Christians that never occurred to me before tonight.

The movie VTN is showing appears to have at least three working titles, none of which appear to be the *actual* title (the film is labeled differently at each of the commercial breaks, which serve exclusively as promos for other VTN programs). However, I can tell that this motion picture is specifically directed at teenagers, and it's one of those films in which the goal is to "scare kids straight." The protagonist is a teen (I believe his name is Steven) who is torn apart by temptation. But what's interesting are the things Steven is tempted to do; he is not tempted to try drugs (even though there are people in this film doing drugs), nor is he tempted to have sex (even though people at this kid's school are having sex), nor is he tempted to get involved with a sect of teenagers dabbling in organized crime (although that's part of this story, too, oddly). Our hero is never involved in any of that shit. Steven's gut-wrenching crisis—i.e., the crux of this whole story and the singular issue that's tearing this kid's life to shreds—is the temptation to *not save* his adolescent peers from doing all of those terrible things. In other words, he is not frayed by a desire to go down on his girlfriend or the desire to get drunk and feel cool; those things are never a problem for Steven. His problem is that he wants to merely ignore all the kids in his school who are going to hell, even though the local youth minister demands that Steven take responsibility for their souls.

And here's what makes this story even more complex: During the film's final 20 minutes, the minister succeeds; Steven realizes that he has to tell his pagan peers the Good News About Jesus. It is his duty as a child of God. And as a result, Steven tries to talk some sense into a local drug dealer and explain that there is a better way to live.

And that drug dealer blows Steven away with a handgun.

And this is how the movie ends.

I'm not gonna lie to you: I did not see this coming. I've been brainwashed by enough Hollywood blockbusters to know teenage heroes are generally not gunned down at the conclusion of most docudramas. And this makes me wonder if hyper-Christian cinema might be a completely untapped bastion of profound originality. It's not like Christian rock, where the artists uncannily attempt to mime mainstream music; Christian film operates as if mainstream film grammar doesn't even exist. I don't know who directs these movies, but these folks are really, *really* "thinking outside the box." It's not that they are simply borrowing different influences, or that they have a different ideological agenda, or that they inexplicably care what Michael Medved thinks of their work. These filmmakers are making movies for an audience that lives *in a wholly different universe*. It's a universe where a movie about a teenager tempted to smoke angel dust would seem wildly implausible; no teen watching the Victory Television Network would possibly consider such a choice. The scenarios most of us grew up watching on the *ABC After School Special* would never apply to these people; in these films, the stakes are much higher. It's not enough to merely avoid delinquency—it's quite possible you may need to die for the sins of everyone at your school.

After a few minutes, another one of these evangelical teen-sploitation movies airs on VTN. This one is called *The Dinosaur Project*, and it's about a precocious 10-year-old who creates controversy at the school science fair by proving that evolution is a fraud and that the world is only 4,000 years old. Had I been born to a family of zealots in McComb, Mississippi, it's entirely possible that this would have been my greatest fifth-grade fantasy: I would have labored away on my diorama, brilliantly illustrating how the Great Flood destroyed the tyrannosaurus before Noah could shuffle its carcass onto the ark. I would have explained how the flood's rapidly rising waters muddled erosion patterns, prompting secular scientists to erroneously claim that fossilized bones were (somehow) millions of years old. I would have saved my class from the evils of knowledge. And if that had been the case, I'm sure my life would be different right now; I'd probably be in the ninth year of my marriage, and I'd have four kids, and I'd be a high school football coach who gives his team ice cubes to keep them from dying of heat stroke. But I certainly wouldn't be *here*; I certainly wouldn't be stoned in a hotel room, thinking about Ronnie Van Zant's corpse and wondering if jokes about dead rock stars really aren't that funny.

THE EIGHTH DAY

Kobe ➤ Nico ➤ Lizzie ➤ Nashville

You know what's the best part about driving by yourself? Talk radio. Talk radio offers no genuine insight about anything, but I always feel like I am learning something; I always feel like I suddenly understand all the people I normally can't relate to at all. At the very least, I feel like I understand what most of America finds interesting. And on this summer day in 2003, America is interested in only two things: Whether or not Kobe Bryant is a rapist, and whether or not the Episcopalian church should have a gay bishop in New Hampshire. So I suppose this means the country is really only interested in *one* thing: The sex lives of people who aren't them.

As I write this, the evidence against Kobe seems damning. This makes for an interesting paradox because—unlike the O. J. Simpson trial—just about everyone I know is hoping Kobe gets off. The single hottest topic on today's omnipresent AM chatter was the identity of Kobe's accuser, and whether her name should be withheld by the media; the staple argument, of course, is that her identity must remain hidden because there's so much social baggage associated with being a rape victim. This strikes me as a peculiar line of reasoning. Certainly, there is a social stigma that comes with being raped; however, there's obviously a far greater stigma with being perceived as a rapist. Bryant's reputation is destroyed forever, regardless of his guilt or innocence in this case. I also can't fathom why rape shield laws don't allow the defense to question the alleged victim's mental condition. I mean, what if this woman is insane? What if she *regularly* accuses people of rape? How can that not matter in a court of law?

That said, Kobe Bryant is a professional basketball player. Therefore, I am certain he is guilty.

Meanwhile, all this business about the gay New Hampshire clergyman makes the Episcopalians sound like marketing representatives; their fear (at least from the antigay contingent) is that electing a homosexual bishop will stop people from going to church. Nothing depresses me more than hearing an organized religion worry about *membership*. Do they think Jesus is somehow impressed by voter turnout? Do they think God gives preference to religions that appear especially popular? It's not like God only allocates federal funding to religious organizations that meet a quota. Several callers also used this issue to moronically rail against the potential legalization of gay marriage. I find this profoundly depressing. In my opinion, we *must* legalize gay marriage. Gay males are the only men in America who still want to be married.

Ten rock 'n' roll casualties nobody ever talks about but probably should, as they are latently educational (and good subjects for dinner parties):

> ➤ **Marc Bolan:** Arguably the most pretentious wizard in glam-rock history, Bolan fronted T. Rex, claimed to author science fiction novels that were never published, and honestly believed it was a good idea to name an album *Zinc Alloy and the Hidden Riders of Tomorrow: A Creamed*

Cage in August. With his signature top hat and solid-gold easy action, Bolan loved to sing about cars: He claims to have driven a Rolls-Royce, apparently because it was good for his voice. He loved his Cadillac. He once pursued a woman named Buick McKane, and he was a jeepster for her love. He even had "highway knees," whatever the fuck that's supposed to signify. And this was all somewhat paradoxical, since Bolan never learned how to drive; the irony is further extended when one considers that he died in a 1977 car accident, two weeks before his 30th birthday (his girlfriend drove them both into a tree). Bolan glorified a machine he could not operate, only to have that same machine spell his doom. The lesson: Be careful what you wish for, lest you get it.

➤ **Steve Clark:** As the insecure lead guitarist for Def Leppard, Clark liked to drink massive amounts of everything. In 1991, while taking prescription painkillers for three broken ribs, Clark came home from an evening at the pub and decided to have a few nightcaps, which—according to his drinking companion, Daniel Van Alphen—ended up being a triple vodka, a quadruple vodka, and a double brandy (all of which he consumed in 30 minutes). This killed him. What's interesting about this episode is that Def Leppard had fired a guitarist named Pete Willis in 1982 *because he had a drinking problem*. The lesson: We *all* have problems, brother.

➤ **Nico:** Born in Nazi Germany in 1938, Christa Päffgen's father died in a concentration camp. She, however, managed to become a model. At the age of 15, a photographer dubbed the six-foot ectomorph "Nico," supposedly to honor his ex-boyfriend. Nico would later move to New

York, take a method-acting class with Marilyn Monroe, make a record for Brian Jones (which was produced by a young Jimmy Page), have a relationship with Bob Dylan, join Andy Warhol's Exploding Plastic Inevitable and sing with the Velvet Underground, only to be kicked out of the band for being too charismatic. She feasted on heroin and cigarettes; she slept with (sadly) Jim Morrison and (oddly) Jackson Browne. When her son fell into a drug-induced coma, she showed up at the hospital to record the haunting beep of his life-support system. Then—at the age of 49, in Spain—she died in a bicycle accident. The lesson: Live weird, die weird.

➤ **Falco:** Everybody in America thinks of Falco as a ridiculous one-hit joke rocker from Vienna who's only remembered for a novelty single, 1986's "Rock Me Amadeus." Europeans, however, thought he was some kind of controversial genius (several of his songs were banned from international radio, including a track called "Jeanny," which certain listeners interpreted as a glorification of rape and murder). In the '90s, he fled the omnipresent Austrian media and lived like a sultan in the Dominican Republic, only to die there in 1998 when his Mitsubishi Pajero was hit by another car. The lesson: Europeans have terrible taste in everything.

➤ **Pete Ham and Tom Evans:** There's something especially poignant about people who hang themselves. Since hanging is understood as a form of capital punishment (and because capital punishment is inevitably a means to mollify the living), one always gets a sense that individuals who commit suicide by this method are literally executing themselves; they want to show society that they deserved to be punished. I am not sure how this applies to the band Badfinger, protégés of the Beatles whose best song ("Come and Get It") was written by Paul McCartney. They signed with the Beatles' label Apple in 1968, and it looked like they were destined for stardom; by the time they released *Ass*, in '73, everything had collapsed. To make matters worse, they mysteriously lost $600,000 from an escrow account. In 1975, lead songwriter Ham hung himself. Three years later, what remained of Badfinger attempted to reunite, but that also failed; in the failure's aftermath, bassist Evans hung himself, too. No other major band has experienced multiple hangings. Everyone likes to lionize Joy Division's Ian Curtis for noosing it up in 1980, but that was his whole aesthetic; Joy Division's singular directive was self-loathing. Every guy in that band should have hung himself, probably; nobody would have missed New Order, except for a bunch of idiots who think taking drugs and dancing is more fun than drinking and feeling melodramatic (which, I suppose, is everybody in the world except me). The lesson: Nobody can be the Beatles, so don't even try.

▶ **Michael Hutchence:** My sister liked INXS. I never understood who they were; I think they existed for 13 years before I knew their name was not pronounced "inks" (as in "rhymes with lynx"). Lead singer Hutchence hung himself like the dudes in Badfinger, but he was a little more straightforward about his intentions: The day before he killed himself in November 1997, he made a bunch of maniacal phone calls, including one to his manager. "I've fucking had enough," he decreed. Hours later, he was found in a Sydney hotel room, kneeling on the floor—he had hung himself from the doorknob with a belt. There were many subsequent tabloid rumors that this was not a suicide and that Hutchence was actually involved in a diabolical autoerotic encounter that went haywire. There is no real evidence of this. There was, however, quite a party happening inside his blood (an internal cocktail composed of booze, coke, Prozac, and just about anything else you could imagine). The main thing I remember about his death was discussing it in the corner booth of Duffy's Tavern in downtown Fargo; Lenore kept insisting that the color of the belt Hutchence hung himself with was brown. "Brown belts are the deadliest kind," she insisted. The lesson: If INXS had covered "Hotel California," that B-side would now seem strangely poignant.

➤ **Mike Patto and "Ollie" Halsall:** As the two driving forces in Patto (a jazz-influenced psychedelic four-piece from the U.K.), nobody really cares that namesake vocalist Patto died from cancer in 1979 or that guitarist Halsall died from a heart attack in '92 (possibly from a heroin overdose). However, consider this: During the 1980s, bassist Clive Griffiths and drummer John Halsey were involved in a car accident. Halsey recovered from his injuries and now walks with a limp; Griffiths, meanwhile, was partially paralyzed and contracted a rare case of partial amnesia. What's so compelling about this amnesia is that Griffiths *no longer remembers being involved with Patto.* He can't remember being in a band whose singer died in the late '70s—which means he can't remember the singer, either. He has not forgotten how to rock; he has forgotten that he *did* rock. The lesson: To live in the hearts of those we leave behind is not to die.

➤ **Randy Rhoads:** "March 19, 1982, is a day that will live with me forever. Not only did I lose my best friend but the greatest musician I had ever known." Ozzy Osbourne wrote these words in the liner notes of the posthumous live album *Tribute*. "Randy Rhoads came into my life in 1979. At that time I was incredibly depressed, and he was what I had dreamed about in a guitar player. He helped make all my dreams come true." Obviously, those dreams ended on March 19, 1982, when Rhoads was riding in a single-engine Beechcraft Bonanza F35 airplane (Ozzy's coke-fueled tour cook was controlling the plane's yoke). An air-traffic controller in Oakland told me that Beechcraft Bonanzas are called "doctor killers" by her coworkers; this is because so many rich physicians decide to become amateur pilots and crash their Bonanzas into the ground. It turns out these planes are also "guitar-god killers," because the idiot flying Rhoads's plane decided to buzz Osbourne's tour bus. He missed. The plane's left wing hit the bus at over 140 mph and flew into a nearby house, exploding on impact. They needed a dentist to identify Randy's 25-year-old corpse. Ozzy never seemed to recover from this accident, and he spent the next 20 years hiring guitar players who looked like Randy's little brother. I recall watching a documentary about Ozzy with Quincy one night in the mid-'90s, and Osbourne was describing how the two fleeting years spent with Rhoads seemed longer than all the years before he met him and all the years that have passed since his death. "That is so sweet," Q said. "I've never heard a man talk about another man like that. I think Ozzy and Randy were in love with each other." For some reason, this made me furious. The lesson: Randy Rhoads was not gay.

Tonight, I sleep with Lizzie.

Lizzie is my lawyer's cat. I am currently scribbling notes in the spare bedroom of my lawyer's Nashville condo with this super furry animal, and I am trying to remember what I did tonight. I'm pretty certain it involved honky-tonks. Here in Nashville, people unironically refer to downtown bars as "honky-tonks." All of these honky-tonks feature live bands that play for free, and it seems like half the songs performed by these bands prominently included the word *honky-tonk* in the chorus. If this was what Los Angeles had been like in the 1980s, all those hair bands that played the Whiskey-a-Go-Go, the Roxy, and the Troubadour would have needed to find a way to jam the words *metal club* into all their lyrics.

There are many attractive females in Nashville (perhaps these were the "honky-tonk women" Mick Jagger once referred to), and they are evidently required to wear tight-fitting skirts whenever they appear in public. I don't think I saw one woman in pants throughout the entire evening; perhaps Nashville has fallen under Taliban rule. Besides the skirted women, the downtown community features elderly Red State tourists who drink PBR and hundreds of 26-year-old men who look like they're auditioning for a Kings of Leon tribute band. On the whole, I found Nashville intensely "authentic" and far more fun then I would have ever anticipated. However, part of me misses the bygone era of country line dancing, which nobody seems to do anymore. It always fascinated me that the people who liked George Strait and Billy Ray Cyrus were equally enamored with linear, highly structured dance choreography that offered no spontaneity whatsoever. Line dancing reminds me of the way Great Britain used to fight land wars.

Perhaps you are wondering why I am staying in my lawyer's guest room; part of the reason is that my lawyer is not really my lawyer. She's an entertainment lawyer, certainly, and she looks over all my legal contracts, certainly, but she is mostly just a friend from my college newspaper who elected to attend Vanderbilt's law school while pursuing her dream of becoming the next Loretta Lynn. She's a multi-tasker. She got me drunk tonight, too. When this woman worked at the college newspaper (way back in the 1900s), she was one of the only women on a male-dominated staff, so many of the guys in our office had unrequited crushes on her. College newspapers tend to have a lot of static sexual energy. My first real girlfriend worked with me at that same newspaper; I was 20 and she was one of those "older than average students." Dee Dee was 29. She reminded me of Debra Winger in *Urban Cowboy*. I had no idea how to interact with her. For several months, Dee Dee flirted with me so aggressively that I assumed she was publicly ridiculing me. The two of us would hang out in the newsroom until 3:00 A.M. on Thursday nights for no reason, and I would somehow perceive this as a strange coincidence. One night in November, she told me that there was something wrong with her left breast.

"What is the problem?" I asked earnestly.

"I don't know," said Dee Dee. "What do you think the problem is?" She slowly reached up to the collar of her T-shirt and pulled it down, maybe one inch above her left nipple. She was not wearing a bra. She took my right hand and placed it on her chest, holding it there with her right hand. Her heart was thumping through her sternum. Her skin was on fire. It was like touching the hood of a black Trans Am that had been parked in the sun.

"I'm not sure what to say," I finally said. "I don't think there's anything wrong with it, actually. But perhaps you should see a physician."

I said good-bye and went home to watch reruns of *Family Ties*.

To this day, I cannot fathom how Dee Dee did not conclude I was gay; maybe she just thought I was soul-crushingly aloof. The truth was that I simply did not know what to do in this type of situation: I found that specific encounter extraordinary, but it still did not seem possible that this sexy, mature woman (who had already *lived an entire life* during the 1980s) would want me to touch her bosom for any reason that was not exclusively medical. My mind and my gut are never simpatico: Every time I think somebody likes me, she doesn't; every time I think somebody doesn't like me, she does. This has never changed, and I'm certain it never will. Fortunately, some people are less defeatist than I. That December, Dee Dee decided I needed to get stoned, because I had never been stoned before. It was 11 degrees below zero, but she still wore a black mini-skirt when she picked me up (she kind of looked like those summer girls from Nashville, now that I think about it). Later that night, she decided I needed to have sex, because I had never done that before, either. All things considered, this was a pretty epic evening. We were romantically involved until the following May. Over those five months, Dee Dee taught me many, many things; it should be mandatory for all men to have their first intimate experiences with someone nine years older than they are. And then—of course—I stoically dumped her, over the telephone, two days before she graduated from college, and for no clear reason. It shattered her. It didn't affect me at all. "Why do guys always say it's so hard to break up with their girlfriends?" I thought to myself. "This is easy. I could do this twice a year for the rest of my life." Two weeks later, I turned 21. I assumed the rest of my life would be a series of (a) meeting cool women, (b) convincing them to fall in love with me, (c) losing interest after six months, and then (d) restarting the process with someone else. Since that time, I have never had any relationship end so easily, nor have I ever met a woman who loved me as unconditionally as Dee Dee. It's taken me a decade to realize that this was no coincidence.

We are always dying, all the time. That's what living is; living is dying, little by little. It's a sequenced collection of individualized deaths. My relationship with Dee Dee ended like a gangland execution: She called me on the telephone and I shot her in the back of the skull. My relationship with Diane is ending like a massive stroke; things were bad immediately, but there's still the slim hope of a total recovery. The death of Lenore has been akin to that of a person in hospice; it's been an agonizing case of bone cancer, but the trauma has pulled us closer. Lenore is like a grandparent I never truly knew until she became terminal. And as for Quincy . . . well, I'm not totally sure how she died out of my life, to be honest. Quincy is like a passenger on a plane that crashed into the North Atlantic, never to be recovered. She *must* be dead. Logic *demands* that she is dead. But until I see a body, the potential for denial remains. Without a proper funeral, I cannot accept her passing. I mean, have we sent a search party to Greenland? Maybe she's living among the musk ox. Maybe she has amnesia. Maybe she's a vampire. These things happen.

I'm too drunk to continue writing. Lizzie the Cat is staring at me; I think she's judging me. "Meow," I say. "Meow meow meow! You know that I am right." When I crawl under the covers, Lizzie bounds off the bed and lies down in the corner of the room, hissing in my general direction. I guess I'm not sleeping with Lizzie after all.

THE NINTH DAY

Bell Bottom Blues ➤ Something That Could Not Happen
Yet Did ➤ The River, the Road, the South ➤
Pole Vault Summer ➤ Satan Lives

Eric Clapton has been inducted into the Rock and Roll Hall of
Fame on three separate occasions. He's been inducted as a
solo artist, as the frontman for Cream, and as original guitarist
for the Yardbirds. He's been inducted on four separate occasions if you count the 2004 inclusion of Traffic, a group he was
not a member of and has no significant connection with beyond
the fact that they suck in the same generalized manner.

With the possible exception of Jim Morrison, Eric Clapton is
(arguably) the most overrated rock musician of all time; he's a
talented, boring guitar player, and he's a workmanlike, boring
vocalist. He also has an abhorrent (and, I suppose, boring)
neck beard. However, he is not terrible in totality; he did
unleash one stellar album: Derek and the Dominos' 1970 LP,
Layla and Other Assorted Love Songs. Part of what made
Derek and the Dominos intriguing was their almost unfathomable self-destructiveness: With the exception of Clapton,
virtually every guy in the band either died or went to prison
(including Duane Allman, a detail I completely overlooked while
in Macon three days ago). Jim Gordon, the Domino drummer

who wrote the astonishing piano coda to "Layla" (best employed in Martin Scorsese's *Goodfellas*) spent his life battling schizophrenic compulsions,[1] ultimately listening to the voices inside his head and murdering his own mother. He was sentenced to 16 years in prison. That shit makes lusting after George Harrison's wife seem almost affable.

Still, the idea of Clapton (Derek?) singing about his love for Harrison's woman (Pattie Boyd) on "Layla" is the single most devastating element of *Layla and Other Assorted Love Songs*. Clapton's soul does seem—for lack of a better term—"tortured." I hate to use a term like *torture* when discussing someone's romantic crush, because it always seems flippant; I'd sooner feel unrequited love for 100 women than spend two hours tasting electricity in the Hanoi Hilton (being in love is not like having your testicles attached to a car battery, even if that's how it sometimes seems). However, I understand what Eric was feeling, sort of. I have to assume part of his heart was simply shocked by the irony of this specific attraction: As one of the best-looking, best-known musicians in the world, Eric Clapton could have immediately had any woman he wanted—but he

---

1. Lucy Chance once told me an anecdote about schizophrenia. There is a particular hypothetical question physicians ask patients they suspect might be suffering from this particular ailment: "A man and a woman are married for 10 years. The husband suddenly dies. At the funeral, the widow meets another man and deeply enjoys his conversation. They talk for two hours, and it's exciting and reassuring. The following week, this same woman murders her own sister. Why do you think she committed this act of violence?" Now, if you ask a normal person this question, they'll usually theorize that the widow was talking to her sister's husband, and that she committed murder out of desperation and loneliness. However, schizophrenics (supposedly) provide a specific (and very disturbing) answer to this query with remarkable consistency; they inevitably say, "Well, she obviously wanted to have another funeral, because that same guy will probably show up again." I find this fascinating. If head-butting Chicago street singer Wesley Willis had not died in 2003, I would ask him this question.

still wasn't *a Beatle*. In 1970, George Harrison was probably one of only 10 people in the universe who was cooler than Eric Clapton, and Harrison happened to be Clapton's best friend. Those are awfully depressing circumstances for a man in love.

"You see, that kind of thinking is precisely your problem, Chuck." This is what Quincy would say if she were in the passenger seat right now, talking about Eric Clapton. If Q were in this car with me, I would still be playing Derek and the Dominos, and I would be casually saying all the thoughts I just wrote to myself, and Quincy would be outraged. "You always dwell on the wrong elements of relationships, Chuck. The reason 'Layla' is moving has nothing to do with the fact that Eric Clapton should—or shouldn't—be able to sleep with Pattie Boyd because he's *almost as cool* as George Harrison. Having an attractive girlfriend is not supposed to be the *reward* for *being cool.*"

"I know, I know," I would say in response. "But still, it must have been hard to think, 'Man, I could have any woman I want—except for the one woman I *really* want.' Remember how it was before you and I finally got together? I spent a year killing myself trying to make you love me, and it was a heartbreaking process. It was like I was singing 'Layla' to you every single night, and all you did was sleep with George Harrison."

"But that's exactly the shit I'm referring to," Q would say. "The year you spent 'killing yourself' to make me love you . . . I thought that was us being best friends. We had all those intimate conversations and you sent me all those long e-mails and we watched all those movies involving Eric Stoltz—I thought that was us *having fun.* But you see that kind of behavior as *the work* you're forced to do in order to sleep with the people you want to sleep with."

"That's not true," I would say. "I would do anything to go back to that year when we *weren't* having sex."

"You say that now, but you'd do the same thing if we went back to 1996."

"I kind of have to agree with Quincy on this point." This is what Lenore would say if she were suddenly in the backseat, listening to Q and me argue about Eric Clapton. "Chuck, you do tend to repeat the same behavior over and over again, and all you really change is the person involved. I remember one night when you kissed me, and you spontaneously said my lips tasted like 'the perfect combination of cigarettes, lip gloss, and Lenore.' That was a really wonderful, really romantic thing to hear from somebody, and I thought about that sentence for a really long time. But then you kissed me two years later, and you 'spontaneously' said that phrase again, almost verbatim. All you did was replace the word *cigarettes* with *gin*!"

"But that sentiment was true on both of those occasions," I would say in my defense. "It's not like I was trying to trick you. That wasn't a lie."

"Oh, I'm not accusing you of lying," Lenore would politely say. "It's just that it's hard not to feel like a character sometimes, instead of a person. It's almost like you're just fitting different women into a script that always stars you in the exact same role."

"Totally," Quincy would say. "And as for your specific concern over Eric Clapton's infatuation with his friend's wife: That is such conventional male idiocy. It's a little insulting, actually. In fact, don't you even have some arcane personal regulation about dating women who've dated your friends?"

"Actually, I do," I would admit. "My policy is that if a woman breaks up with a guy I consider a friend, I will never date that woman under any circumstances. However, if one of my male friends actively breaks up with a woman I find appealing, I become eligible to date her—with his unspoken permission—when the amount of time following the break is equal to twice the length of the original relationship. For example, if they were together for seven weeks, I could not ask the woman on a date until three months and one week had passed since he dumped her. These rules are nonnegotiable."

"That makes me think you're either a moron or a guy who's trying way too hard to create a persona for himself," Q would say. "What you're essentially saying is that even though you alleged that you were hopelessly in love with me for two years, and that even though you never loved anyone as fiercely as you loved me, and that even though you often claimed you fell in love with me during our *very first* conversation, you would have never even pursued me if I had happened to dump one of your stupid friends from college? That makes me question the sincerity of your emotions. Moreover, it strikes me as a tad hypocritical, considering I was still involved in a five-year relationship with someone else when you first told me you loved me."

"I never really knew that dude," I would say.

"But *I* knew him!" Quincy would say. "That relationship was important *to me*. Shouldn't that have mattered to you at all?"

"Ha!" Lenore would add. "You got off easy. Chuck once kissed me at a point in my life when I thought I was going to *marry* someone else. The most desirable thing I could ever do was be desirable to people he didn't know."

"That is not completely true," I would protest.

"Ah, Charles," Lenore would coo. "I understand. I didn't mind. It was sweet, kind of. I loved how cocky you seemed whenever we would walk into a bar and every guy in the room stared at my chest like a pack of wolverines. I know that made you feel cool. And I was glad I could make you feel that way."

"Well, you did make me feel cool," I would say. "Both of you did."

"You see, this is what worries me." Suddenly, an imaginary Diane is sitting in the backseat with the imaginary Lenore.

Diane has just removed her imaginary iPod and joined our imaginary conversation. "Chuck, it really bothers me that you seem fixated on beautiful women in problematic situations, particularly women who are already in serious relationships. It makes me uncomfortable, and it makes me question why you ever started talking to me. It makes me feel like you were writing this book before you ever met me, and I was just added because you needed a third character. And I find it almost as troubling that you're using such a clumsy literary device to make your internal monologue seem like dialogue, and I hate the way you're making us all talk with identical syntax. Inside your own mind, we all talk exactly like you!"

"Ah, Christ," I would say, suddenly trapped in a no-win situation within my own superego. "Diane, I talk to you because I love talking to you."

"Yes, but why did you *start* talking to me? And if I gained 40 pounds and cut my hair, how long would it be before you *stopped* talking to me?"

"That is a completely unfair question," I would say, which is interesting, because—technically—I'm unfairly asking it of myself. "I have no idea what would happen if you suddenly looked different. What would happen if I stopped being funny? What if I became retarded? What if I decided to stop listening to you whenever you talk about why you like shopping for boots? How long would it be before you stopped talking *to me*?"

"That, in a nutshell, is why you don't understand what 'Layla' is about," Quincy would interject. "Diane brought up qualities that make someone physically unattractive. You are bringing up qualities that make someone unlikable. And you don't seem to see any difference between those two ideas."

Quincy is making a valid point, if I do say so myself.

"You know, this is probably why you're visiting all these places where people died, yet all you're thinking about are the women you've slept with," Q might continue. "You don't understand love or death, so you compensate by becoming inappropriately obsessed with both—and probably for the same exact reason. You're conflating unlike idioms in the hope that they will accidentally take on symbolic meaning. It's like this thing with the drummer from Derek and the Dominos going fucknuts and killing his mother: For some fucked-up reason, knowing that factoid is making you appreciate 'Layla' even more, as if a piano coda written by a sociopath is inherently more interesting than a piano coda written by Elton John or Michael McDonald or anybody who's not clinically insane. Can't you see that someone losing his mind and killing his mom is not *interesting*? It's *tragic*."

The voices inside my head never make me want to kill my mother. However, they sometimes make me want to kill myself.

So here is the big question: Is dying good for your career? Cynics always assume that it is, but I'm not so sure anymore. And now that I've been to Memphis, I'm not even sure if I care.

Memphis offers two key points of investigation for rock 'n' roll forensic experts. The first is Graceland, where Elvis Presley's heart stopped on a toilet. The second is Mud Island Harbor on the Mississippi River, where Jeff Buckley went for a swim and did not succeed. One could argue that both of these artists significantly benefited from dying: Presley's career was collapsing when he died in 1977, so dying ended that slide and—in all likelihood—kept his legacy from becoming a sad joke (it is virtually impossible to imagine a "noble" 70-year-old Elvis, had Presley somehow managed to live into the present). Meanwhile, Buckley's death is precisely what made him into a star; he was a well-regarded—but relatively unfamous—avant-garde rock musician until he drowned on May 29, 1997. Almost immediately, he became a messianic figure (and his album *Grace* instantly evolved from "slightly better than good" to "totally classic").

I walked around Graceland this morning, and it kind of made me embarrassed to be American. I have always sided with Chuck D's original take on the King: Elvis never meant shit to me. I don't like any of his songs except "Suspicious Minds," his only good movie is *Roustabout*, and his whole career seems like some kind of sociological experiment. But the main thing I dislike about Elvis Presley is the *idea* of Elvis Presley, and that idea is what keeps Graceland in business. It's the religiosity of garbage culture; it validates the import of tabloid aesthetics, and it makes our society look stupid. Presley fanatics are worse than the dopes who still care about JFK Jr. and Princess Di. For some reason, there is a stunning number of Americans who desperately want celebrity royalty and cultural dogma, and that's all Graceland is. Oh . . . and karaoke. There was also some karaoke.

But those were my thoughts three hours ago; now, things are different. I'm typing on my laptop computer, next to the Mississippi River, and I'm starting to rethink my thoughts on Graceland (and maybe my thoughts about EAP and his TCB ways). The water is green, and it's as calm as a cookie sheet. I remember reading that Jeff Buckley's mother believed there was a conspiracy surrounding her son's death, because she insists he was too strong a swimmer to die in these waters. I don't know how I feel about this supposition, as I cannot swim (I can't even float). I'm like that crazy bitch from *Swimfan*. The über-calm Mississippi still looks plenty deadly to me; as far as I'm concerned, it may as well be a Burmese tiger trap filled with electric porcupines. However, I must agree that the water does not flow very fast in Mud Island Harbor, and—though it certainly seems like a *strange* place to swim—it's hard to believe a guy who (supposedly) wasn't drunk or high managed to disappear beneath anything so tranquil.

But how or why Buckley died really doesn't matter at this point; what matters it how his death is perceived by the rest of the world. And—as far as I can tell—Buckley's demise is viewed 100 percent positively (at least from an artistic standpoint). There is an entire cult of disciples (led, I believe, by Minnie Driver) who inject the knowledge of Buckley's demise back into his work, and what they then hear on songs like "Drown in My Own Tears" is something that couldn't exist if he were still alive. It's a simple equation: Buckley is dead, so *Grace* is profound. But this is reverse engineering; this says more about the people who like Buckley than it does about his music. Much like Alice Cooper, we love the dead. Even when it's merely an accident, dying somehow proves you weren't kidding.

Which bring us back to Elvis. Whenever I see footage of an old Elvis film or his '68 comeback special, I get the distinct feeling that he *was* kidding. But now that he's dead, everyone is able to pretend that all his goofiness was somehow seminal, because dead men tell no jokes. We have to take him seriously, because it's disrespectful to do otherwise. America is a confusing place, both for the living and for the dead. That's why Graceland exists, and that's why 20 million Elvis fans can, in fact, be wrong.

Just north of Clarksdale, Mississippi, at the intersection of Highways 61 and 49, the soul of rock 'n' roll was spawned from Satan's wheeling and dealing. This is the "crossroads" where Robert Johnson sold his soul to the devil, thereby accepting eternity in hell in exchange for the ability to play the guitar like no man before him. Satan's overpriced guitar lesson became the birth of modern blues . . . and by extension, the building blocks of every hard-rock song ever recorded.

This, of course, never actually happened. Robert Johnson met the devil about as many times as Jimmy Page, King Diamond, and Marilyn Manson did, which is to say "never." But this doesn't mean rock 'n' roll wasn't invented here. Rock 'n' roll is only superficially about guitar chords; it's really about myth. And the fact that people still like to pretend a young black male could be granted Lucifer's darkest powers on the back roads of Coahoma County (and then employ this demonic perversity through *music*) makes Johnson's bargain as real as anything else. It would also indicate that the devil is lazy, since Johnson's entire musical career is a paltry 29 songs. Hydroelectric brainiac Greil Marcus has written some amazing thoughts about Mr. Johnson, particularly about his discovery of Johnson's music in January 1970, a few weeks after seeing the death and destruction of the Rolling Stones' doomed free concert at Altamont Speedway. Marcus compared the experience of hearing songs like "Stones in My Passway" and "Four Until Late" to a phenomenon Herman Melville referred to as "the shock of recognition": Marcus found himself relating to something he had absolutely no relationship with. He says Robert Johnson made him realize he was sick of rock 'n' roll. This fascinates me, because those same Robert Johnson songs only make me sleepy. In 1995, I gave Quincy the Robert Johnson box set for Christmas (augmented with a disco ball) and we immediately tried to listen to it, only to realize that (a) the box set includes two takes of almost every song, sequenced back-to-back, and (b) even the songs that are technically different sounded identical to all the others. I like blues-based rock, but I hate the fucking blues; it was more fun to play *Let It Bleed* and look at Johnson's photograph on the front of the box. He certainly had a stellar hat.

Much like the site of Duane Allman's demise, this present-day crossroads doesn't look like anything: It looks like (duh) two roads. There are fragments of spilled barley on the shoulder of each road, so this must be a thoroughfare for local grain trucks.

The only thing marking the site is a billboard aggressively pro-moting microsurgical vasectomy reversal. What strikes me as most ironic is the fact that I was able to find Robert Johnson's crossroads with the Tauntaun's GPS: Somehow, it seems like satellite technology should not allow you to find the origin of America's most visceral, organic art form. You'd think the devil would have blown up my transmission. Then again, Satan might be secretly happy with me, because I played AC/DC's "Highway to Hell" for the duration of the 40-minute drive from downtown Memphis. Which only made sense, because that's what this highway is supposed to be.

Since I know I'm going to have to write about these cross-roads for my *Spin* story, I wander around the area in the hope of finding anything I might be able to classify as metaphoric. There's nothing here. As I walk up 49, it strikes me that this entire road trip is a peculiar thing to be doing and that I'm hav-ing an awfully strange summer, all things considered. I used to have strange summers semi-annually, but strange summers tend to dissipate as you get older. In 1991, I lived with two guys, one of whom was a collegiate pole-vaulter; we had pole-vaulting poles laying across the floor of our living room for three months, and we tripped over them constantly. I played video games all night and never had any money. There was a Mexican guy in our apartment complex who worked on his van 11 hours a day, and we referred to him as "Van Guy." We would play Skid Row on maximum volume at 2:00 A.M., and nobody complained. This was the kind of housing development where nobody complained about anything, ever. Van Guy would actually ask us to turn our stereo *up* if we happened to be playing "Monkey Business." One night, a drunk girl broke into our apartment while I was sleep-ing on the couch, but it turned out she was simply confused (she thought she was breaking into her ex-boyfriend's apartment). I fell in love with one of our neighbors; her name was Heather, and she would rush over to our apartment every time MTV showed the Alice in Chains video for "Man in the Box," coquettishly claiming that the video's imagery terrified her. We went to see *Point Break* together, but nothing happened. That, obviously, was a weird summer. The summer of 1993 was almost as weird; I was living with two very short men who liked to smoke cigars and wrestle on the carpet, and (somehow) we had a swimming pool. Every afternoon, a perfect-looking woman would come over to our pool and try to teach me how to swim, but I never learned; all we ever did was drink Coors in the sun and get heatstroke. Nothing ever happened between us; neither of us even tried. I'd watch two syndicated hours of *Saved by the Bell* at suppertime (two episodes on USA and two episodes on TBS) before driving over to a house on a street called Dyke Avenue (really!) and drinking Boone's Farm wine with seven alcoholic slackers who were somehow even lazier than me. Radiohead's "Creep" was on MTV constantly, and we universally agreed that Jonny Greenwood's guitar tones sounded like a lawnmower. We used to argue about the U.S. Constitution, although I can't recall if we actually cared. Every person in that Dyke Ave house was depressed about nothing in particular. And it was *weird*. And it's weird how it all seemed normal at the time, and that it never occurred to me that this was not how normal people lived, and that there would eventually be a day in my future when I would look back on that summer and realize I spent the most compelling period of my life sleepwalking through reality. Because—right now, in the present tense—I know I'm experiencing the third-weirdest summer of my life. I'm wholly aware of that fact. I am wholly aware that hopelessly tromping through road ditches in rural Mississippi in the hope of understanding the satanic majesty of Robert Johnson will be hard to explain to someone when I'm 50. The context will be unthinkable. In the distant future, this afternoon will probably seem weirder than living with a pole-vaulter in 1991.

Or maybe they'll just seem the same.

Somehow, I always assumed the Deep South would be similar to the not-so-deep Midwest. I'm not sure why I have always assumed this; perhaps it's because—whenever I meet displaced Southerners in New York City—they remind me of what I miss about the United States (a nation that Manhattan is not part of). But it turns out Mississippi is not like North Dakota. It's not even like Ohio. People here are inflexibly obsessed with "being Southern," and that self-adoration manifests itself in completely unpredictable ways. For example: As I drive away from Satan's Crossroads, the man on 94.1 FM "the Buzz" tells me it's almost five o'clock, and then he says, "And you know what that means!" And I *do* know what that means; it means he is about to play whatever song this radio station always plays at five o'clock on Friday, which will signal that the workweek is over and it's time for everyone to drink Corona (a beverage "the Buzz" seems to advertise every seven minutes). In Cleveland, the song they always played at 5:00 P.M. on Fridays was Bruce Springsteen's "Born to Run." In Fargo, it was Loverboy's "Working for the Weekend." These both seemed like obvious choices (especially the latter). However, "the Buzz" plays "Camel Walk" by Southern Culture on the Skids, a commercially insignificant band that looks like a cross between the B-52's, the Jon Spencer Blues Explosion, and the kind of U.S. citizens usually described as "the unemployable." When performing live, Southern Culture on the Skids periodically throws pieces of fried chicken into the audience. "Camel Walk" is a song about the erotic qualities of oatmeal-pie consumption. Somehow, this is the song that represents philosophical freedom in Mississippi; this is the universal metaphor for escaping the

127

workaday clutches of The Man. But it is *their* song, you know? Cleveland co-opted Springsteen from Jersey, abashedly pretending that he's actually a part of Ohio culture; Fargo picked Canada's Loverboy simply because they sang the most expository lyrics. But the South doesn't want to co-op anything. They like who they are.

THE TENTH DAY

Onward to Iowa ➤ A Coincidence of Consequence ➤
The Life I Forgot I Had

There is a certain emotion we all have the potential to experience, and it is an emotion that can only be described as "terrifying nostalgia." I briefly felt it yesterday afternoon, but it
smothered me in totality at 11:30 last night. I was watching a
movie on the Sundance Channel called *Security, Colorado*,
which is a city I've never been to and which probably does not
exist. It was a cheap, rudimentary film (slow-moving, shot on
video, mostly improvised) that was clearly made by people in
their very early twenties. The plot involved a 21-year-old
woman from Denver who relocated to Security, Colorado, to be
with her new boyfriend and quickly became depressed by her
alien surroundings. The pacing of this movie was shockingly
deliberate: In one scene, the woman just sat at a desk and
wordlessly updated her résumé; later, we watched her drive to
the post office and mail the résumé to prospective employers.
Within the reality of *Security, Colorado*, this sequence constitutes "action." And I'm not sure if this was supposed to be
entertaining or insightful, but it was certainly arresting. I
could have watched that scene five times in a row.

Now, here's what's so terrifying about *Security, Colorado*:

The stark, pedestrian images used by the filmmakers (probably out of financial necessity) expressed nothing, symbolically or metaphorically. The only purpose they served was to remind me that a huge chunk of my life is *completely over,* even though I will probably live 60 more years. There are so many things that will never happen to me again, and I never even noticed when those things stopped occurring. And this does not mean I wish I had my old life back, because I like my new life better; I was just shocked to discover how much of what used to be central to my existence doesn't even matter *to me* anymore.

There is a scene in *Security, Colorado* where the female protagonist ("Karen") is working at a record store, and an acquaintance comes into the store and invites her to a house party. A few hours later, Karen drives to a home that looks likes a cross between a private residence and a dive bar; she walks down to the cement-laden basement and stands around uncomfortably, thoughtlessly chatting with people she barely knows while listening to an amateur garage band playing at a ridiculous volume in a very small space. After the party, she returns to her spartan apartment. Her TV is broken. I think she sleeps on a mattress on the floor, but maybe it's just a bad futon; she has some sporadic sex (but not much), and it only makes her life worse. Karen worries about everything, but she can only express her worry through uncreative clichés. Her whole life has an excessively casual, excessively melodramatic ambience.

What's so disquieting to me is how this kind of life—a life of going to joyless keg parties and having intense temporary acquaintances and spending most of one's time in basements and tiny apartments and crappy rented houses with five bedrooms— was once my life completely (as it probably was for many people like me). Those were the only things I *ever* did. That wasn't part of how I lived; that was everything. But now it's like those experiences never happened *at all*. I can recall having conversations with people during college that would seem impossible to have today (both in subject matter and in overall tone). I vaguely recall a person from Stillwater, Minnesota; I can't remember her name. She had black hair and pointy eyebrows. She was flat-chested and pretty. One night in November, we sat in her bedroom and spent 45 minutes intensely discussing how Pearl Jam's *Ten* was undeniably good, but not as life-altering as *Nevermind* or *Screaming Life* (this Minnesota chick adored Soundgarden, so I pretended they were electrifying). Nothing romantic happened; we weren't drunk, and we weren't close friends. I just happened to be there, and we just talked. Pedestrian as those details may seem, I honestly cannot imagine falling into that kind of situation ever again. I mean, how did I possibly end up sitting on this woman's bed? What were the circumstances that led me there? Was Eddie Vedder really that significant to us? And why did this seemingly intimate encounter lead absolutely nowhere? Why didn't we (at the very least) become friends? The whole episode now strikes me as inappropriate and random and completely inexplicable. *But that used to be my life, all the time.* That used to be normalcy, and now that normalcy is completely over. Things like that will never happen to me again, even if I want them to. And I did not choose to *stop* living that life, nor did I try to *continue* living that life. I just didn't notice when it stopped.

When you start thinking about what your life was like 10 years ago—and not in general terms, but in highly specific detail—it's disturbing to realize how certain elements of your being are completely dead. They die long before you do. It's astonishing to consider all the things from your past that used to happen all the time but (a) never happen anymore, and (b) never even cross your mind. It's almost like those things didn't happen. Or maybe it seems like they just happened to someone else. To someone you don't really know. To someone you just hung out with for one night, and now you can't even remember her name.

Flipping back and forth on the car radio between an "'80s Retro Weekend" and an über-conventional classic-rock station, I hear the following three songs in sequence: "Mr. Roboto," "Jumpin' Jack Flash," and a popular ballad from the defunct hair-metal band Extreme.

Well, that settles it: Styx and Stones may break my bones, but "More Than Words" will never hurt me.

The caller ID on my vibrating cell phone reads "Diane." It makes me nervous to answer my phone while driving across a bridge, but this is something I must do.

"Hey hey," I say say.

"How's tricks?" asks Diane. "Where are you?"

"Over the water," I say. "I miss you."

"I miss you too," Diane says. "It's boring here without you. There's nobody to talk to."

"What's going on in the office? What am I missing?"

"We had a meeting yesterday, and we accomplished nothing. Marc Spitz accused Ultragrrl of being retarded," says Diane. "That was the whole meeting. The big news around the office is that Jon Dolan has been beating Chris Ryan at billiards, and this is controversial, somehow."

"Really? That's fucking crazy! How many times have they played? That's insane." Diane does not seem to recognize how shocking this information is; you see, Chris Ryan is a good pool player, and Jon Dolan is merely okay.

"I have no idea how many times they've played. Why is anyone even talking about this? I don't understand you people." It sounds as if Diane is waiting for a train or a bus (or possibly a rickshaw). "How have you been eating? You should try to eat a salad or something. Or some soup. Don't just eat chicken-fried steak every meal."

"How much mail have I received in my absence?" I ask.

"A shitload," says Diane.

Mail is something I have been thinking about a lot: One of the best things about working at a rock magazine is the amount of mail you receive. As I mentioned earlier, your entire existence as a rock critic is built around the process of reviewing one's mail. Pretty much every day, you get dozens of free CDs, a few free DVDs, a book or two, and random letters from random people making random requests. The most compelling piece of mail I ever received was from a prison inmate named Wayne Lo. The letter was an obsessively scribbled four-page manifesto about heavy metal (specifically the band Europe), as Wayne Lo had read a book I wrote about hair bands from the 1980s. When I first opened his letter, I had no idea who Wayne Lo was, and I suspected he was just some faceless Asian dude who had likely been busted for dealing acid, since most incarcerated fans of my writing seem to be acid dealers. But then I got to the bottom of page two, where Lo had off-handedly written the following paragraph: "*I came to prison in '92 . . . people thought I was some hardcore-loving punk when I was arrested because I had a Sick of It All T-shirt on when I was arrested. That was just a crazy coincidence. Sometimes I wonder what would have happened if I had a Poison or a Warrant shirt on. Would they have asked whether the music made me do it? If you didn't know, I was the first school shooter of the '90s. I killed two people and wounded four at Simon Rock's College in December of '92. I was a sophomore then. Just turned 18 a month earlier.*" He then wrote "18 and Life," which was the breakthrough single for Skid Row and which (I think) was supposed to strike me as ironic. And then he casually returned to writing about the relationship between the country song

"What Might Have Been" by Little Texas and the White Lion power ballad "When the Children Cry." I was mildly freaked out by all this, so I immediately Googled his name and discovered that Wayne Lo believed God had told him to kill those innocent people and that there's actually a book (Gregory Gibson's *Gone Boy*) written by the father of one of Lo's victims. This book tries to reconcile the senseless, perverse murder of the author's son.

Sometimes it's difficult when you discover what kind of people appreciate your work.

"Be careful when you drive," Diane interjects. "Keep both hands on the wheel. And make sure you get enough sleep at night, otherwise you might get highway hypnosis."

"Man, I bet Chris Ryan must be pissed."

"What? Why?"

"Was Dolan just playing especially well?"

"Are we still talking about pool?"

"Was Chris Ryan playing poorly, or was Dolan just playing great? What bar were they at? Were they very drunk? Were they listening to 'Werewolves of London' by Warren Zevon?"

"I have to get back to work, Chuck."

"But I want to keep talking," I say.

"I know you do," Diane says. "I know you do."

Four hours ago, I was looking for a motel. Then I heard something over the radio waves of rural Iowa: A scant 36 miles away, Great White was performing a benefit concert in Cedar Rapids to raise money for victims of the Station fire. I do not believe that luck exists, but sometimes I still get lucky.

After turning the car around and driving to Cedar Rapids (at speeds upwards of 90 mph, listening to Soundgarden's *Badmotorfinger* and still thinking about nameless, pointy-eyebrowed girls from Minnesota), I was faced with a logistical conundrum: I had no idea whatsoever about where this concert was going to happen. I knew which city it was in, but not the specific club that was hosting it. This is a bigger problem than one might think, because the kind of bar that hosts Great White shows in 2003 is not exactly a big-ticket establishment. I decide to just walk into a HandiMart gas station and ask the kid working the Slushee machine if he knows where this show is going to happen; he does not. In fact, he has no idea such a show has even been planned. He thinks Great White has broken up. He says he likes the Offspring. I then ask him a follow-up question: "Well, where do you *think* a band like Great White would play, assuming they were to perform in Cedar Rapids?" He briefly plays with the hoop in his nose and then takes a guess: "Probably the Cabo Sports Bar." Apparently, this is a brand-new place, right next to the shopping mall.

And you know what? His guess is completely fucking right.

The show is outside the bar on the club's sand volleyball courts. It's $15 to get inside, and all the money is going to the Station Family Fund. When I get there, the opening band, Skin Candy, is doing a cover of Tesla's "Modern Day Cowboy." There are maybe 1,000 people waiting for Great White, and it's a rough crowd: When you look into the eyes of this audience, you can see the hardness of their lives. At this show, there aren't many people with a job that includes air-conditioning. More than a few of them are complaining about the fact that a 16-ounce Budweiser costs $3.50. It is impossible to stare at these people and not imagine that this is exactly what the crowd in West Warwick must have looked like.

I get backstage (which is really just the other side of the parking lot) and find Great White vocalist Jack Russell; he's wearing a sleeveless T-shirt and pants with an inordinate number of zippers, and he's got quite the little paunch. Somebody walks by and stealthily hands him a handful of tablets, but it turns out they're merely Halls cough drops. I ask him what he remembers about the fire in Rhode Island, but he balks. "I can't talk about any of that stuff because there is an ongoing investigation and I don't want to interfere with anything the attorney general is doing." This is understandable, but I ask him the same question again, 30 seconds later.

"Well, it changed my life," he says the second time around. "Of course it changed my life. But I had to make a choice between sitting in my house and moping forever or doing the one thing I know how to do."

Russell tells me he can't talk any further. However, Great White guitarist Mark Kendall is less reticent. He's wearing Bono sunglasses and a black do-rag, and he fingers his axe throughout the duration of our conversation. He seems considerably less concerned about the Rhode Island attorney general.

"That night was just really confusing," Kendall says. "I was totally numb. I didn't know what was going on. I had my sunglasses on, so I really couldn't see what was happening. But it didn't look that bad at first. It was when the door opened that things became chaos."

I tell him that there are people in Rhode Island who will never forgive him for what happened, even if it wasn't his fault. Even if it was no one's fault.

"Oh, I totally understand that. That is a completely understandable reaction on their behalf," Kendall says. "I mean, I've never gotten over losing my grandfather, and he died 15 years ago. On the day of that show, I met five different people during the day who ended up dying that night. I feel really, really bad about what happened. But no blame should be cast."

Supposedly, Great White now donates almost all of their tour revenue to charity. I ask Kendall how they manage to donate everything to charity and still afford to live. "Well, we did sell over 12 million records," he tells me with mild annoyance. Sometimes it's easy to forget that there was once an era when "Once Bitten, Twice Shy" was considered the epitome of pop music, and that era was only 15 years ago. Twenty minutes later, the band opens with "Red Light," and—much to my surprise—they sound pretty great. Visually, the 2003 version of Great White is unlike any band I've ever seen; this is because the original drummer, bassist, and second guitarist have been replaced with punk kids who can't be over the age of 25. It looks like Russell and Kendall have formed a blues super-group with Green Day. After the first song, Russell asks for 100 seconds of silence to commemorate the West Warwick victims. It works for maybe a minute, but then some bonehead standing in front of me holds up a Japanese import CD and screams, "Great White rules!"

"Lucy? This is Chuck. Are you sleeping?"

"I'm never sleeping. What are you calling about? Where are you?"

"Why are you awake? It must be something like 3:30 A.M. in New York."

"It's past 3:30. I can't sleep. I keep thinking my eyes are going to roll back into my skull."

"What?"

"You know how your eyes roll back when you start to fall asleep? I can feel them doing that every time I close my eyes, but I don't think they're going to stop. I think my eyes are going to roll back into my head and disappear."

"Lucy, that makes no sense."

"I know! It's like some kind of Chinese torture. I'm going to see an ophthalmologist tomorrow. It's freakish."

"Perhaps you have early-onset Cotard's syndrome."

"Perhaps I do! What is that, exactly?"

"It's a psychotic condition associated with nihilistic delusions. People who are still alive become convinced that they're actually dead."

"That doesn't sound anything like what I just described to you, Chuck. Where are you?"

"Iowa. I just saw Great White, and they were not bad."

"How much have you had to drink tonight?"

"Not much. But some."

"Are you calling about Diane?"

"Why would I be calling about Diane?"

"I don't know. You tell me, Chuck. You're the one who called."

"But I never said I was calling about Diane. I never even implied that I was."

"That's true."

"Diane doesn't love me because I love her. That's all it is, isn't it? The fact that I love her makes me completely unappealing."

"I don't know, Chuck. But . . . yes. That is most likely accurate."

"Why is she like that?"

"I don't know. Why is everybody like that? Why are *you* like that?"

"You know, I suddenly don't want to talk about this. And now I'm faced with the additional concern of your eyes rolling back inside your skull. I don't even know how to address this issue. Do you think maybe you're losing your goddamn mind?"

"That's certainly what my mom thinks."

"You better get to sleep, Lucy. You'll be exhausted tomorrow. Sorry I called so late. I don't know what I was thinking."

"No worries. I was just lying here, pretending to be hooked up to an IV needle."

"Lucy, I absolutely cannot fathom why you would be pretending that."

"That's what I do when I can't fall asleep. I pretend I'm in a hospital, hooked up to an IV—except that I imagine the IV is actually draining the life out of me, drip by drip."

"Oh, yeah. I guess you told me that once before. Well, good night. Have fun pretending to die, Lucy Chance."

"You too, Chuck Klosterman."

THE ELEVENTH DAY

Planes That Land Quickly and Accidentally ➤
The Truth About Lying ➤ I'm Worried, I'm Always in Love

The sky blinds me through my still-cracked windshield this morning as I listen to my favorite album of the 1970s: *Rumours* by Fleetwood Mac. *Rumours* was the best-selling studio album of that decade and remains the sixth most successful record of all time, and I always love it when my own personal taste perfectly dovetails with that of mainstream-rock consumers from a bygone era; it's like finding common ground with the bones in a graveyard. Maybe I'll follow up *Rumours* with the Eagles' *Their Greatest Hits 1971–1975*, Michael Jackson's *Thriller*, Shania Twain's *Come on Over*, and the 1976 debut record from Boston. Maybe all music sucks until it sells 17 million copies.

As anyone who watches VH1 surely knows, nearly every song on *Rumours* is about breaking up with people, as it was written and recorded while (a) guitarist-songwriter Lindsey Buckingham ended a lengthy romance with shawl-clad singer Stevie Nicks, (b) bassist John McVie divorced singer-keyboardist Christine McVie, and (c) drummer Mick Fleetwood began mentally preparing himself to nail Stevie, which finally happened during (I think) the making of 1979's *Tusk*. *Rumours* became a very metaphoric album for Quincy and me. We wasted a lot of time debating the song "Go Your Own Way," specifically over who had the moral high ground in the lyrical argument between Buckingham and Nicks. Predictably, Q always took Stevie Nicks's side in this debate, and I always aligned myself with control freak Lindsey. "The fact that Lindsey Buckingham even wrote a song like this proves he's a jackass," Q would say. "What kind of asshole forces his ex-girlfriend to sing backing vocals on a song that accuses her of being a slut?" In retrospect, this does seem egocentrically vindictive. Still, I think Stevie Nicks totally had it coming, especially in light of the fact that she later shacked up with Don Henley.

Rumours is supposedly Bill Clinton's favorite album, and that makes complete sense (Hillary is his gold dust woman, I guess, and I'm sure she would verify that rulers make bad lovers). The songs on *Rumours* make me think about myriad things, particularly about how complicated it will be to reconcile my relationship with Diane if I see Lenore in two days and suddenly decide that I want to drop everything and spend the rest of my life with her. This is probably not going to happen, but it's also not impossible; the thing about Lenore is that I cannot say no to her. Whenever we're apart, it's remarkably easy for me to detach myself from her life. However, if we're in the same room—and if I have to look into her doe eyes and if I'm close enough to smell her neck—I am as weak as Jack Lemmon in *Glengarry Glen Ross*. The same thing happens when I talk to Diane on the telephone: Somehow, her language always obliterates my logic. Like Ron Artest in the open floor, Diane can always break me down. It would be interesting to see what would happen if Diane called me while I was looking directly at Lenore; I have no idea who is the unstoppable force and who is the immovable object. I have no control over the things that thrill me.

But you know what? Wishing for control is like wishing for

the rapture, and *Rumours* sometimes reminds me of this. I once interviewed Jeff Tweedy of Wilco, arguably the least pretentious semi-genius of the modern rock age. We started talking about how the best parts of songs are usually accidents; Tweedy mentioned that the most transcendent moments in pop music are inevitably unintentional, because listeners reinvent those mistakes and give them a personal meaning no artist could ever create on purpose. This segued into a conversation about Fleetwood Mac, and I told him about the way Quincy and I would incessantly play the opening five seconds of "I Don't Want to Know" at maximum volume. This is because—if you play the song loudly enough—you can hear Lindsey Buckingham's fingers sliding down the strings of his acoustic guitar. His sliding phalanges make this unspeakably cool squeak; it sounds organic and raw and impossible to fake. Q and I would play this opening sequence over and over and over again, and we were convinced that this was the definitive illustration of what we both loved about music; we loved hearing the *inside* of a song. And when I told that story to Tweedy, I was surprised how inexplicably happy it made him.

"It's so great to hear you say that," Tweedy said. "I don't know Lindsey Buckingham personally, but—from what I know about him—I would assume he's the kind of artist who wants to control every single element of how his music is perceived. Yet the one moment off *Rumours* that was most important to you and your friend is a little crack he couldn't spackle over. Nobody can control anything, really."

This is true. In fact, the day after Tweedy told me this, he checked himself into a rehabilitation clinic for an addiction to painkillers. I never saw it coming. We had talked in his backyard for three hours, and nothing seemed wrong; Tweedy seemed totally reasonable and devoid of delusion. He seemed completely in command of his life. Now, maybe he was pretending. But maybe we're all pretending. And maybe that's why I've convinced myself that I love "I Don't Want to Know" for its five seconds of squeak. Nobody can control anything, really.

Clear Lake, Iowa, is a town with a wonderfully expository name: it's a little community next to a lake, and the water in that sumbitch is way clear. Almost 45 years ago, a small plane crashed in a frozen soybean field 4.7 miles north of this town, and its cabin held the Big Bopper (best known for "Chantilly Lace"), Ritchie Valens (best known for Lou Diamond Phillips's winning portrayal in *La Bamba*) and Buddy Holly (best known as the precursor to Rivers Cuomo, at least according to 15-year-old emo girls currently living in Omaha). Don McLean felt this crash was the day the music died, inadvertently prompting many drunk U.S. males to symbolically drive Chevys to levies. Thirty-two years later (and despite Madonna's effort to prove otherwise), "American Pie" remains a stunning musical achievement. There are only two *really* long songs that get played on classic-rock radio every single day: "American Pie" (whose album version clocks in at 8 minutes and 38 seconds) and "Stairway to Heaven" (recently remastered to 8 minutes exactly). I've noticed that nobody changes the station when "American Pie" comes on; they always listen to the whole thing and sing along with the chorus. However, almost no one listens to "Stairway to Heaven" all the way through. We need some sociology grad students to look into this.

But ANYWAY, it takes maybe 15 minutes to drive out to the gravel road near the crash location (nice little maps are provided at the Clear Lake visitors' bureau), and then it's a half-mile walk through a bean field. As I walk along the fence line toward the unknown marker, I find myself considering the relationship between plane crashes and rock 'n' roll. If you're a dead rock star and you weren't a heroin addict, odds are you died in a plane. As you (hopefully) noticed on page 97, I visited the Skynyrd disaster just four days before this one. As stated on page 109, heterosexual guitarist Randy Rhoads died in a plane crash in Florida. Otis Redding's plane went down in Madison, Wisconsin. Rick Nelson's DC-3 crashed on the way to Dallas in 1985, and everybody on board was burned alive when the cabin caught on fire (except for the pilot and the copilot, which is something that *never* seems to happen). Stevie Ray Vaughan didn't die in a plane crash, but a helicopter is close enough; I suppose Patsy Cline wasn't a "rock star," but her 1963 death near Camden, Tennessee, falls into this same idiom.

For unadulterated freak-out potential, nothing usurps death by plane crash. In a car accident, there's never more than an instant of recognition—if you have any more time than that, you can usually slam on the brakes and avoid the part where you die. When you die in a car, there is no time to think—it's like the bullet you never hear. But when you die in an airplane, you *totally* know it's coming. There is going to be—at the very minimum—a solid 20 to 30 seconds when you will be struck with one overwhelming realization: "I am falling out of the sky and I am going to die. This seat belt is worthless. I have no other options, and there is nothing I can do." Those 30 seconds must feel longer than listening to "American Pie" *and* "Stairway to Heaven," even if they were played back-to-back by Carlos Santana.

When I look down at my Nikes, I see semi-fresh shoe prints in the powder-black dirt. People must make this walk regularly. These are people I can relate to. I would estimate that this is probably the 15,000th time I've walked through a bean field. In southeast North Dakota, beans are one of the more popular "row crops" (so called because they are planted in parallel rows). North Dakota farmers take an unreasonable amount of pride in their ability to plant beans in relentlessly straight lines; perfect rows prove that you can drive a tractor without oversteering, and this proof is satisfying, somehow. The straightness of the rows is visible from the road as you drive past the field; if the rows are truly straight, the field looks like a tall stick figure running alongside your car when you cruise past the crops. In the middle of every summer, there comes a point when the bean fields become populated with large weeds, but it's too late in the growing season to spray them with herbicide or to remove them with a cultivator. The only option is to "walk the beans." What that means is that you get a bunch of teenagers together. Each kid takes responsibility for eight rows and the entire group walks up and down the field, manually removing any rogue plant that isn't supposed to be there. It's exhaustive, mindless work; you are constantly bending over to pull up ragweeds by their roots, and if you walk the beans all day long, you can easily meander between 15 and 25 miles (during the hottest part of the year). Rich farmers would hire Mexican migrant workers to do the job, but middle-class farmers just made their own kids do it, as children work even cheaper than migrants (this was also supposedly "safer" than hiring Mexicans, since everyone in my hometown assumed that Mexicans were definitely thieves and possibly rapists). The first summer I walked the beans, my older brother paid me and my sister $25 apiece for a combined 80 hours of work. That may seem like a rip-off, but it was totally okay at the time; he advanced me $12.50 up front, thereby allowing me to buy Mötley Crüe's *Theatre of Pain* the week it was released. As I grew older, I joined forces with two other teenagers, and we would walk the beans for other area farmers; they paid us real money (usually $15 per acre), and the whole process became borderline enjoyable. It was like going for a stroll that never seemed to end; every single conversation lasted a minimum of 90 minutes. I was about to enter 10th grade. The three of us mostly talked about girls we wanted to have sex with and guys we wanted to kill. This kind of talk was not uncommon in my social circle. When you are a male entering the 10th grade, there are only four kinds of people on the planet: girls you want to fuck, girls who are unfuckable, guys you want to kill, and guys who generally seem okay. For a 10th grader, those are the only four demographics for the entire world population. Obviously, that worldview changes as you become an adult; now that I'm 31, I realize there are at least six categories.

However, there is no one to talk to today, there are no killable dudes or unfuckable women occupying my mind, and there are no weeds that need to be pulled. I am the only soul in this bean field. At one point, I start to think I must have made a miscalculation, because I've walked a helluva long way and I still don't see anything on the horizon except more beans. Maybe I'm in the wrong field. Maybe I took the wrong road. I consider turning around. But then—seconds before I surrender and go back to the car—I find the spot where three legends died in one depressing coincidence.

In fact, I find myself looming directly above this spot.

This memorial is small.

Without question, the craziest aspect of the Holly-Valens-Bopper death memorial is that nobody could *ever* find it by accident; it's just a tiny metal cross in the middle of deep nothingness, decorated with Bud Light beer cans and empty cigarette lighters and somebody's Blockbuster card. It's sort of like getting to the summit of K2 and realizing it's littered with dozens of empty oxygen tanks. I stand in front of the metal cross for maybe 10 minutes (probably nine minutes more than necessary), and then I walk the half-mile back to the Tauntaun. While driving away, I play the Radiohead song "Lucky" off *OK Computer,* a beautiful track about trying to understand if surviving an air crash is an illustration of good fortune (because you lived) or misfortune (because you were in a plane that fucking crashed). This made me think of Waylon Jennings, the member of Buddy Holly's band who famously did not board that ill-fated aircraft bound for Moorhead, Minnesota; he gave up his plane seat and drove. As a result, Waylon saw the 1970s. Waylon saw the 1980s. Waylon saw the 1990s. Of course, he still died in 2002 (just after having his foot amputated because of an illness). He had a long life that Holly never knew. But now that they're *both* dead, I'm not sure being remembered as the narrator for *The Dukes of Hazzard* is a better legacy than being the unofficial namesake for an entire genre of eyeglasses. In an unspecific, mostly intangible way, Buddy Holly will always be around. So—depending on how you view the afterlife—it's difficult to deduce how Thom Yorke would classify Buddy Holly's final destiny; if there is no afterlife, Holly is having the closest possible equivalent. Maybe Buddy Holly was luckier than we want to believe. Which, of course, raises another question: Why do we want to live?

I'm driving north again, heading to Rochester, Minnesota, to see two of my closest friends from college and their lovely wives. I adore seeing these guys, and they are among the 15 people in all America whom I trust. But there's one thing that makes me nervous about seeing them: I'm always afraid that they suspect I've become a drug addict, and I'm sometimes afraid they are not-so-secretly judging me for this. However, they are wrong. Here's how to tell if you (or someone you know) has a drug problem: Pay attention to what CD they use for drug maintenance.

When separating the seeds out of marijuana or chopping up freshly purchased cocaine, you generally use the jewel case of a compact disc as the base of operations. Jewel cases were *designed* for this process. And when you're young and enthusiastic and entirely recreational about your drug use, you always pick a CD that is somehow symbolic of the experience: With marijuana, you will select Pink Floyd's *Wish You Were Here* or My Bloody Valentine's *Loveless* or Thin Lizzy's *Jailbreak*. If you're chopping up coke with your Capital One VISA card, you'll use the jewel case from Sabbath's *Vol. 4* or Neil Young's *Tonight's the Night* or *Be Here Now* by Oasis. But if you ever reach a point where you no longer care about the aesthetic of the album you select, and you don't even consider what album you're pulling off the rack, and you find yourself pouring $70 of cocaine onto Men at Work's *Business as Usual*, you have a drug problem. Get help.

THE TWELFTH DAY

"Slow Ride" *v.* "Free Ride"

A comparative study of classic-rock tropes placed
within the context of American road travel, examining the merits
(or lack thereof) of metaphorically (or literally) riding unnamed
objects of unknown size

Musical structures define the process of motion. There are particular words and melodies that lend themselves to transportation; often, pop songs of this nature *only* sound good to humans who are actively operating motorized vehicles. There are myriad examples of this: Judas Priest's "Better by You, Better than Me," the Scorpions' "Lovedrive," Tom Cochrane's "Life Is a Highway," and anything ever recorded by REO Speedwagon. However, the two clearest examples of this phenomenon are Foghat's 1976 song "Slow Ride" and Edgar Winter's 1973 hit "Free Ride." These songs are so philosophically intertwined that they're often conflated by certain subsets of Americans, namely (a) gargantuan men with mustaches who put money into jukeboxes when they drink Coors, and (b) unemployed film historians who are never quite sure which of these songs appears on the soundtrack to Richard Linklater's *Dazed and*

Confused[1] and which one was used in the film but wasn't included on the official soundtrack release.[2] However, those who make this mistake are not merely juxtaposing a smoked-out heavy rocker with a mid-tempo boogie rocker; those who make this mistake are misguided patriots and shortsighted moral relativists. The sonic differences between "Slow Ride" and "Free Ride" pale in comparison to their idealistic dissonance: While "Slow Ride" advocates a worldview that accepts and understands life as it is, "Free Ride" demands its listener to actively change the world and take a proactive, self-reliant approach to everyday existence. "Slow Ride" is a more visceral song, but "Free Ride" outlines a more optimistic way to live. This is probably because Edgar Winter—almost without question—is the most successful albino "keytar" enthusiast of the late 20th century. He had a lot to be happy about.

"Slow Ride" opens with a repetitive bass drum that (momentarily) creates an atmosphere of utter doom; it is as if we are all enslaved in the belly of a pirate ship and Foghat drummer Roger Earl is going to force us to methodically row until we reach the end of a pre-Copernican earth. However, this is ultimately not the case. In truth, we are about to take a "slow ride," and we are implored to "take it easy." But what does Foghat mean when they say *slow*? What truly constitutes *easy*? Though Foghat was from England, their perspective mirrored the constructs of many Eastern religions: parallels can be drawn between Foghat vocalist "Lonesome" Dave Peverett and Vietnamese monk Thich Nhat Hanh, author of *Peace Is Every Step: The Path of Mindfulness in Everyday Life*. Thich Nhat Hanh's principles are based on the idea that every moment is an existence upon itself and there is no action devoid of merit; eat-

1. The former
2. The latter.

ing a bowl of rice can be as satisfying and self-actualizing as completing a triathlon. "Lonesome" Dave Peverett takes the same stance, although it's possible he's actually talking about having sex with strippers from Brixton.

Conversely, "Free Ride" paints the portrait of a society of extremes: Mountains are described as "high," valleys are classified as "low," and no one seems to know how to grapple with this paradox. Here, Winter takes a classically American posture: The answer, he tells us, comes "from within." His conception of a "free ride"—in other words, his conception of *freedom*—is founded on individuality and personal responsibility. A slow rider appreciates the world, but he's also shackled to a static reality; meanwhile, a free rider is a wholly creative force. Edgar Winter personifies the cowboy spirit: He is not trying to find comfort within the present; he is reengineering a living future.

That said, "Slow Ride" is better live.

There are a lot of disenfranchised cool kids in downtown Minneapolis, and a lot of them seem to have a general idea of where Replacements guitarist Bob Stinson drank himself to death in December 1995. They all know it was on the 800 block of West Lake Street, and they all seem to think it was next to a bowling alley called Bryant-Lake Bowl. The kids are all right: Stinson died in a dilapidated upstairs apartment situated above a small-time leather shop that's directly across from the Bryant-Lake lanes. "I remember that night," says BLB cook Holly Morris, a bowling-alley employee of nine years. "Everybody was looking out the window at the ambulances. But I didn't even know who he was at the time. He wasn't that famous."

Morris claims I am probably the first person who ever came looking for the location of Stinson's demise (or at least the only one she can remember). As such, I am unsure which of the two upstairs apartments actually housed Minneapolis's finest alcoholic guitar hero. I walk around to the back of the building and scamper up the wooden steps that lead to the two flats (it occurs to me that these would be hard stairs for a drunk to handle, especially in wintertime). The door on the right has a sign that says BEWARE OF DOG and no sign of activity inside; the door on the left is unmarked, but when I peer through the screen door, I can see a child's drawing of Jesus on the refrigerator.

I knock on the door to the left. No answer. I knock again. Again, no answer. This is strange, because I know (for certain) that somebody is in this apartment: As I circled around to the stairs, I saw a pudgy white arm ashing a cigarette out of the window. Granted, I don't really have a plan here—I'm not exactly sure what I should ask this person if and when he opens the door ("Um . . . do you ever play 'Bastards of Young' and stare at your stereo speakers?"). But I feel like I should at least see the inside of this apartment (or something), so I keep knocking. And knocking. I knock for 10 minutes. No one ever comes out. I try to peep into the same window where I witnessed "the cigarette incident," but now the shade is down and I'm starting to feel like a stalker. I ultimately decide to walk away, having learned zero about a dead musician I really knew nothing about to begin with.

Actually, that's not true; there's at least one thing I know about the Replacements. In January 2000, a friend of mine died from cancer. When I started writing this book, I vowed that I would not mention any of this, because I feel guilty enough about exploiting people in my life who are still alive; I can't fathom feeling as though I took advantage of someone who actually died. But I feel like I need to mention this anyway, because his death was all I could think about when I walked down Stinson's back stairs. I still don't know what it means. Because he was sick for more than a year, I had plenty of time to reconcile my friend's passing—I was able to think about his death for months before it happened. There were no surprises. Nothing—not even the final news—was remotely shocking. But a few weeks after the funeral, I was driving through rural Ohio, and "Bastards of Young" came on my car stereo, and I started crying uncontrollably. And I know why that happened; it happened because my friend—a brilliant, lovable goofball named Thad Holen—adored the Replacements, and he once told me that this was his favorite Replacements song, and it just so happens that the lyrics of "Bastards of Young" talk about burying people and struggling with the memory of when they were around. I comprehend how (and why) I had a relationship with Thad through this song. But what's disturbing is how my relationship with that song kept getting larger and larger. I played it when I got home that night, and I cried again. After a while, other Replacements songs made me want to cry because those other songs suddenly reminded me of "Bastards of Young." And as months and years passed, I didn't even have to play the music of the Replacements; I could just read about the band or imagine what their songs sound like, and I would feel my throat tighten and my pupils moisten. Even as I type this paragraph, I feel extremely close to tears, just because I'm thinking of the Replacements. And that is what I don't understand. When did crying about my friend evolve into crying about a rock band? I mean, I am not thinking about Thad right now. Honestly, I am not. I am thinking about Paul Westerberg, who is a singer I like. I am thinking about *Let It Be* and *Don't Tell a Soul*, which are albums I like. I am thinking about having seen Bob Stinson's unremarkable apartment, which I neither liked nor disliked. I'm not unhappy. But my chest feels like the inside of a frozen cave, and I can't help but wonder if my sincere love for Thad has become an excuse to be insincerely miserable about something else entirely.

Seeing no resolution to my existential recognition of loss, I decide to eat lunch.

Not many people know this, but I lived in Minneapolis in the summer of 1994. The reason not many people know this is because I only lived there for five weeks. As such, there's not much in Minneapolis for me to be nostalgic about; I didn't even live there long enough to keep from getting lost every single time I left my apartment. However, I did saunter into the Uptown Bar and Grill twice a week (always for supper on Sunday night), so this place serves as my emotive ground zero by default. The Uptown Bar and Grill is interesting, because it's almost like two wholly different establishments: One half of the room is like a dive bar–rock club, and the other half is a nice little Midwestern restaurant. The night before the '94 Lollapalooza, I was able to eat a delicious hot turkey sandwich with mashed potatoes and gravy while listening to a semi-hard rock band called Hester Moffet. Everybody in the place was drinking Rolling Rock, and two girls told me it was because *Rolling Rock* is like the phrase *Rock 'n' Roll* in reverse. We were all pretty stupid in the good old days.

While I inhale my lunch (another hot turkey sandwich, although not as tasty as the one I recall from '94), I call Quincy. No answer. There was no answer when I called yesterday, either. What the fuck is going on? For the second time today, I don't leave a message. Maybe she's just out of sorts. Besides, it's not like this is particularly strange behavior; Q is not exactly punctual. The first time Quincy ever came over to my apartment, she was 15 minutes late. "That's one thing you'll have to accept about me," she said as she removed her scarf and threw it on my futon. "Everywhere I go, I'm always 15 minutes early or 15 minutes late." This turned out to be a half-truth. For the next two years, she was 15 minutes late for almost everything we

ever did together. She was never 15 minutes early for anything; once, she arrived exactly on time and mysteriously
elected to count that as being 10 minutes early, which still con-
fuses me. Our nation's relationship with time is something I will
never understand. "You are a foolish man," Quincy would
often tell me. "You show up too early for everything. Don't you
understand that when people say a party is starting at 9:00, they
actually mean the guests are supposed to come at 10:00? That's
just common sense." I will never buy that logic. In America,
parties that are supposed to start at 9:00 P.M. actually start at
10:00 P.M. However, rock concerts that are supposed to start at
9:00 P.M. actually start at 9:45. Movies that are scheduled for
9:00 P.M. don't begin until 9:09. Sporting events set for 9:00 P.M.
begin at 9:05. However, television shows that are set for 9:00 P.M.
do start at 9:00 P.M., unless they're being broadcast on TBS. So
what's crazier: That I show up for things when they're supposed
to begin, or that everyone else in the entire world has somehow
come to accept that every activity operates within its own
unspoken, individual schedule? How is everyone else's wrong-
ness understood to be right?

If Quincy is avoiding me on purpose, I will spend a lot of
time staring at my hands.

The day is warm, but the day is disappearing. I've just arrived
at the apartment of My Nemesis. I am sitting beneath a mammoth poster of the film *Blow Up*, and My Nemesis is sitting in
front of a computer that looks like two computers. We're drinking beer and talking about mutual friends we've completely lost
contact with. Something is going to happen tonight.

I met My Nemesis in November 1990. I walked into somebody's dorm room to play Nintendo, and he was sitting on the
bed, holding an acoustic guitar on which he could play only one
note—the opening note of Tesla's "Love Song." He was wearing

a denim jacket, and he had used a black Magic Marker to draw the symbol for anarchy on the back. It was just about the silliest thing I had ever seen. We immediately became friends. One night, we were driving down Demers Avenue in Grand Forks, North Dakota, and I was sitting in the passenger seat of his Buick Somerset. I made a joke about the likelihood of My Nemesis having anal sex with his high school girlfriend, which was a reference I made 30 or 40 times a day. He pulled over the car and hit me in the face. Soon after, we decided to live together. Every interaction we had was based on arguing, drinking, or both. Usually both. For the first two years we knew each other, it was the most creative friendship I had ever experienced. Over the next two years, it became the most self-destructive, unhealthily competitive relationship I would ever have with anyone. Though we remained close friends for four years, I'm fairly certain we hated each other. At the conclusion of those four years, I graduated from college and immediately got a great job at the largest daily paper in North Dakota's largest city; now, this actually means I got a normal job at a tiny newspaper in a small American town. But it *seemed* like a big deal at the time because I was writing a high-profile column for this publication, and I suddenly became a mini-celebrity in downtown Fargo.[3] This seemed to annoy My Nemesis. Around that same time, a few unsuccessful goofballs I knew from college started an alternative newspaper, and My Nemesis—who was probably my closest friend at the time—used this irrelevant alternative publication as a vehicle to publicly attack me. I responded poorly to this. It prompted me to drive back to Grand Forks, drink about 27 beers, and punch him in the face in front of all our friends. My Nemesis seemed to oddly accept my drunken haymaker, and I suspect he felt as though

3. Which is kind of like being the hottest guy in the Traveling Wilburys.

he (kind of) deserved to get punched at least once. Sadly, I was under the impression that hitting him in the face once would not be as effective as hitting him in the face, say, 1,000 times. And more unfortunately, My Nemesis had consumed somewhere in the vicinity of zero beers, and he had spent his formative years fighting all the people from his hometown who didn't like his anarchy jacket. And most unfortunately, this was the only fight I'd ever been in. Consequently, my career fighting record remains 0–1–0. Afterward, we stood on opposite sides of the street and yelled at each other for so long that the partygoers who happened to witness the debacle actually got bored; they slowly filtered back inside the house to listen to the new Pavement album. I assumed My Nemesis and I would never speak again, and for three years we didn't. But then I ran into him in a bar, and we both wanted to pretend we were cooler than Steve McQueen, so we spoke casually, almost as if we had just seen each other two days ago. Slowly, we started communicating again (usually via e-mail). He's an interesting character, and he's very smart and charismatic, and I suppose I love him. And it's weird, because now we *never* fight. We don't fully trust each other, we aren't emotionally close, and I suspect he would secretly feel like he "won" if I became a failure and my career collapsed. But I'm still staying at his apartment tonight, because he is My Nemesis. And Your Nemesis can't be Your Nemesis unless he is also Your Friend.

My Nemesis asks me a few questions about why I am driving across America, but he is only mildly interested in my answers. He has a job that involves the Internet, and it sounds difficult and boring; I ask him questions, too, but barely listen to his answers. He's had this job for at least five years, and I still have no idea what he does. After four drinks, we drive to some hipster Minneapolis restaurant for dinner, and we talk about the strengths and weaknesses of our respective cell phones. Our larger plan is to meet three other people at a poofy college bar called the Kitty Cat Club; we get there before nine bells. The first of these three people to arrive is a local rock critic, and he likes to drink. He's Drinking Guy. The second of these three people is another local rock critic, but he only orders Coca-Cola. He's Non-Drinking Guy. The third person is yet another local rock critic, and she has an astounding skeletal structure; she looks like Uma Thurman. I think we talk for maybe 33 seconds before I become obsessed with engineering a scenario that will result in me kissing her. So now I am in a bar with three rock critics (one of whom I want to kiss) and My Nemesis, a guy who probably *should* have become a rock critic.[4] I have traveled 2,000 miles to do precisely what I do four nights a week in Manhattan. The beginning is the end is the beginning.

I go outside the bar and attempt to contact Quincy for the sixth time, and she still doesn't answer my call. For the sixth time, I leave no message. Fuck. I guess she doesn't want to see me. My posse of rock critics has moved to the bar's patio, so I join them for some Midwestern Power Drinking. There are a lot of drunks in this world, but people in the Midwest drink differently than everywhere else I've ever been; it's far less recreational. You have to stay focused, you have to work fast, and you have to swallow constantly. Uma, Drinking Guy, My Nemesis, and myself are like pirates. I can't believe Non-Drinking Guy is comfortable with this, but he seems cool with our self-destruction (this impresses me—personally, I despise being around drunk people whenever I'm sober). We all kind of talk like we're doing impersonations of Camille Paglia, assuming she

4. This actually isn't as coincidental as it might seem: Per capita, Minneapolis produces more rock critics than any city on earth. If you meet a rock critic who isn't from New York, there's a 33 percent chance they were raised (or once worked) in the Twin Cities. This loose critical collective is sometimes referred to as "the Vinyl Mafia."

had snorted a lot of Ritalin. Liz Phair has just released a much-maligned comeback album, and it seems like we analyze this record for two fucking hours (or maybe ten fucking minutes). Uma Thurman keeps giving me cigarettes that I'm not even asking for. Every cigarette makes me excited. Something is going to happen tonight.

Now, here's the rub: Going into this evening, My Nemesis had given me the impression that he and Uma Thurman were (potentially) a romantic item. He never directly said that, but it was implied (or at least that's what I chose to infer). But now that we're drinking, it is obvious that this is not the case; My Nemesis merely *wants* them to be an item. The reason I can tell they're not dating is because he's being really, *really* nice to her. So suddenly, I feel cool: My Nemesis and I used to be strikingly similar personalities, but now we're not; now he's just a guy she knows in Minneapolis, and I'm somebody else from someplace different who won't be here tomorrow. Uma Thurman is giving me a lot of attention. Her insights about OutKast and Neil Young are trenchant. She is laughing at my jokes, even when they are not funny. Her laughter is irritating My Nemesis, and I am a little ecstatic. You see, My Nemesis also knows Lenore; they met at a party a few years ago. Since that meeting, My Nemesis has unsuccessfully tried to kiss Lenore on no less than three separate occasions. He doesn't know that I know this, but I know this. And I would like to say this is not on my mind, but it kind of is.

In Minneapolis, the bars close early. We decide to go back to My Nemesis's apartment to drink more booze and get high and continue arguing about whether or not Boston had three great songs or no great songs (the jury remains split). Drinking Guy wants to go to his home and sleep, but it's not difficult to change Drinking Guy's mind. I ride in My Nemesis's Ford Mustang, and I'm shocked by how well he drives when he's dangerously intoxicated; that's another skill set I've lost since moving to New York.

For five minutes, Uma Thurman drunkenly (but purposefully) paces the apartment. She's like this long, sexy snow leopard, hunting for vodka and ice cubes and possibly a lighter. It is shocking how fast physical attraction makes you forget everything else in your life; my despair over not connecting with Quincy (and my apprehension about seeing Lenore in less than 24 hours) evaporates like boiled milk. Everything Uma says sounds flirtatious, even when she asks me where the bathroom is and I don't know. I'm trying to remember anything I've ever casually said to a woman that made her like me, and I'm saying them all at once. This is going to be complicated, but I have a legitimate shot here. I can see a window of opportunity.

But then Uma Thurman does something I could not have anticipated. She (literally) sees a window of opportunity and climbs out onto the roof.

Something is going to happen tonight.

My Nemesis has a palatial apartment; the building was once owned by the heir to the Pillsbury dough fortune. If you crawl out a certain window, you land on the roof of a smaller apartment building that's directly next to it. From there, you can jump back onto My Nemesis's building and ascend to the summit of its roof. But this maneuver is not safe; I suppose it's never safe to climb on any roof, but this roof is very steep and very, very high. So is Uma. She's also been drinking heavily for four hours, and she's wearing heels.

At this point, it becomes abundantly obvious that My Nemesis is pursuing Uma Thurman, because he (literally) pursues her onto this roof. My Nemesis has always been an agile billy goat. This turn of events makes Non-Drinking Guy extremely angry, as he is certain Uma Thurman is going to fall to her death. It is times like these when being Non-Drinking Guy must profoundly suck. Meanwhile, me and Drinking Guy are trying to ascertain the relative danger of the situation, but we're too stoned; we can't tell if this behavior is incredibly grave or incredibly normal. This is the single-biggest problem with taking drugs: What's normal seems crazy, and what's crazy seems normal.

"Do you think we should call the police?" asks Drinking Guy.

"Oh, I don't think so," I say, "unless you think we should. Because if we should, we should do so immediately."

"I don't think we should call the police," Drinking Guy replies. "Although it is going to be pretty bad if she falls off, as she will likely be killed on impact."

"Maybe she does this all the time," I say. "She seems pretty good at climbing."

"She's always been good at climbing."

"Oh, excellent," I say. "So this *is* normal. You've obviously seen her climb things before."

"Yeah, but I think it might have been a staircase."

Non-Drinking Guy is now officially "enraged with concern." He starts yelling at Uma Thurman, demanding that she come down posthaste, insisting that he is going to leave the scene if she does not, because he is not in the mood to watch her die. Uma is straddling the peak of the roof. Damn, she looks so fuckable up there, kicking her head back in laughter, drunkenly risking death for no apparent reason. It's like watching Grace Kelly climb Raymond Burr's fire escape in *Rear Window*. Non-Drinking Guy is so pissed that he's actually balling up his fists in anger. "She is going to kill herself," he pleads to me and Drinking Guy. "Don't you guys care that she will *die* if she falls off? She will not get hurt. She will be fucking *dead*."

I start to imagine what it would be like if Uma Thurman fell to earth. Would she plummet in the blink of an eye, or would it feel like slow motion? Would watching her death haunt me forever? Would I still leave Minneapolis tomorrow morning, no differently than if we had never met? Would I have to include this episode in my narrative, since I'm already doing a story about death? Would this night become the most interesting anecdote of my entire life? Would I spend the next 40 years recounting the night I met a foxy rock chick, smoked a few of her cigarettes, spent four hours trying to kiss her, and then watched her plummet 60 feet to the pavement? Would the final image of her smashed, bloody face completely erase the image of her perfect cheekbones that currently inhabits my consciousness? Would her death become the *only* thing I remember about this person?

But then Uma climbs down.

Uma climbs down from the roof, and so does My Nemesis, and then everybody goes into the living room for two more beers. Non-Drinking Guy immediately returns to his traditionally unenraged self. We start asking each other hypothetical questions, and suddenly it's 4:30 A.M. Uma Thurman hugs me good-bye, and we agree to become Friendsters. People don't die. People go home, and people go to bed, and Quincy never leaves me a voice mail.

Nothing is going to happen tonight.

THE THIRTEENTH DAY

Lenore ➤ The Situation With The Eyeglasses ➤
The Worst Decision I Ever Made on Purpose ➤
Ryan Adams, Somehow

I'm still half wasted when I awake, which is better than being hung over (but just barely). It's 9:05 A.M. I roll over and see a little book on the floor; it's Thomas De Quincey's *Confessions of an English Opium-Eater*. It occurs to me that—since leaving for this trip—I have read nothing except the occasional newspaper (and usually just the sports section). Surprisingly, I don't miss it. I've always been envious of friends who claim to have some kind of profound, erotized relationship with literature, because I don't feel that way at all. My apartment is filled with books, but I secretly suspect I hate reading; sometimes it feels like something I'm forever forcing myself to do (and for reasons I never quite understand). Part of this might have to do with the fact that I write at roughly the same speed I read, so I always feel like I should be making better use of my time. Nobody's paying me to *read*, you know? And I realize voicing this perspective in print is precisely why certain intellectuals consider me irrelevant, and I realize that the proliferation of this style of thinking is probably what makes America a nation of imbeciles, and I realize this sentiment would break the heart of my eighth-grade English teacher. But it's also 85 percent true. And I'm not sure how this happened, because when I was in high school, all I ever did was read; it wasn't until I spent thousands of dollars to pursue higher education that I discovered reading was kind of a neutral, reactive way to spend an evening. At this point, I almost have to force myself to read, which is what I do now; I pick up *Confessions of an English Opium-Eater* and read the first 20 pages. It's not bad. Maybe those 20 pages made me smarter, and maybe they did not. Actually, I just find myself wishing I could eat opium for breakfast, so I'm guessing they did not.

I take a boozy shower in a less-than-sparkling bathroom; it appears My Nemesis still owns the same towels he had in college, although that's probably impossible. Today my drive will be relatively short: I'm going up to see Lenore, who now operates an import store in a little town called Herschel, three hours north of downtown Minneapolis. She opened this store after traveling around the Eastern Hemisphere for nine months, eventually concluding that the people of rural Minnesota needed more opportunities to buy silk products from Thailand. I'm still trying to get my boozy head around that business model.

The reason Lenore was in Asia is the crux of why this three-hour trip is going to be incredibly uncomfortable. I suppose I need to describe what happened between us, lest this story seem incomplete; I am reticent to do so, as it is not something I particularly enjoy recounting, nor is it something Lenore would be very thrilled with me commenting upon. There are times when Lenore enjoys when I write about her, and there are times when she does not; very often, I think she feels like we're having an argument in which she is not allowed to talk back.[1] As

1. Or, as on page 118, she feels like we're having an argument where I talk back *for her*, which is probably worse.

a consequence, I am going to be both brief and vague about all this, and you'll just have to make up the plot points on your own. Sometimes your fiction needs to be somebody else's fact.

Lenore and I were together for five years, but we were never really together at all. For the first six months of our relationship, we were both in Fargo, but it was always understood that Lenore was going to relocate to Minneapolis the week after she graduated from college; as such, things never became serious. After she moved to Minneapolis, I moved to Ohio. For the next four and a half years, we were never in the same city. I dated a few people, but she would always call me on the telephone and inadvertently convince me to walk away from them (which was always easy for me to do). During this four-and-a-half-year stretch, Lenore dated lots of people. She even reconciled with her high school sweetheart and appeared destined for marriage; this man despised me, as he was certain I was consciously trying to sabotage their relationship. This is because I was (and because I did). But the singular aspect of our affair that defied all logic was that—somehow, against all odds—it always worked. We had an unspoken pact: When we were together, we were together; when we were apart, we were apart. I suppose lots of people make similar pacts at different points in their lives, but Lenore and I were especially well-suited for such an agreement. We were remarkably successful at this venture. It was absolutely the most successful entanglement I've ever had with anyone, and it never failed. Until, of course, it failed. And then it failed spectacularly.

As for the details of this failure . . . well, you will not get to read about them. Here is all you need to know: Some time ago, Lenore decided to embark on a nomadic odyssey through Australia and Southeast Asia, ostensibly to "find herself" (why Lenore thought she might "find herself" in Laos has never made sense to me, but I am not a sensible person). A mutual friend was throwing a going-away party for her in Minneapolis, and I flew in from Akron to attend said party and to say my good-byes. Things at this party did not go as planned; even if I wanted to write about the specific events of that night, I don't think I could. My friend Nick Chase was an eyewitness to this debacle, and he still refers to this party as "Chuck's 9/11." He likes to use the events of that night as the ultimate example of humiliation; for example, whenever a pro athlete chokes in the clutch, or whenever a political figure is devastated by scandal, or whenever any overconfident celebrity is delivered a crushing comeuppance by the media, Nick Chase is apt to call my office the following morning and leave a voice mail message such as, "Not since Chuck's 9/11 have I seen a man so emotionally obliterated in public." Nick Chase is very witty.

But ANYWAY, I was pretty sure that particular weekend was the last time I would ever see Lenore. It was not. We reconnected at a wedding in Washington just one month ago, and it was a perfect three days. When she arrived in town, the entire wedding party was rendezvousing at a karaoke bar; the moment I saw her walk through the tinted-glass door, I knew we would wake up together. When I looked into her eyes, I could see the word *yes*. It's like the word *yes* is stenciled into her pupils. And *yes* has always been my favorite word.

Perhaps you are wondering, So what's the problem here? Why don't you just marry this person? I have certainly considered those two questions myself, thousands and thousands of times. But there *is* a problem here. It's not an obvious problem, but it's always around. And the only way I can really describe this problem is by explaining The Situation With The Eyeglasses.

Lenore always hated my eyeglasses. She demanded that I get new frames, and I never did. In 2001, I was on a tour after the release of my first book, and one of the stops was in Minneapolis (where she was living at the time). Lenore saw this as an opportunity to reinvent my face. She took me to the hippest eyeglass outlet in town (and—amazingly—there actually is such a place) and immediately made me try on a pair of $725 frames. The ultra-pushy salesclerk told Lenore that they were hand-made frames from Italy and that I should also get high-density lenses (which were $200) so that the size of my pupils would not be distorted by the thickness of the plastic. Now, it is important to note that I *liked* my old glasses. I didn't love them, but I certainly didn't hate them. They made me look the way I was supposed to look. In theory, I could have argued this point, and I'm sure I would have won. Nobody can make me do anything. But you know what? I suddenly realized that saying no to these glasses would merely result in us going to another eyeglass store and having the same argument. And I was only going to be in Minneapolis one more night, and I didn't want my unwillingness to waste $1,000 on eyeglasses to interfere with the possibility of ripping off Lenore's clothes in six hours. So I wordlessly surrendered my credit card to the salesclerk, and now I have a pair of eyeglasses that are worth more than the combined value of every piece of clothing in my entire wardrobe. Now, Lenore saw this purchase as a major victory. She loves my new glasses because she thinks they make me look fashionable, even though I am not. Meanwhile, I saw this as a minor victory, because the rest of the evening went exactly as I had hoped.

That, in a nutshell, is The Situation With The Eyeglasses. And that, as an allegory, is the problem that has always been between us: Lenore wants me to be a slightly different person than who I actually am, and I can't force myself to care about the things that are important to her. So even when we both "win," nothing really changes.

I will probably wear these glasses for the rest of my life.

➤   ➤   ➤

Herschel is the kind of town that could only exist in Minnesota Lake Country; it's a tourist trap in the middle of nowhere, nestled next to a popular lake you've almost certainly never heard of. There is nothing to do here, figuratively speaking. However, a town like Herschel seems fabulous compared to life on the Minnesota Iron Range (or pretty much anywhere in rural North Dakota), since those places offer nothing to do, *literally* speaking. Assuming they have enough money to own (or rent) a rudimentary lake cabin, semi-affluent people in North Dakota drive three hours to "the Lakes" every weekend from Memorial Day until Labor Day. Growing up, my parents thought people who did this were foolish and immature and irrationally obsessed with water-skiing; this was one of the myriad ways I was trained to despise (and envy) rich people. My family never went anywhere. Like most farm families from the '70s, we never took vacations; to this day, I still haven't traveled recreationally for more than three days in a row. I never want to go anywhere. However, Lenore grew up in the kind of North Dakotan family that went to the Lakes constantly; they occasionally flew to their lake cabin in her father's private plane. Lenore's dad is a banker. This is more difficult for me to reconcile than I would like to admit.

Herschel is a town that survives on the spending habits of weekend travelers; it's very small (population 1,069) and doesn't get MTV, but it has lots of shops and gas stations and a better-than-average Hardee's. When people go to the Lakes, they often like to purchase items that prove they have been there, such as a T-shirt that says GONE FISHIN' or a coffee mug that features a cartoon walleye. Having returned from her recent world travels, Lenore has opened her own store in Herschel. I'm still confused as to why someone would spend a weekend on the shore of a Minnesota lake and then decide to purchase a handcrafted Laotian chess set, but Lenore is evidently making a nice little profit (or at least breaking even). It seems that she is a savvy businesswoman. And when I finally arrive in Herschel, I discover she is not alone—there are somehow *three* separate import stores on the town's main drag. I will never understand what people want out of life.

I've never been to Herschel before today, but it takes maybe 90 seconds to find Lenore's store. It's 3:30 P.M., and she's working by herself. She smiles when I walk in, but she's dealing with actual customers, so I mill around. Among the things she sells are fallen tree branches she has spray-painted gold; these four-foot wooden sticks now cost $50 because they sit inside a vase that costs $200. Lenore is surreptitiously crafty. She's also the talk of the town; apparently, every single farmer in the Herschel area has asked her on a date over the past two months. Her life is like a poorly written romantic comedy starring Julia Roberts: An uncommonly beautiful young woman inexplicably relocates to a small town and opens an impractical store for no plausible reason, and every blue-collar man in town simultaneously fights for her affections. She was flattered by this for the first two weeks; after that, she started lying about a fiancé who doesn't exist. Years ago, Lenore told me that she would go on one date with almost anyone who asked her; she felt any man who had enough guts to approach a total stranger always deserved at least one dinner. Upon moving to Herschel, this policy has changed.

When her store patrons leave, we hug. Things already seem tense. Lenore closes the store early, and I follow behind as she drives to her parents' cabin. I'm listening to "Dancefloors" by My Morning Jacket and having a panic attack. Part of me assumed this would be easy; I had convinced myself that visiting Lenore would *always* be easy, regardless of what was at stake. When we reach her cabin, I immediately decide to go jogging, and she seems almost relieved. The air is filled with mosquitoes and my run is terrible. I wish I was still running in North Carolina so I could just fantasize about the *idea* of Lenore. I'm much better at that.

I'm only outside for 30 minutes; Lenore is reading when I return. I take a shower and we drive 20 minutes to the best steak house in the county; she has white wine and blackened catfish while I consume five beers and 85 percent of a cow. The conversation improves as the sun disappears. There are so many things I forget about Lenore when I don't see her. She is one of those people who has never taken a bad photograph in her entire life, so my memories of her always resemble the way she looks in pictures; my memories are all posed. I always forget how funny she is and how good she is at keeping secrets. Every time I see her, I notice this cute little scar on her shoulder, and I always find myself thinking, "When did she get that scar? How did that scar happen? How could I have never seen this scar before? Who is this unknown person with this unknown scar?" I've asked her about that scar 200 times, and I still can't remember how it happened. And I remember everything.

It's full-on night when we exit the restaurant; we're holding hands, but it doesn't feel like the kind of organic hand-holding that makes people secure. We drive back to her cabin and sit on the back porch, staring into the endless black water and listening to the miniature waves lapping up against the rocks. The moon has menacing clouds slowly drifting in front of its orange face; it's like the opening shot from a 1950s werewolf movie. Everything is inappropriately romantic.

"I suppose we need to talk about some things," I say. And the way I say this gives away everything, because Lenore immediately says she knows that we aren't going to be together and that the weekend at the wedding was probably just an unconscious way for us to finally say good-bye to each other. She doesn't say this with much conviction, but I agree with her. This is a complex situation. Part of the intricacy comes from the fact that—at the wedding, which was in June—I gave her an early copy of an essay collection called *Sex, Drugs, and Cocoa Puffs*. This was a book I had written that was due for release in early August (i.e., this same week). The opening essay in that book was written the week immediately following her going-away party in Minneapolis (i.e., Chuck's 9/11), so it's all about her. A few months prior, I had also written a piece about Lenore that ran in *GQ*, because that's the kind of thing self-indulgent, first-person writers inevitably do. I have no idea what compels me to do these things; I will never understand why I need to write about the events that other people merely experience. And even though Lenore understands that this is how I am, she remains uncomfortable about having thousands of people read about my personal feelings toward her, particularly when the things I write are often things I would never say.

"Why didn't you tell me you loved me?" she asks by the lake. "It's on the second page of your book, but you never actually said it to me. Not even once."

"That's not true," I say. "I told you I loved you seven times." This is technically accurate but intellectually fraudulent; I've told Lenore I loved her on seven occasions, but three times were in handwritten letters, three times were in e-mails, and once was when I was drunk.

Still, I was never lying.

"I hate living here," Lenore says after a disquieting silence. "I'm moving to Minneapolis after Thanksgiving."

"You should definitely do that," I say.

"And I'm moving on," says Lenore. "I'm serious. This is the last time we're doing this."

I have never really known what "this" is, but I suspect she's right.

It's cold for August, so we go inside and snuggle on the couch. She's playing a Ryan Adams CD, which is (apparently) all she ever listens to these days. In New York, I sometimes catch glimpses of Ryan Adams at a bar called Hi-Fi, and he seems to be living the most stereotypically hipsterish life imaginable (i.e., always rumored to be addicted to drugs, always rumored to be dating Parker Posey, always falling off the stage in Liverpool, always leaving angry voice mails for rock critics in Chicago, etc.). His life is almost imaginary, and it seems like his feelings and emotions should not relate to anyone, except for maybe Courtney Love. But Lenore thinks his songs are perfect. She thinks *all of them* are perfect. She's playing something obscure off of either *Heartbreaker* or *Demolition*, and it's slowly making her face fall sad, and I can tell that this sadness is why she loves Ryan Adams. She gingerly asks if I want to watch a movie in which Robin Williams plays a deranged photoshop employee, because she rented such a film two weeks ago and still hasn't watched it. I can see the VHS tape sitting on top of the TV. I say no. We're holding hands again, but this time it feels intimate. Dangerously intimate. I do not like the current image of Lenore's life; I don't like the idea of her not watching movies and not dating local farmers and listening to Ryan Adams in the dark.

"Let's just go to bed," she says. "But let's not get all crazy."

I hug her for the next seven hours on a very small bed, each of us facing the same wall. I kiss her neck for maybe 15 minutes, and she falls asleep halfway through. Clothing is never removed. Nobody gets crazy. Tomorrow, I will take a shower and leave before her digital clock reads 9:05 A.M. We will exchange cordial good-byes. Later that day, Lenore will send me the nicest e-mail I've ever received from anyone, and reading it will make me want to hide in a cave for 10,000 years. It will make me feel like I am reading Lenore's obituary in the newspaper. I will send her an e-mail in return, and I will pray that she finds endless happiness in life, and I will always secretly hope that she never likes another man as much as she likes me, even if she ultimately loves that man more. And we will never see each other again.

THE FOURTEENTH DAY

Broken Bones ➤ Throwing Rocks ➤ "Up North" ➤
Poor, Poor Helen ➤ Some Guys Have All the Luck

The single-greatest male singing voice of the rock era belongs to
Rod Stewart. Nobody at *Spin* believes me when I make this
argument, and many of my coworkers assume I am trying to be
ironic when I insist that Rod Stewart's whiskey-soaked throat
is more moving than Sinatra's. Here again, I find myself confused: Why would I want other people to think I like someone
I do not actually like? What possible purpose would that serve?
Why would *anyone* pretend to like things they actually hate?
These are questions that haunt me every time I listen to the Rod
Stewart box set *Storyteller*, which I'm doing (right now) as I
slouch toward Fargo.

Storyteller is a four-disc, 64-song set, but you can get the
entire Rod Stewart experience simply by listening to track six
on each of the four CDs. The sixth track on the first disc is "I've
Been Drinking," which is the first cornerstone of Stewart's
iconography; he is the lovable drunk who always chooses alcohol over everything else, and you can't tell if it's admirable or
pathetic. The sixth track on the second disc is "Stay with Me,"
a Faces tune where Rod convinces a woman to have sex with

him, only to beg her to leave his flat before he wakes up the following morning (although he does offer cab fare and cologne). That's the second component of Rod's persona: He is a male tart and a bad boyfriend, probably because he makes a lot of decisions when he's drunk (as explained on disc one). The sixth track on disc three is "The First Cut Is the Deepest," where we all learn *why* he drinks and carouses; he can't get over the first woman who broke his heart. But maybe he never loved her at all; maybe that's his whole problem; maybe it was just an "Infatuation," which is the sixth track on disc four. I have never understood the song "Infatuation," just as I have never understood the *concept* of infatuation. It has always been my understanding that being "infatuated" with someone means you *think* you are in love, but you're actually not; infatuation is (supposedly) just a foolish, fleeting feeling. But if being "in love" is an abstract notion, and it's not tangible, and there is no way to physically prove it to anyone else . . . well, how is being in love any different than having an infatuation? They're both human constructions. If you *think* you're in love with someone and you *feel* like you're in love with someone, then you obviously are; thinking and feeling is the sum total of what love is. Why do we feel an obligation to certify emotions with some kind of retrospective, self-imposed authenticity? For the first 30 years of my life, I had no idea that Stewart didn't write "The First Cut Is the Deepest." It turns out that song was actually written by Cat Stevens. Am I now supposed to rethink my previous appreciation for those sentiments? Should I now question their validity, since it turns out that Rod Stewart was just *pretending* to embody that worldview? If my only way to understand the world is through what I think and what I feel, how can *thinking* that I'm in love and *feeling* that I'm in love be relegated into the category of "infatuation"? What's the fucking difference?

People always criticize Rod Stewart for having bad taste, and I guess I can understand why; "Tonight's the Night" is a pretty wretched song, as was his cover of "Downtown Train." His version of "Cigarettes and Alcohol" was ludicrous. But maybe there is a larger point to all those bad decisions; maybe Rod Stewart is just trying to explain that he doesn't understand the world and that he's just trying to figure it out through the things that matter to him personally, even if they suck (and even if they involve Jeff Beck). If all you ever do is drink brandy and chase women and miss those women when they leave (and then question why they were even there in the first place), that becomes the way you understand existence; consequently, that's how you try to understand everything else. And that's completely valid, if not necessarily universal. Rod Stewart may be a blond clown with bad judgment, but everything he says is true.

I reach Moorhead, Minnesota, at 12:02 P.M., which means I will reach Fargo at 12:10; Fargo and Moorhead are basically one town, split by the Red River and connected by the Main Avenue Bridge. It's difficult to understand why anyone would choose to live in Moorhead instead of Fargo, since the only upside to Moorhead is higher taxes. I suppose people have their reasons.

It's been five years since I lived in Fargo, and I was only a citizen of that community for four years. Somehow, it still feels like I lived there for two decades (it's like the way Ozzy used to talk about Randy Rhoads, which I mentioned on page 109; in my mind, it seems like those four years in Fargo were longer than the 22 years before I got there and longer than all the years that have passed since I left). Whenever I return, I want to drive past all the things that defined my subsistence there: the newspaper I worked at; a bar called Duffy's Tavern; the house where Quincy's parents still live; my $160 a month apartment on the south side of town; a dilapidated house behind St. Luke's hospital where we would drink sangria in the summer; a frontage road by the airport where you can sit in your car and listen to the Cardigans while watching Northwest Airlines jets land in the moonlight. I always want to return to these places, and sometimes I do. It's always a mistake. It's funny how vividly I remember those specific locations, but how quickly I forget that they're all surrounded by strip malls.

There are probably 100 people in Fargo I'd like to visit, but I can't see any of them; I promised my mother I would visit her on this trip, and she said she'd have lunch ready for me at 1:00 P.M. If I am not at my parents' house by 1:00 P.M., my mother will assume I have hit a deer (this is always her first assumption when anybody is late for anything). From Fargo, it's a 65-mile trip to my hometown. I will make it home in time, but just barely.

I grew up on a farm five miles outside of a town called Wyndmere, but my parents don't live there anymore; they moved into Wyndmere proper 10 years ago. My parents are considerably older than most people's parents: I'm 31, but I'm the seventh child in a relentlessly Catholic family. In fact, one of my sisters is almost 18 years older than me (I was born in June of 1972, and she left for college that August—we only lived in the same house for 75 days). Though it did not seem strange at the time, the way my parents moved into Wyndmere was a little bizarre: My oldest brother took over the farm when my dad retired, and they just switched houses; my brother and his family moved out to the farm, and my parents moved into his house in town. They just completely switched lives in the span of one weekend; they literally "traded spaces." I doubt if this kind of domestic exchange is common in places that are not rural North Dakota. But that's not even the weirdest part; the weirdest part is that my brother eventually decided to build a new house on our farmstead, and he intended to level the home we all grew up in; this made sense, because the roof leaked and it only had one bathroom and it vaguely resembled a middle-class residence in Appalachia. However, my mother insisted he should try to sell the house, because she is not one to waste anything, even if it has no value. This seemed like a ridiculous plan, but my brother begrudgingly agreed to advertise: Anybody could buy our house if they (a) paid $2,000, and (b) were willing to move the building off its foundation. Well, some optimistic carpenter actually did this; he and his young wife bought our $2,000 house and moved it 20 miles away. So now—if I drive down a certain road, near a certain neighboring town called Hankinson—I can see the house where I spent the first 18 years of my life . . . except it's now in a totally different location. It looks the same, but everything around it is completely alien, and I don't know any of the people who are living inside. And because the owner is a carpenter, he's fixed everything, so it looks new; it looks the way it did in 1975, when I was three years old. Have you ever had a dream where someone looks completely different than they do in everyday life, but—because it's *your* dream—you still know who they are and what they represent? Seeing my house is like having that dream when I'm still awake.

I careen toward Wyndmere on Highway 18, driving fast but on the lookout for deer. Everything is flat as a pancake; not coincidentally, I listen to Head East's *Flat as a Pancake.* The reason North Dakota is so flat is because it was crushed by a glacier during the ice age; as that glacier crept over the plains, it deposited soil sediments from prehistoric Canada, which is why the Red River Valley has some of the richest, most fertile dirt in the world. North Dakota doesn't have a great deal of political or social history, but it has shitloads of earth science.

At 12:42, I pass some land my family used to rent for farming purposes; because this land was a few miles north of town, we referred to this patch of land as Up North. This became a proper geographic designation, as in, "Your brother is working Up North this afternoon." We also rented some land closer to home that was always called Butter Bushes, despite the fact that it had no relationship to dairy products or shrubbery. It has never occurred to me to ask why Butter Bushes was called Butter Bushes. I don't think anyone knows. But ANYWAY, every time I drive by Up North, I think about deer having their necks broken by my brother's bare hands.

This is actually a semi-amazing story.

Deer hunting is tremendously popular in North Dakota. In fact, on the first day of deer-hunting season each year, students with hunting licenses are excused from high school at noon. Hunting for deer is seen as a totally acceptable excuse for not going to class. Many boys in my school did this every autumn; they'd drive to school with rifles in their Dodge pickup trucks, wearing blaze-orange hunting vests to U.S. History. One year we went to the play-offs in football, so all the guys who left at noon to hunt deer were required to return at 4:00 P.M. for football practice. In other words, they spent the totality of the day hunting mammals and tackling mammals. As I've grown older, I have come to realize that academics were not much of a priority at Wyndmere High School. Sometimes I am surprised I can read.

Now, I was never a deer hunter. I have no ethical problem with deer being killed for human consumption, especially since the only social purpose deer serve is to make my mom nervous about driving on the highway. If I ever assassinated a whitetail, I would lose no sleep whatsoever. However, shooting animals is not the kind of skill at which I excel; Men shoot animals, and I'm just a Guy. My two older brothers, on the other hand, are veteran deer slayers. My brothers are Men. This was especially true one October, when my oldest brother (Bill) was harvesting corn Up North.

Like many Midwestern states, North Dakota has a real frontier spirit; if something happens on your property, you can pretty much do whatever the hell you desire. All laws become void. As a consequence, you can hunt deer on your own land, even if you don't have a license; all you need is something called a "gratis tag," which that state will give you for free. I guess the burden of responsibility falls on the deer (or something like that). ANYWAY, my brother was harvesting corn with our combine, which is a massive piece of farm machinery that cuts, threshes, and cleans grain. It's like a tractor, only bigger and more complicated; it's like operating a Cobra gunship, except it doesn't fly and it gathers food (as opposed to annihilating Vietnamese villages). Bill kept a deer rifle in the combine's cockpit, just in case he happened to see a deer.

Which he did.

Bill saw a mammoth eight-point buck. However, the buck was way off in the distance—maybe an eighth of a mile, and it was running toward the neighbor's land (and if it got across the border, we couldn't kill it). Moreover, Bill knew there was only one bullet in the rifle. So my brother—who kind of looks like Clint Eastwood, at least in the neck area—opened the door of the combine (while it was still moving) and shot this buck at a distance of at least 250 yards. And he dropped it. With one shot.

This is pretty impressive shooting, all things considered.

However, there was still one problem. He didn't kill it. The deer lived, somehow. It was laying there on the ground, slowly bleeding to death. And—as I noted earlier—there was only one bullet in the gun. There was nothing my brother could do, except stare at this hemorrhaging creature and wonder how he could put it out of its misery before it had a seizure.

Fortunately, my other brother (Paul) arrived minutes later.

Paul reads Louis L'Amour novels and played defensive tackle in college. He was (and is) a pretty powerful manimal; at the time, I think he weighed about 240. Bill and Paul both looked at this deer for a few moments, quietly wondering how they could end its suffering. This is a problem few Americans ever face: How do you execute a wounded deer? Do you hit it with a ball-peen hammer? With a shovel? Do you try to stab it to death with a pocket knife? There is no protocol for this kind of situation. Which is why Paul walked over to the deer, grabbed an antler in each hand, twisted it clockwise, and wordlessly broke its neck.

This is pretty impressive spine snapping, all things considered.

I did not witness this event firsthand, but it still taught me an important lesson: We turned that buck into sausage, and he was delicious. However, Paul refused to eat any of this venison, even though he had killed deer before (and would kill deer again). He could not eat *this* particular deer, always saying, "Every time I smell that sausage, I think of that deer's big brown eyes staring up at me, just before I heard its neck crack."

The lesson? America's relationship to hunting would be far different if it always involved hand-to-hand combat.

When I arrive at my parents' house, it's 12:55. My mom is nervously looking out the kitchen window. I walk through the door and immediately see my father, my aforementioned brother (the one with Eastwood's neck), my brother's wife, and their three daughters (all of whom are smiling like cheerleaders for an SEC football team). My mother hugs me and mentions that I need a haircut; my father shakes my hand (perhaps he thinks I am running for town alderman). My mother has prepared roast beef, baked chicken, corn on the cob, squash, a blueberry pie, and 13,000 pounds of mashed potatoes. The universe appears to be in order.

We finish eating in less than 15 minutes (everybody in my family eats as fast as humanly possible). For the next hour and a half, we sit around the kitchen table while I answer remarkably random questions about my life; these queries range from "Do you have a girlfriend?" to "Does your office at *Spin* use electric heat?" My family is proud of me, but they honestly have no idea what I do for a living (I tell them about the dead rock stars I've visited, and the only one my dad has heard of is Elvis, whom he considers a yippie). I am informed of a recent tractor accident and about all the local high school kids who have suddenly developed insane drinking problems. At one point, my mom calls me a "crazy bugger," which makes me happy. My mother has only three terms she uses for all criticism, and each epithet has a starkly unique connotation. The first level of criticism is to call someone a "bugger." This is a minor insult that indicates you have probably eaten too many cookies or spilled a glass of Kool-Aid on the kitchen tile (in fact, *bugger* can even be used positively; if you give my mom a nice Christmas present, she is apt to refer to you as a "nice bugger"). The second level is "dumb bunny," which was something I was called quite often; the dumb-bunny classification is levied on anyone who has indisputably made a mistake, such as getting a speeding ticket or going outside in wintertime with a wet head. Being called a "dumb bunny" is kind of like being charged with a misdemeanor. Her felony designation is to call someone an "idiot," but this is rarely employed; in the 18 years I lived at home, I was only referred to as an "idiot" once, and that was when I hit the mailbox with a pickup truck.

After dinner (and in North Dakota, "dinner" is the meal you have at noon), I sit in the living room for 20 minutes, talking with my father about what he's been reading (first-person accounts of World War II) and what he's been watching on PBS (something about the history of the circus). My mom tells me she was hoping I could spend the night but that she knows I have to pursue my "business." I mention that I just visited Lenore, who remains the only woman I've dated that either of my parents ever met (for five minutes at 9:00 A.M. on Thanksgiving Day 2000—and my mom hugged her). They still remember Lenore and mention that she is extremely pretty. I agree with them, and then I leave. All told, I spend only two hours with my parents, which probably makes me a relatively shameful son. However, I am so unbelievably glad my parents don't mind that they don't know any details about my life. They don't understand me, but they understand me.

I drove into Wyndmere on Highway 18, but I'll drive out on Highway 13. Filling up the Tauntaun's gas tank at the Wyndmere Cenex station, I can look to the north and see my high school football field (and the grassy, overgrown practice field that sits next to it). The practice field is at least 40 yards from Highway 13, a roadway punctuated by the Wyndmere overpass; the Wyndmere overpass is a mammoth concrete bridge that towers 50 feet above two lines of railroad tracks. When I was a seventh grader, I witnessed the greatest athletic achievement of my lifetime on that practice field, and it involved that overpass. It was track season, 4:09 P.M., 1985. A group of us were sitting on the grass in the middle of the practice field, pretending to stretch our hamstrings, dourly waiting for track practice to officially commence. Somebody spotted a sedan on Highway 13, crawling up the overpass. A jovial, sandy-haired high school junior—a fellow nicknamed Bubba, who also happened to play quarterback on the football team—was inexplicably holding a little rock in his right hand; he had picked it off the gravel running track that circumvented the practice field. For no real reason, some moron (I can't recall who) casually said, "Hey, Bubba, I bet you can't hit that fucking car with that fucking rock." Without even considering the ramifications, Bubba whirled around and side-armed the stone at least 200 feet; it was like he fired one of those SAM surface-to-air shoulder rockets terrorists use to knock down helicopters. And he hit that fucking car with that fucking rock. It sounded like a roman candle when it smacked off the trunk. Nobody could believe it. We were all writhing on the ground, speaking in tongues, rejoicing like those kids in Portugal who saw the Lady of Fatima. It was akin to witnessing something that could only happen inside a video game. I saw Michael Jordan score 63 points in a losing effort against the Celtics in 1986. I saw Doug Flutie beat University of Miami on a 48-yard Hail Mary pass to Gerard Phelan in 1984. I heard about my brother shooting a deer out of a combine, and I heard about my other brother breaking its neck. However, those things will always seem easy, at least when compared to casually hitting a moving vehicle at a distance of 70 yards *with a rock*.

Some things can only happen when you're young.

Flying through Bismarck, a city I've (strangely) only visited twice in my life. As I drive, Def Leppard is describing what—at least within the worldview of vocalist Joe Elliott—was the ideal Saturday night in 1981: They have their whiskey, they have their wine, they have their women, and (this time) the lights are going out. The particular album I'm playing (*High 'n' Dry*) is from the era of Def Lep when the drummer still had two arms; Leppard percussionist Rick Allen lost his arm in a car wreck on New Year's Eve, 1984 (which is probably the one thing about Def Leppard just about everyone knows). I wonder what Allen would think about people who suffer from Body Integrity Identity Disorder (BIID), an extremely rare psychological disorder that makes otherwise sane people amputate their own limbs for no apparent reason. Due to motives that remain completely unfathomable, individuals with BIID feel as though they can only be normal if they lose a certain part of their body; there was a case in England in which a man packed his healthy left leg in dry ice for hours, consequently forcing doctors to chop it off. Another BIID victim in Chicago built a homemade guillotine and took off his own arm. This made them happy, somehow.

I have no way to verify this, but there must be some connection between Body Integrity Identity Disorder and Cotard's syndrome. On the surface, they're partial opposites: People with Cotard's syndrome believe they don't exist, while people with BIID think they can't be normal unless they make part of themselves nonexistent. Still, there seems to be a similarity between how both patients view the world; they both seem confused over what constitutes reality, and they both respond to an illogical urge with an even more illogical action.

Maybe I'll listen to "Pour Some Sugar on Me" from 1987. No drum rolls, obviously, but at least I'll be able to stop thinking about crashing this car and losing my arm (and then being theoretically happy about it).

"Who the Sam Hell are these people?"

This is not me talking; the person asking this question is sitting two stools away from me at the bar inside the Best Western Inn in Dickinson, North Dakota. It should be noted, however, that I was thinking a remarkably similar thought when this strange man started talking to me.

"I have no idea," I say in response, "but they seem to be having a good time."

For the second time today, it is 8:05 P.M.; I changed time zones a few miles back. Dickinson (population 16,101) is maybe 75 miles from the Montana border, and it's one of the unsexiest towns in North America: There was a time when there was oil out here, but now there are just big empty spaces and dudes who can run fast (Dickinson High has a consistently dominant track-and-field team, for some reason). I checked into the Best Western and immediately found its bar, assuming there might be (at most) two or three interesting locals drinking Yukon Jack and complaining about their lives. Much to my surprise, the bar is half full: On the other side of the room, a small crowd of casually dressed insurance agents appear to be having a going-away party for a coworker, and these insurance agents (mysteriously) decided to have said party in the cocktail lounge of a $102-a-night hotel. Every person in attendance is completely obliterated. It's a collection of ten 27-year-old guys and six 31-year-old women, and they're all doing body shots and singing along with the jukebox (Jimmy Buffet, Van Morrison, AC/DC). It's like watching soccer hooligans: I would place the odds of someone getting into a fight at 3-to-1 and the odds of someone getting date-raped at 7-to-1. I'm tempted to just finish my drink and watch some HBO, but the aforementioned person sitting two bar stools to my right starts asking me questions.

"What the hell is going on tonight?" the old man asks, nodding toward the dancing idiots. "What a bunch of drunken fools. They should go downtown."

I agree with the man. He is roughly 60 years old and wears a short-sleeved dress shirt and a tie. He looks a little like Johnny Carson, but his voice is more like Tone-Lōc's. I like him immediately.

"Those people should be in a damn zoo," he says. "Throw 'em in with the gorillas and see how much they wanna dance. Crazy batch of goddamn lunatics. You with them?"

"No," I say.

"I didn't think so. You seem halfway reasonable. You live around here?"

"No, I'm a reporter. I'm driving to Seattle."

"A newspaper reporter?"

"Not really, but I used to be," I say.

"I wouldn't have guessed that you were a reporter, since you're wearing short pants," he says. "Do you wear a tie to work?"

"Do I wear a tie to work? No. Why would I wear a tie to work?"

"Why? What do you mean, *'Why?'* Why the hell not?" says the man in short sleeves. "Always put a tie on. Always. It only takes an extra 30 seconds in the morning, and it's always the smart move. Old-timers will think you're an up-and-comer, young folks will know you mean business, and ladies will think you're the kind of guy who might suddenly take them out to a decent restaurant. It's always the smart move. Are you married?"

"No."

"Well, you have time. You'll get married. Everybody gets married, one way or another. And that's important. Getting married was the best decision I ever made. A man's wife is more important than his parents and his children combined."

For the next 45 minutes, this short-sleeved man gives me *a lot* of advice. Most of it dwells on (a) the importance of loving your wife,[1] (b) the importance of hunting-dog ownership,[2] (c) why we have fewer windmills than we used to,[3] (d) what's wrong with the American League,[4] (e) how to properly fire an employee,[5] (f) why life insurance is a sham,[6] (g) how to buy or

1. Women need to feel loved in order to feel free, so withholding love from your wife is like sentencing her to prison.
2. Even if you lose your job, your hunting dog will respect you. In life, this quality is rare.
3. Something about aquifers.
4. "It's become goddamn slow-pitch softball."
5. Concede that you've both made mistakes, but stoically admit that you can't fire yourself.
6. Insurance salesman are no different than chiropractors, whatever the fuck that means.

sell a race horse,[7] and (h) the complexity of human relationships, particularly when placed in a business setting. I do not
understand what this man does for a living and I never ask his
name (and he never asks for mine), but he has innumerable the-
ories on dealing with thorny personalities and finding financial
success. The theory I like best is his "Anger Scheme." This old
man is of the opinion that you can never really know someone
until you've seen them positively enraged.

"People never show you what they're truly like until you see
them go ape-shit," he says. "That's the only time people say the
things they really feel. Anger makes people honest. No matter
how reasonable someone might seem, you never know for sure
until they get mad. You, for example. You seem halfway reasonable, but you might be the type who'd go home and get a
shotgun if I pissed you off."

"Actually, I never get mad," I say. "Every time I feel myself
becoming angry, I suddenly become depressed. I don't think I
have the potential to get mad."

"Oh, you could get mad," laughs the man. "In 10 minutes, I
could probably make you mad enough to shoot me in the back.
And that's important. That's the kind of thing you need to
know about anyone you want to do business with. So anytime
I'm considering a new partner, I always take the man out, get
him drunk, and piss him off on purpose."

"You can't be serious."

"Oh, absolutely," he says. "I just figure out whatever makes
him uncomfortable, and then I keep bringing it up over and
over and over again—religion, politics, the Indian casinos,
whatever. Everybody eventually loses their shit, especially if
they've been drinking, and especially if they've been drinking
gin. But that's the only way to see a person's true colors before

7. Something about looking at certain bones.

191

it's too late. I mean, I don't want to end up associating with a damn sociopath. I even did this with my wife, way back when we were dating."

"You angered your wife on purpose?"

"Yes," he says.

" Why would you possibly want to do that?"

"Actually, it was just before I proposed," he continues, stirring the ice in his drink with his ring finger. "We were out one night—I can't remember where, I think it was either Bismarck or Mandan—and I was already pretty certain Helen was the girl for me. That's her name: *Helen*. But I had to make sure she could handle adversity. That's really important in a marriage. Really, truly important. Your wife needs to be able to deal with some degree of adversity, because there is always going to be adversity along the way. That's just part of being alive. I know that sounds like a helluva quality to look for in a woman, because it seems more like a quality you'd look for in a governor. But trust me on this. It's important. Dealing with adversity is important. So I had to see how Helen would react when she got mad."

"What did you do to her?"

"Well, Helen has this great-lookin' younger sister," he says, "and I knew she always felt threatened by her sister's looks, so I just kept asking her all these questions about her sister—nothing dirty, of course, but I just acted real interested in what her sister's personality was like and what kind of men her sister dated. Casual questions, but *pointed* questions. Well, after maybe two hours of this, and after two hours of gin and tonics, Helen finally lost it. She just went bonkers. She threatened to throw her glass at my goddamn head!"

"And this relationship worked out?"

"Well, she never threw that glass. And then I explained the

whole thing and proposed a week later. She's one helluva woman."

The going-away party appears to be breaking up. People are hugging each other. These insurance agents now seem slightly less disturbing than the gentleman I am sitting alongside. I pay for my drinks and excuse myself from the old man, and he shakes my hand. "Give my regards to Helen," I say.

"You know that I will," he says in response, and I know that he will.

THE FIFTEENTH DAY

Mastodons

MONTANA (Thursday, August 14, 11:11 A.M.): Thomas Jefferson is, hands down, the coolest president in American history. Now, this is not because he wrote the Declaration of Independence, although I will concede that has merit; Thomas Jefferson is history's coolest president because of the advice he gave Meriwether Lewis and William Clark before they explored the Northwest Territory in 1804. One of the many things that Jefferson warned Lewis and Clark about was mastodons. "You dudes need to watch out for potential mastodon herds," he told them (I'm paraphrasing). "If you see any mastodons, make sure you tell me about them, because I need to know." Tragically, mastodons had become extinct 10,000 years before the expedition started. However, this is still solid advice. I mean, I'm taking the same path Lewis and Clark took (more or less), but nobody told me to watch out for mastodons. Where is the love?

I am developing a boyhood crush on the stereo in this car. It seems to understand me. Steve Miller keeps calling me "baby" and insists that I should keep on rocking him, which seems completely reasonable. I insist on taking rock lyrics literally.

For example, it occurs to me that whoever organized tour itineraries for the Steve Miller Band must have been a dolt: Miller says he went from Phoenix, Arizona, all the way to Tacoma, then to Philadelphia, down to Atlanta, and then crossed back to L.A. (before finally concluding with some one-off dates in Northern California, where girls were said to be "warm"). This is terribly inefficient. It seems that even Space Cowboys need travel agents.

Perhaps you've heard that Montana has no speed limit. Perhaps you've heard that Montana has a speed limit, but only at night. Perhaps you've heard that Montana has a speed limit, but the speeding fine is only five dollars and it's rarely enforced. I had heard all these things before coming here, and it turns out none of them are true. I get a speeding ticket less than an hour after crossing the North Dakota–Montana border. The highway patrolman is inquisitive, but generally polite; he apparently reads *Spin*. His favorite band is Audioslave. I mention to him that I was once in a low-rent Chinese restaurant in SoHo and Audioslave's "Show Me How to Live" came over the in-house stereo, and two youngish policemen at the next table started loudly talking about how Audioslave had made the best album of the year. This is a true story; perhaps Audioslave is inadvertently Cop Rock. The highwayman tells me he's not surprised that other members of law enforcement dig Audioslave, because "they're damn heavy." I mildly agree. Still, I do not weasel out of this ticket. And in Montana, you have to pay the speeding fine on the spot, so I hand him a $20 bill. This is a remarkably reasonable fine—but what do they do if they pick up someone who doesn't have any cash in their wallet? Maybe police cars in Montana have ATMs built into the dashboard.

For two weeks, I've been ostensibly following a westerly trajectory. However, today is the first day I truly feel like I am driving *west*. Montana feels like the West. The rest areas have signs next to the bathrooms that read: RATTLESNAKES HAVE BEEN OBSERVED. PLEASE STAY ON THE SIDEWALKS. I wonder how many rattlesnakes need to be observed before the state legislature decides to erect signposts. I also wonder what it must have been like to come out here on a wagon train in 1870. What could have prompted someone to think that this was a good place to live? I completely understand why someone might want to live in eastern Montana *today*, but what could have possibly seemed like an upside in the 19th century? It's 90 degrees in the summer, it's 30 below in the winter, there are hardly any trees, and rattlesnakes have been observed (please stay on the sidewalk). Was life in the 19th century so painful that living wasn't even desirable? Existence itself must have seemed like punishment. Pioneers worked for 13 hours a day, slept as soon as it got dark, bathed in their own sweat for six months, shivered and fought pneumonia for the six months that followed, and inevitably starved to death. That was as much as you could ever hope for; it was their version of a satisfying life. I have to assume that pioneers saw the inhospitable landscape of Montana and immediately realized that most of their settlement would die within a year, which actually seemed reassuring. "This is perfect," they no doubt concluded. "Maybe I'll be dead before Christmas!"

This, I surmise, is How the West Was Won. Which is (not coincidentally) what I've just slid into the stereo; I'm playing *How the West Was Won* by Led Zeppelin, a recently released collection of live Led Zep recordings from the year of my birth. I've been saving this CD for rural Montana, since Montana seems like the only state where a 23-minute version of "Whole Lotta Love" would feel completely necessary. Whenever I find myself in an argument about the greatest rock bands of all time, I always place Zeppelin third, behind the Beatles and the Rolling Stones. This sentiment is incredibly common; if we polled everyone in North America who likes rock music, those three bands would almost certainly be the consensus selections (and in that order). But Zeppelin is far and away the most *popular* rock band of all time, and they're popular in a way the Beatles and Stones cannot possibly compete with; this is because every straight man born after the year 1958 has at least one transitory period in his life when he believes Led Zeppelin is the *only* good band that ever existed. And there is no other rock group that generates that experience.

A few years ago, I was an on-air guest for a morning radio show in Akron. I was on the air with the librarian from the Akron public library, and we were discussing either John Cheever or Guided by Voices, or possibly both. Talk radio in Akron is fucking crazy. While we were walking out of the studio, the librarian noticed the show's 19-year-old producer; the producer had a blond mullet, his blank eyes were beyond bloodshot, and he was wearing ripped jeans and a black Swan Song T-shirt with all the runes from the *Zoso* album. The librarian turned to me and said, "You know, I went to high school with that guy." This librarian was 42. But he was right. He *did* go to high school with that guy. So did I. Everyone in America went to high school with that guy. Right now, there are boys in fourth grade who do not even realize that they will become "that guy" as soon as they finish reading *The Hobbit* in eighth grade. There are people having unprotected sex at this very moment, and the fetus spawned from that union will become "that guy" in two decades. Led Zeppelin is the most legitimately timeless musical entity of the past half century; they are the only group in the history of rock 'n' roll that every male rock fan seems to experience in exactly the same way.

You are probably wondering why that happens; I'm not sure,

either. I've put a lot of thought into this subject (certainly more than any human should), but it never becomes totally clear; it only seems more and more true. For a time, I thought it was Robert Plant's overt misogyny fused with Jimmy Page's obsession with the occult, since that combination allows adolescent males to reconcile the alienation of unhinged teenage sexuality with their own inescapable geekiness. However, this theory strikes me as "probably stupid." It would be easy to argue that Zeppelin simply out-rocks all other bands, but that's not really true; AC/DC completely out-rocks Led Zeppelin, and AC/DC is mostly ridiculous. Whatever quality makes Led Zep so eternally archetypal must be "intangible," but even that argument seems weak; here in Big Sky Country, I'm listening to "Heartbreaker" at rib-crushing volume, and everything that's perfect about Led Zeppelin seems completely palpable. There is nothing intangible about the invisible nitroglycerin pouring out of the Tauntaun's woofers. Everything is real. And what that everything is—*maybe*—is this: Led Zeppelin sounds like who they are, but they also sound like who they are not. They sound like an English blues band. They sound like a warm-blooded brachiosaur. They sound like Hannibal's assault across the Alps. They sound sexy and sexist and sexless. They sound dark but stoned; they sound smart but dumb; they seem older than you, but just barely. Led Zeppelin *sounds* like the way a cool guy *acts*. Or—more specifically—Led Zeppelin sounds like a certain kind of cool guy; they sound like the kind of cool guy every man vaguely thinks he has the potential to be, if just a few things about the world were somehow different. And the experience this creates is unique to Led Zeppelin because its manifestation is entirely sonic: There is a point in your life when you hear songs like "The Ocean" and "Out on the Tiles" and "Kashmir," and you suddenly find yourself feeling like these songs are *actively making you into the person you want to be*. It does not matter if you've heard those songs 100 times and felt nothing in the past, and it does not matter if you don't normally like rock 'n' roll and just happened to overhear it in somebody else's dorm room. We all still meet at the same vortex: For whatever the reason, there is a point in the male maturation process when the music of Led Zeppelin sounds like the perfect actualization of the perfectly cool you. You will hear the intro to "When the Levee Breaks," and it will feel like your brain is stuffed inside the kick drum. You will hear the opening howl of "Immigrant Song," and you will imagine standing on the bow of a Viking ship and screaming about Valhalla. But when these things happen, you don't think about *Physical Graffiti* or *Houses of the Holy* in those abstract, metaphysical terms; you simply think, "Wow. I just realized something: This shit is perfect. In fact, this record is vastly superior to all other forms of music on the entire planet, so this is all I will ever listen to, all the time." And you do this for six days or six weeks or six years. This is your Zeppelin Phase, and it has as much to do with your own personal psychology as it does with the way John Paul Jones played the organ on "Trampled Under Foot." It has to do with sociobiology, and with Aleister Crowley, and possibly with mastodons. And you will grow out of it, probably. But this is why Led Zeppelin is the most beloved rock band of all time, even though most people (including myself) think the Beatles and the Rolling Stones are better. Those two bands are appreciated in myriad ways and for myriad reasons, and the criteria for doing so changes with every generation. But Led Zeppelin is only loved one way, and that will never evolve. They are the one thing all young men share, and we shall share it forever. Led Zeppelin is unkillable, even if John Bonham was not.

Today's lunch is ideal; it includes enough white gravy to choke a wildebeest. Note to self: You can't get good gravy in New

York, so quit trying. I take on fuel and Mountain Dew at another low-rent gas station and point the Tauntaun west, still acclimating myself to the size of Montana. It's a veritable subcontinent. I look at a map, and I realize I've only moved an inch across the state. I'm something like three and a half inches from Washington. Geographic ratios hate me.

One thing everyone tells you about driving through Montana is that you can't receive any radio stations, which shouldn't be a problem for a man with 604 albums in the backseat of his car (I bought four more CDs in Bismarck, one of which was Garth Brooks's very-popular-yet-still-underrated *No Fences*). However, things like this always become an unwinnable eternal contest with me; the fact that it's hard to find radio stations is precisely what makes me want to hear the radio. I find one on the AM side, and it's a talk show hosted by Sean Hannity, one of the many automatons on the Fox News Channel. I can tell immediately that he's dealing with some sort of breaking news, because his voice has that "I'm actually being serious right now" inflection. My first thought is that Dick Cheney must have died from a heart attack. However, Hannity is talking about people who are trapped on the subway and smoke that's rising from Staten Island, so my next thought is that somebody blew up the Statue of Liberty. "Fuck," I think for a moment, "tomorrow, a thousand shitty newspaper columnists are going to write thinly veiled metaphoric eulogies about the death of Lady Liberty." However, Hannity says everything appears to be under control and that this is merely a citywide blackout. "There appears to be no connection to terrorism," he says, which immediately makes me assume it *must* be connected to terrorism (it's strange how we've all become accustomed to not believing anyone paid to keep us informed). I try to call Diane on my cell phone, but cell phones don't work in Montana. The reports coming over the radio are confusing; nobody seems to know why this blackout is happening. I pull into the first rest area I see (rattlesnakes have evidently been observed at this one, too) and try to call Diane from a pay phone. It goes straight to her voice mail. I leave a rambling message that asks a bunch of questions, all of which I know she could never possibly answer. When I get back in the car, Mr. Hannity is taking calls from listeners in Manhattan. All the callers are describing the scene like it's Mardi Gras; people seem to be wildly enjoying this blackout. Hannity says everyone should buy bottled water and open their apartment windows. He congratulates the people of New York for remaining calm during this period of hardship, and he salutes them for not looting the stores and initiating a race riot. Christ. We have low standards in this country.

Since I can't use my cell phone (and since even this AM station is starting to fade as I pass through the mountains), it's impossible to remain engaged with what's happening across the street and 3,000 miles to the east. Giving up hope, I listen to the White Stripes' *De Stijl*, and it doesn't remind me of anything that's ever happened to me in real life. I play the Pet Shop Boys' *Discography*, and all their seamless, flawless songs make me feel vapid and lonely (except for their cover of "Always on My Mind"—that makes me imagine I'm driving with a gay Willie Nelson). I play the Eagles, and I take it easy. Sometimes I find myself driving way over 100 mph, but there is no one around to care. This is what traveling is, I suppose.

My goal is to get to Missoula by 6:00 P.M. I get there just before 7:00. There is a hotel called the Campus Inn off the first exit, and that sounds ideal. Part of me irrationally fantasizes that it will be attached to a bar called the Campus Tavern. But (of course) it's not, and—even if it was—it's August. Right now, it would be easier to find uranium than college kids.

I check in and turn on the television; CNN is explaining the details behind the New York blackout and explaining how (and why) it's affecting places as far away as Cleveland. It turns out this situation really isn't the spawn of terrorism, but maybe the terrorists should have considered something like this; it certainly seems like an easy way to fuck with people. After changing clothes, I go for a run, and the sky is darker than common sense would dictate. It's because of the smoke. Montana is burning; there are massive forest fires across the entire western half of the state. America has a lot of problems tonight. I sprint past a few restaurants and a strip club, edging toward the outskirts of Missoula, wishing I was in ever-darkening New York and wishing mastodons still walked the earth.

After showering with hard water and eating shrimp at a Bennigan's, I decide to settle in and watch the news. There are images of drunk people in Times Square, wordlessly expressing carefree bewilderment while dancing to silence. Here in Montana, I understand everything that is happening in Manhattan . . . but everybody who's actually there remains completely clueless as to why there is no electricity. I know that the power is expected to return tomorrow afternoon; they have no idea if this will last a day or a week or a year. It's like looking down from heaven and watching all the mortals majoring in philosophy.

This peculiar detachment entertains me for maybe 15 minutes; after that, it becomes abundantly obvious that CNN and MSNBC are just repeating the same information over and over and over again. I look into my overnight bag to see if I have any dope left, but all that remains are superfine granular crumbs; this is what we in the getting-high business refer to as "shake." I have enough shake for (maybe) a fifth of a joint. Everything seems hopeless. But then I remember a girl from college who had dated a drug dealer in high school; this girl claimed you could smoke shake by using the cigarette lighter from a car. According to this chick, you push in the cigarette lighter until the coils get hot, and then you sprinkle the shake onto the lighter's exposed head and inhale the smoke that floats off the coils through a drinking straw.

(READER'S NOTE: I concede that pouring morsels of pot onto a car lighter and hunching over the rising smoke—with a cocktail straw between my teeth—must resemble the pathetic actions of a desperate drug addict. But I was in Montana. The rules are different there.)

I steal a straw from the hotel bar, exit the hotel, unlock the driver's side door of the Tauntaun, and attempt to get high via my dashboard. The coils of the lighter grow electric orange, not unlike the home uniforms the Denver Broncos wore in 1977. Much to my surprise, this trick completely works: I'm totally fucking stoned, and I'm totally fucking shocked. I feel like I just figured out how to make fire on *Survivor*. I repeat this process until all my drugs are gone, and then I listen to "Dazed and Confused" for 14 minutes. Robert Plant claims the soul of a woman was created below, and—for the first time in my life—it dawns on me that Plant is suggesting that women's souls are made in hell. That seems harsh.

As I meander back to the hotel, my spirits are soaring; like a phoenix rising from the ashes, I am a phoenix rising from the cigarette lighter. I notice a 17-year-old male at the front desk without any luggage. He checks into the room directly across from mine, and then he goes down the back stairs and opens the rear exit. Nine other high school kids pile into the hotel (five guys and four girls). They all have duffel bags, most of which are filled with Budweiser, Lord Calvert, and Malibu. This is apparently how you have fun when you're a high school kid in Missoula: You rent a single hotel room and see who gets to die from alcohol poisoning. These teenagers are wildly enthusiastic about drinking, but they're enthusiastic in a bizarrely expository manner: They all seem to be repeating the same exact phrase. "We are *so* going to party," they gleefully say to each other. I find myself shocked by the unyielding repetition of this sentiment. Nobody says "We are totally going to get wasted" or "We are going to party hard" or "We are going to get crazy." They all say the same six words with exactly the same syntax: "We are *so* going to party." I almost get the feeling they're mocking somebody who isn't there; maybe they have a semi-uncool friend named Rob who is wont to say "We are *so* going to party," and now his personal catchphrase has become an inside joke. When I was in high school, we all knew a guy named Scott who was prone to exaggeration, and it became common to exclaim "Scott!" whenever you wanted to accuse anyone else of lying; for example, if someone said, "I think I drank 14 beers last night and I wasn't even buzzed," six skeptics would immediately say "Scott!" This joke lasted three years. I don't miss high school at all.

Because I've just spent 20 minutes freebasing cannabis in the front seat of a rental car, I mysteriously decide to do my laundry. There is a laundry room right next to the ice machine, and I spend an inordinate amount of time choosing between Tide and Cheer. I go down to the front desk to get change for two dollars. I later realize I need three dollars, so I go down again and get ten dollars in quarters. I gingerly walk back up the stairs with 40 quarters cupped in my hands. Drugs are so bad.

Suddenly, I hear the ice machine running, and I look over my shoulder. It's one of those high school girls, and she's filling up a wastebasket with ice cubes. She is a white girl wearing a Fubu jersey, and she has braces. I have nothing to say, but I can't stop myself from talking.

"I bet you are going to put that ice in the bathtub," I say. This is what you do when you're drinking in a hotel room; you chill the beer in the bathtub. I know these things.

"Right on," she says.

"So what are you guys doing tonight," I ask, simply because

I want to see if she'll say "We are *so* going to party." But she doesn't.

"Oh, you know, nothing. Just playing drinking games—Up and Down the River, Asshole, stuff like that. We won't be too loud. We just wanna get fucked up."

It's hard for me to relate to this premise, because I never *just* wanna get fucked up; I always want something else to happen while I'm doing it. *Just* being fucked up is never enough. Nonetheless, I assure her that this is not a problem.

"Hey, don't worry about me. Be as loud as you want. What do I care? I will just be watching the TV, as they say on the street. There's that big blackout in New York, you know. It's really something. No chaos, though, so that's good. Society is ultimately good. I really believe that. But as for your party—don't mind me. I won't complain. Just don't run up and down the hallways. Actually, let me rescind that: Run up and down the hallways, but only if you must. I guess what I'm saying is that I am not your enemy. Together, we can beat this thing."

"Right on," she says.

We walk back to our respective rooms, and the girl tells me to have a nice evening. "Watch out for mastodons," I say, and she looks at me like we've been friends for 20 years. The kids are all right.

In my room, the TV is showing HBO's *Project Greenlight*, which I love. I watch it for maybe five minutes, and I'm starting to think *The Battle of Shaker Heights* might have the potential to be at least as good as *Vision Quest*. But then there is a knock at my door; I look through the peephole. It's the teenage girl from the ice machine. I open the door halfway.

"Hey," she says. "Hey, I . . . Can I ask you a question?"

"Certainly," I respond.

"Are you, like, high?"

"What?"

"You're high right now, right?"

For no valid reason, I am terrified.

"It's totally okay," the girl says. "It's awesome, actually. Because I was talking to my friends, and we will totally buy some pot from you, if you have it. Even if it's just a little. But no pressure."

"Well . . . I can't do that," I say. "Because, for one thing, I'm not a drug dealer. And for another thing, I don't have any marijuana. What makes you think I had marijuana?"

"Oh, fuck, sorry. Oh, fuck. I'm so sorry," she says. "I must be drunk. I just got confused or something. I'm so sorry. We were just talking by the ice machine, and then you said that shit about the mastodons, and . . . I'm so sorry."

Suddenly, I feel terrible, because this girl has every reason to think I am stoned, inasmuch as I am. My conscience breaks me down.

"Relax, my friend. Don't worry. You're right. You're smart. I *am* high," I say. And then I tell a lie that makes no sense whatsoever. "But I can't give you any, because it's not mine. It's my girlfriend's, and she will be back from the store in like five minutes, and she'd go fucking nuts if I gave any of our drugs away. She's kind of a bitch, actually. I should probably break up with her. I probably will, actually."

"Oh, that's totally no problem. My boyfriend just thought I should ask if you had any, in case that you had any."

"I'm really, really sorry," I say, as if I were somehow obligated to provide drugs to minors in Montana whom I've never met before. "But this is bad shit, anyway. It just makes you hungry. And nostalgic."

"Oh. Well, good then," she says. "I don't really smoke that much, anyway. Only when I'm partying."

"That's an excellent policy," I say. "In fact, I would suggest not smoking marijuana at all until you get to college. It will destroy your ambition, and it will make you fat. And if you smoke it all the time, you'll eventually stop dreaming at night, so you'll always wake up tired."

"Right on," she says unconvincingly. We exchange terse good-byes, and then she walks back into her room. I can hear three teenagers groan through the wooden door. They are *so* not going to party.

After this traumatic encounter with the young female stranger, I lay back on the bed and prepare not to dream. I flip back to CNN for images of New York, engulfed by the night. There is no power in eight states and part of Canada, but the only place that's getting any attention is Manhattan. Pundits are telling me that the present situation is more akin to the Good Blackout (November 9, 1965) than the Bad Blackout (July 13, 1977). The social order is not collapsing, even though the extent of the power failure is massive. "The East Coast continues to suffer through the biggest blackout in U.S. history," reiterates bearded jackass Wolf Blitzer. Whatever, Wolfman. I bet all my friends at *Spin* are really suffering right now; I bet they're suffering from sublime drunkenness. I bet they're all talking about how they will never forget this night for the rest of their lives, because This Is Living History. I bet they are telling secrets about their childhood. I bet they are holding hands while they walk across the Brooklyn Bridge. I bet they are eating complimentary Snickers bars. I bet they are sitting on darkened fire escapes, confessing their secret crushes on each other. I bet unrequited romances are ending in candlelight futon sex. And I wonder who Diane is kissing right now, and I am certain it must be *somebody*, even though logic would suggest she probably isn't kissing anyone. And I wonder whether she would be kissing me if I were there, or if we'd just be fighting about bullshit that doesn't matter, such as why mastodons were better than woolly mammoths.

I always miss the desirable disasters.

There is darkness on the streets of NYC, but there is light in the hallway outside my hotel room; I can see it through the crack under the door. When I was five years old, I used to pretend I was afraid of the dark; I thought little kids were *supposed* to be afraid of the dark, and I wanted to be normal. Being afraid of the dark seemed like a five-year-old's job. I would always insist that my mom leave the hallway light on after she tucked me in, but then I'd just lie there and wait for my older brother to go to bed an hour later and turn it off. I was always relieved when he finally flipped the switch, because that stupid hall light always kept me awake. Twenty years later, I tried to explain a very specific emotion to Quincy, and—as a metaphor—I said, "I feel like a five-year-old who's pretending that he's afraid of the dark." Prior to this conversation, I'd always assumed every child had done this; I assumed every kid had pretended to be afraid of the dark out of social obligation, because this was just part of growing up.

Quincy looked at me for a long time after I told her this.

"You," she said, "have interesting concerns."

THE SIXTEENTH DAY

"There's going to be people turning up in canyons
and there are going to be people being shot in Salt Lake City,
because the police there aren't willing to accept what I think
they know, and they know that I didn't do these things."

Friday morning in Missoula, and the sky glows electric gray.
The air on my tongue feels like smoke, but in a good way (it's
like the taste bacon leaves in your mouth after you've sucked on
the fat). I'm particularly groggy this morning, and it's the first
time I've felt "morning tired" in days: For most of this trip, I've
slept with a soundness that reminded me of high school; prior
to this trip, it had been at least 13 years since I slept soundly on
two consecutive nights, which makes me wonder if it's been 13
years since I've truly worked hard at anything. However, last
night was an exception: I laid in bed and found myself longing
to be in the blackness of New York, where I could have felt nostalgic for something that was happening in the living present. I
wanted to be where things were worse, yet better.

I pull out of the Campus Inn parking lot and immediately
make a U-turn, veering into a gas station. According to my best
estimates, driving through the rest of Montana should take
somewhere between four and 44,000 hours. When I walk into
the service station to pay the man the $16.18 I owe him for the

fuel, I ask how long it will take before I get to Seattle. He asks me how fast I drive. I say, "88." He laughs. I laugh. I have no idea why this is humorous. He asks me where I am from, and I say, "North Dakota, but also New York." He tells me I missed the blackout. I agree that I did in fact miss it. "It's pretty funny," he says. "New York doesn't have air-conditioning for 12 hours, and it's the biggest story of the year. Meanwhile, this entire state is *burning down*, and nobody notices. It wasn't even on the news last night."

You don't have to be away from Manhattan for very long to remember why everyone else in America hates New York.

It's only 11 minutes to the I-94 on-ramp, which is where I will begin today's mission. Generally, I am not a goal-oriented person. I tend to be more task-oriented, and I can only do one task at a time (I can't read two books at once, for example, nor can I eat french fries while driving; for these reasons, I would never actively pursue a *ménage à trois*). If you only concern yourself with singular tasks, it's impossible to set up meaningful long-term goals; that process requires the ability to imagine many tasks in sequence, which is another skill I struggle with (this is why I suck at chess and nine-ball and *Risk* and cleaning the bathroom). However, today I have a goal, and I'm optimistic about my potential success: Today, I am going to listen to all four KISS solo albums in their entirety, including the one by Peter Criss.

This is something I need to do.

When people discuss the 1978 KISS solo records (and granted, this does not happen often), they are usually being employed as a metaphor for everything stupid about KISS, and/or what was stupid about the late '70s, and/or what was stupid about people who bought KISS records in the late '70s. At the time, KISS were working under the premise that they were the Beatles of their generation, but that they could do something the Beatles never even considered: They would make individual solo albums while still remaining in KISS. Their logic was as follows: If (a) a normal KISS record sold three million copies, then (b) making four solo records would allow them to sell 12 million records, and (c) this would allow them to work independent of each other, since (d) they never really liked each other to begin with. Each album was intended to reflect the individual persona each member had created for himself; each album cover would be a beautifully painted portrait by artist Eraldo Carugati, and each portrait was highlighted by a color that would (ahem) "reflect the musician's aura" (blood red for Gene Simmons, royal purple for Paul Stanley, ice blue for Ace Frehley, and kitty-cat green for Criss).

When these four albums came out in September '78, Casablanca Records shipped 5 million of them at once; this was done so that Casablanca could publicize how all four albums "shipped platinum," which is kind of like mathematically arguing I've had 4 million "potential sexual encounters" since moving to New York. Each opus sold in the neighborhood of 700,000 copies, which—if multiplied by four—would have roughly equated to one conventional KISS record. Nobody remembers any of the music off these records, except for Frehley's disco-lacquered cover of "New York Groove," which peaked at number 13 on the singles chart. The modifier most often used when reviewing these projects is "bloated." Almost without exception, they are unloved.

And, obviously, I am that exception.

I think Frehley's solo effort is exceptional, Stanley's is somewhere between "good" and "quite good," Simmons's is sporadically transcendent, and Criss's totally has the right to exist. There are several moments of quasi-genius, most notably Ace's unbridled guitar solo on "Rip It Out," Paul's (admittedly specious) argument for casual sex on "It's Alright," and Gene's willingness to rhyme the phrase *Living in Sin* with *Holiday Inn*. These are all KISS records that don't sound like KISS records, which always tend to be the best KISS records (i.e., *Destroyer, The Elder,* side four of *Alive II,* etc.). And as I listen to these recordings while rumbling across rural Montana, something is starting to scare me, and it's not the demonic laughter at the beginning of "Radioactive" (which is the lead track off *Gene Simmons,* featuring guitar work from Aerosmith's Joe Perry). What is frightening me on this particular morning is the realization that the only way I can intellectually organize the women I have loved is by thinking about the members of KISS.

Has it really come to this? Have I become so reliant on popular culture that it's the only way I can understand anything? If wolves killed my mother, would I try to eulogize her with lyrics off *Blood on the Tracks*? If I had to describe genocide in Rwanda, would I compare the atrocity to the muscular drop-D riffing on Helmet's debut album *Strap It On*? I'd like to think I would not. Yet here I am in Montana, and this is what is on my mind: Diane is sort of my own personal Gene Simmons, because she's all about the bottom line. She demands attention. She's an atheist who's obsessed with her own Jewishness. She's self-interested and intelligent, and that's why I love her. Lenore is more like Paul Stanley—less overt about sex, but sexier. Perfect-looking. Fragile. Not necessarily immune to believing astrological bullshit. Seemingly happy all the time, but somehow more melancholy underneath. Quincy is, of course, Ace: stoned, cool, and the personality I secretly want to be. Dee Dee would be Peter, just because it seems like she deserves to be classified as an original member (metaphorically, I don't think you can relegate the first person you ever slept with anywhere outside of any "classic" lineup; for example, if I was using Fleetwood Mac as the incarnation for every important feeling I've ever had, then Dee Dee would always get to be Christine McVie, regardless of who else I met later in my life). And this process does not end with those four, either; I once had an extended fling with an actress named Siouxie, and our e-mail interaction preceding said fling was so integral to my view of romance that I mentally compare her to Eric Carr, a man who actually played drums for KISS longer than Peter Criss (10 years, ending with Carr's death from lung cancer in 1990). Eric Carr was a much better drummer than Peter Criss, and they both knew it; similarly, this actress was one of the those people who was completely aware that she was a phenomenal kisser. The second time she kissed me, it felt like somebody dropped a piano on my chest. But Siouxie came late in the game; she wasn't part of the original group, and her technical virtuosity at power-smooching could never change that (for the same reason, it's difficult to find vintage KISS posters featuring Eric Carr). I dated a photographer in Ohio who was incredibly earnest about liking me, but I never appreciated her when she was around and probably took advantage of her sexually; she was like guitarist Bruce Kulick (who played on *Crazy Nights* and *Revenge* and a few other sans-makeup records that nobody likes but me). There was a woman in Fargo whom I met at the mall, and she was a chain-smoking lunatic; Tina was tall (six foot one), eccentric (she used to ask me whether I was a "gentleman or a rogue" whenever we were flirting, and this was always some kind of undefined test), erotically ridiculous (she tried to get me to have anal sex with her *on our second date!*), and inexplicably mean-spirited (when we were breaking up over the phone, she flatly said, "You can't satisfy me physically"). Tina was always a case of good news/bad news (for instance, she was a part-time swimsuit model . . . but only for Target). Tina was my Vinnie Vincent (Ace Frehley's virtuoso replacement for *Creatures of the Night* and *Lick It Up,* and a self-destructive egomaniac who would later get kicked out of a different band that was specifically named after him). I had a minor affair with an Akron divorcée who had read my column in the local newspaper and wanted to kiss me before we ever actually met (she was like Eric Singer, Eric Carr's replacement who had attended a KISS concert as a youth). There's a female friend whom I once hooked up with, wrongly, and we've never spoken of it since; she is my Anton Fig (the house drummer on *Late Night with David Letterman* who served as the uncredited percussionist on the KISS album *Unmasked*). I am also 99 percent positive there is also a smiley, bookish girl I'm completely forgetting about from the early '90s, but I probably couldn't pick her out of a police lineup at this point (she's like Mark St. John, the guitar wizard who only played on *Animalize* before contracting a form of inflammatory arthritis called Reiter's syndrome). That's more or less everybody. That's the history of KISS, and those are the contents of my heart. I suppose there was also the aforementioned Heather (from my weird summer with the pole-vaulter), a woman I loved for two long years at college but never came remotely *close* to dating . . . and if you have a grasp on the history of KISS (i.e., "Kisstory"), you've already realized that Heather is Bob Kulick, the older brother of Bruce, who was vaguely involved with Paul and Gene's original band, Wicked Lester.

It is a miracle any woman has ever kissed me.

Still, there is a frozen logic to all this, and it's something I've always understood (but never consciously considered until today). It is no accident that I can see every woman I've ever cared about through KISS, the one rock band I have cared about more than any other. Sadly, this is my savant-like skill. It's like the way a carpenter can look at a pile of wood and see a bookshelf, or the way Gutzon Borglum could look at the side of a South Dakota mountain and see Teddy Roosevelt's face. I did not have to *try* to find a way to compare those women to KISS; it just seemed obvious. That notion had never occurred to me before this morning, but the moment it did, the entire backstory was already in place. Every blank was complete. That girl Tina? She was my Vinnie Vincent before I ever considered what that meant. And you know what? *This is love.* This is why we love things. For years, I have tried to explain to people why I like KISS, and I've inevitably used words like *pretty cool* (when I was 8) and *fucking awesome* (when I was 15) and *culturally interesting* (when I was 22) and *archetypally essential* (when I was 29). I was never wrong with any of those arguments. But I also wasn't right. Those are reasons *for other people* to love KISS, and I honestly never cared if they did or if they didn't. Those reasons were never why I loved KISS; I love KISS because the world makes sense when I think about them. Art and love are the same thing: It's the process of seeing yourself in things that are not you. It's understanding the unreasonable. And although the theory I am proposing is completely unreasonable, it is something I completely understand. Obviously, these connections aren't tangible; Quincy wasn't my favorite person because she sang "Shock Me" or drank cold gin, and Ace wasn't my favorite guitarist because he slept on his tummy or claimed to have "gooey paws" whenever his palms would sweat from nervousness. I didn't love one because I happened to love the other. They are not equals, and my specific feelings for each are completely different. But—somehow—the way I understand KISS has become the way I understand life, and I never even had to try. Which is why it would be a waste of my time to try to explain what's good about Ace Frehley's 1978 solo record. On paper, the songs would be meaningless. But if you had my brain and if you had my ears and if you had ever spent an autumn afternoon on a balcony with Quincy, talking about how our day-to-day life would be different if werewolves were real . . . well, you would love "New York Groove" more than you would love yourself.

Under the right circumstances, disco metal can make you cry. It can make you walk into walls.

Ace is singing "Snowblind," which seems to be his depiction of a bad drug experience. I've never had a bad drug experience. Actually, that's not true; I've had two bad experiences, although one of them was only bad "symbolically."

The first bad experience was last winter. It had been a hard week of drinking in *Spin* City; I think Lucy Chance and I went to the bar on Monday, Tuesday, and Thursday, and I'm pretty sure we stayed out past 3:00 A.M. on all three occasions. It was rather exhausting, and I really could have used a night off from trying to kill myself. However, one of our coworkers was throwing a housewarming party in Brooklyn that Friday, and I still wanted to have at least one more good time without being exhausted, so I took the Dexedrine that Lucy's affable boyfriend had given me as a Christmas present (Dexedrine is a very rock-'n'-rollish pill, mostly because of the band Dexys Midnight Runners but also because it's the prescription drug the Stones sing about in "Mother's Little Helper"). Having never taken Dexedrine before, I expected big things; unfortunately, nothing happened. And since I was drinking beer quite heavily at this party, I decided to take two Ritalins as well. After I swallowed the Ritalin, the host of the party began serving some kind of elaborate rum punch, of which I consumed several glasses. Around midnight, a woman named Sharon showed up, and she told me she had a great deal of cocaine in her purse; not surprisingly, a few of us went into the bathroom and did rails of coke every 20 minutes for the next three hours. I also switched over to brandy and ginger ale, ostensibly so I'd be better at arguing. At 3:00 A.M., someone decided we all needed to chill out, so everyone who was still partying stood around the kitchen and smoked four bowls of dope. At 4:15, a group of us called a car service and started to head back to Manhattan. I thought I was going to go home with Diane, because cocaine makes you believe you are dynamic and attractive. But that didn't happen. Diane rejected me, in front of five of our mutual friends. When I finally got home and went to bed, the sun started coming up, and I went mildly insane. I had to go to the bathroom constantly (this, I assume, was because of the Dexedrine and the Ritalin), and I was dehydrated (from all the booze), and I was depressed about Diane (probably because of the cocaine), and I could not sleep (from the pot). Every 10 minutes, I was pissing like a diplodocus; every 11 minutes, I would get explosive charley horses in my calves from the dehydration. I tried to play sooth- ing music (Rod Stewart's *Never a Dull Moment*), but all the lyrics made me want to weep. And that's when I realized I couldn't weep, even though I wanted to; I was too dehydrated. It felt like my eyes were having dry heaves; my tear ducts were completely barren. And lying there in my bed, unable to cry, feeling the sun through the blinds and vainly trying to uncurl my toes during another round of excruciating muscle cramps, I found myself relating to Demi Moore's character from *St. Elmo's Fire*.

So that was bad experience No. 1.

The second situation was less physically damaging but slightly more depressing: One day in May, Diane and I played Frisbee in Prospect Park. It was a fine afternoon. But then we took a walk and started talking about our relationship, and it imme- diately became awful. We eventually went back to her apart- ment and embarked on one of those terrible discussions where it feels like you'll never speak again, so you just keep recycling the same gut-wrenching conversation over and over and over, because even a redundant discussion is better than losing some- one forever. And just as I was finally about to leave, and just when things seemed like they could not be any more melodramatic or irrevocable, Diane stopped me at the door and said, "Since I can't seem to find a way to love you, let me give you the closest chemical equivalent."

She handed me a sandwich bag containing one hit of ecstasy.

This was a painful thing to hear, but it was mostly just disenchanting. I spent the subway ride home wondering if Diane had rehearsed that line. I mean, who says things like that in real life? It almost seemed like she said it on purpose, just so I'd have something interesting to write about at a later date.

Three weeks later, I took that ecstasy at the Bronx Zoo. It didn't do anything to me. The tigers still looked like tigers. But I was back in love with Diane.

THE DAY BEFORE THE LAST DAY

And We Die Young ➤ Albinos, Mulattos, Etc. ➤
Fuck Me Gently with a Chain Saw

At long last, Seattle. Lots of dead people here. If rock musicians were 16-ton ivory-bearing pachyderms, Seattle would be America's elephant graveyard. And I suppose that could still happen, assuming Elefant lead singer Diego Garcia gets assassinated on top of the Space Needle.

There's quite an impressive list of corpses in this extremely modern town. First you have Mia Zapata, the female punk who represented liberation and self-reliance before being abducted by a sociopath, raped, and then strangled to death with the string of her hoodie sweatshirt. There's Kristen Pfaff, the Hole bassist and professional smack addict who died in her bathtub on Capitol Hill, Seattle's coolie gay district. You have Scott Jernigan, drummer for Karp and the Whip (not really a rock "star," I realize, but close enough) who had just died in June; his liver exploded after a bizarre boating accident on the dock of Union Bay. And one cannot forget the (entirely predictable) demise of Alice in Chains singer Layne Staley, a man who OD'd in perhaps the least rock 'n' roll spot in all of Washington: He lived and died in a generic, five-story teal condo in an area widely considered to be the least-hip neighborhood in Seattle (it's a block from a Petco). Then again, Staley's condo on the 4500 block of Eighth Avenue NE might have been ideal for the hermitlike lifestyle of the typical junk-shooter, since there are lots of teenage dealers hanging out on nearby University Way. It's also possible that heroin didn't even play a role in his death—the big (albeit unsubstantiated) rumor in Seattle these days is that Staley actually died from huffing paint.

Perhaps you are wondering how I knew where all these people happened to perish; the truth is that I did not. A guided Seattle death tour was given to me by Hannah Levin, a rock writer for that city's alternative newspaper *The Stranger* and a freewheeling expert on local tragedies. And of course, all these aforementioned deaths were really just a precursor to the Xanadu of modern rock deaths: the mighty K.C. That memory is what Levin and I discuss as we maneuver down the long and winding Lake Washington Boulevard, finally arriving in what used to be Kurt Cobain's backyard.

"In the weeks before he killed himself, there was this litany of rumors about local singers dying," Hannah tells me. Back in '94, she was working at Planned Parenthood but already engulfed in the grunge culture. "There was a rumor that Chris Cornell had died, and then there was a rumor that Eddie Vedder had died. So even though a bunch of my friends called me at work that day and said Kurt was dead, I didn't really believe them. That kind of shit happened constantly. But then I went out to my car at lunch; I used to go out to my car at lunch to smoke cigarettes and listen to the radio. And—for some crazy reason—my radio was on 107.7 'the End,' which was Seattle's conventional 'modern rock' station. And as soon as I turned the ignition key back, I heard the song 'Something in the Way.' That's when I knew it was true, because the End would have never fucking played that song otherwise. It wasn't even a single."

The greenhouse where Cobain swallowed a shotgun shell was torn down in 1996; now it's just a garden. One especially tall sunflower appears to signify where the Nirvana frontman died, but that might be coincidence. When we arrive at the site, there are four guys staring at the sunflower. One of them is a 24-year-old goateed musician named Brant Colella; he's wearing a Glassjaw sweatshirt, and it has been a long time since I've met someone this earnest. Colella makes Chris Carrabba seem like Jack Black.

"I'm from New York, but I moved to Portland to make music. I'm a solo artist. I used to be in a band, but my band didn't have it in them to go all the way, and that's where I'm going," he tells me, and then looks longingly toward the sunflower. "His heart is here. My heart is here, too. I wanted to see where Kurt lived and hung out. I wanted to see where he was normal. The night before he died, I had a dream where Kurt came to me and told me that he was passing the torch on to me. Then we played some music together."

Colella was 15 when Cobain died. Last night, he and his three friends attended a Mariners game—Ichiro hit a grand slam to beat the BoSox—but Colella wants to make it *very* clear that seeing Cobain's house was his primary motivation for visiting Seattle. He also wanted to make it very clear that (a) he hates people who wear Abercrombie & Fitch, and (b) Kurt probably didn't kill himself.

"There are some people who assume he was completely suicide-driven, but he wasn't like that," Colella tells me. "I don't want to stir up waves and get killed myself, but the information that indicates Kurt was murdered actually makes way more sense than the concept of him committing suicide. But I'm not here to point fingers and say Courtney Love did it. Only God knows the answer to this question. And I realize there are people who *want* to believe Kurt Cobain committed suicide.

People are kind of broken into two factions: There are right-wingers who want to use his death to point out that this is what happens when you listen to rock 'n' roll, and there are also all his crazy fans who want to glorify depression and have Kurt be their icon forever."

When Colella first said this to me, I thought it was reductionist, simplistic, immature, and a little stupid. But the more I think it over, the more I suspect he's completely right.

The life and death of Kurt Cobain has been (almost without rival) the most poorly remembered cultural event of my lifetime. It's normal for someone's death to change how we recall what a celebrity was like, but the situation with Cobain is more complex; this is a situation in which a celebrity died, and many private citizens—including countless individuals who were wholly unconnected to Kurt or Seattle or grunge or even popular music—suddenly chose to remember *themselves* in a completely different way. Kurt Cobain didn't need to die in order to get integrity, because he already had it. However, his dying seemed to give total strangers a sense of integrity they had never wanted while he was alive.

Do I remember the day Cobain's electrician found him dead? I suppose that I do. Kurt Loder reported the news on MTV, seemingly every six minutes. People were surprised, but nobody seemed that shocked; I played in an amateur basketball tournament in Devils Lake, North Dakota, the weekend it happened, and whenever it came up in conversations at post-game hotel parties, people merely said things like, "That's so weird" or "That's so wild" or "That's so pathetic." I recall a lot of speculation over how many copycat suicides would occur in the coming days (a number that falls somewhere between two and 68, depending on which conspiratorial data you want to believe). It was sad, but everybody seemed to keep themselves together. Andy Rooney went on *60 Minutes* and essentially argued that

Cobain was a degenerate who deserved to die, but this just made us think Andy Rooney was an out-of-touch moron (more so).

What I seem to remember more were the months just prior to Kurt's suicide, and sometimes I feel like I'm the only person who does. And what I remember were people attacking Cobain at every turn. Everybody had purchased *In Utero* that fall, but not many people seemed to love it; the mainstream, man-on-the-street consensus was that Pearl Jam's *Vs.* was a little better. This is the biggest thing pop historians revise when talking about Nirvana: They never seem willing to admit that, by the spring of 1994, Pearl Jam was *way more popular*. It wasn't even that close. The week of its release, *Vs.* sold more than 900,000 copies, a seven-day record that seemed unbreakable at the time. Pearl Jam was seen as the people's band; Nirvana was seen as the band that hated its own people. Nirvana dropped off the schedule for Lollapalooza '94, and everyone blamed Kurt (except the insiders, who blamed his wife). Jokes were made when he almost killed himself in Rome. Kids were confused and insulted by his liner notes for *Incesticide*, where Kurt expressed annoyance over uncool people liking his songs. There was just this widespread sentiment that Kurt Cobain was a self-absorbed complainer and that if he hated being famous, he should just disappear forever.

Which he did. And then everything immediately changed for everyone.

Now, I'm not going to try and pretend like I never cared about Nirvana, because I really, really did. For a six-month period in 1992, they were absolutely my favorite thing to talk about. I have emotions tied up with *Nevermind* that are so stupidly clichéd I am ashamed to recognize their existence; I can remember the first time we all played that cassette in a dorm room. I can vividly recall My Nemesis telling me that he had figured out how "Lithium" was about bipolar disorder, which was as exciting as breaking a Soviet code during the Cold War. I briefly tried to wear cardigans after watching Nirvana on *Unplugged*. I unconsciously relive an entire three-year span of my collegiate life every single time I hear the opening nine seconds of "Smells Like Teen Spirit." All of that is true. But they were just a rock band, you know? And I have loved *a lot* of rock bands. When I say that Nirvana was my favorite thing to talk about in 1992, my liking them was pretty much the whole conversation: "I like Nirvana. You say you don't? Well, I do." This would be followed by a debate over the merits and minutia of songs and songwriters and fashion decisions, but it was really just a process of self-definition: I listened to Nirvana, so I viewed myself as "the kind of person who listens to Nirvana." Tangibly, that's as far as it went. I never thought Kurt Cobain represented me; I choose to represent *him* as a way to explain what kind of person I thought I was. It didn't seem like that big of a deal; I briefly did the same thing with King Missile.

Then, of course, Kurt killed himself. Soon after, the reverse engineering began in earnest. Slowly, the memory of Cobain evolved; weeks after his death, people who hadn't seemed especially jarred by his passing started to claim they were finally feeling okay. The memory of the recent Nirvana backlash completely disappeared; suddenly, Nirvana had always been everyone's favorite band. *Nevermind* was no longer the soundtrack to living in the early '90s—now it was that experience *in totality*. Kurt Cobain had not merely made culturally important music—suddenly, he had *made culture*. His death became a catchall event for anyone who wanted their adolescence to have depth: It was now possible to achieve credibility simply by mourning retrospectively. Cobain's iconography hadn't changed that much, really; what changed was the number of people who suddenly thought Cobain's iconography said something about themselves.

The week following Cobain's suicide, a group of my friends rented the movie *Heathers* (which—if nothing else—indisputably proves that we must have been handling the whole tragedy rather comfortably). Released in 1989, *Heathers* seemed pretentious in '94; it actually seems smarter today than it did that particular spring, for some reason. However, there is a voice-over in this movie that was mildly ironic in '94 but aggressively metaphoric a decade later: It's a journal entry Winona Ryder scribbles after the deaths of the high school superbitch ("Heather") and two muscle-bound troglodytes from the football team ("Kurt" and "Ram") . . .

> *Dear Diary: My teen-angst bullshit has a body count. The most popular kids in school are dead. Everybody is sad, but it's a weird kind of sad. Suicide gave Heather depth; Kurt, a soul; Ram, a brain. I don't know what it's getting me . . .*

Within the context of *Heathers*, suicide gave the dead qualities they never possessed in life. This is not a shocking revelation; suicide made Judas sympathetic, Sylvia Plath irrefutable, and Marilyn Monroe unfortunate. However, Cobain's suicide was of the postmodern variety; his death changed the history of the living. Suicide gave sorority girls depth; nihilistic punk kids, a soul; reformed metalheads, a brain. All you had to do was remember caring about Nirvana, even if you did not. And it's not that these self-styled revisionists were consciously lying; it's more that they really, really needed that notion to be true. Kurt Cobain was that popular-yet-unpopular kid who died for the sins of your personality.

In *Heathers*, Winona Ryder said she didn't know what the suicide of other people was going to get her. Little pre-shoplifting Winona was clearly the last of her breed.

THE LAST DAY

.08

I don't know why I'm in the logging community of Aberdeen, Washington. Nobody famous died here; I guess I just wanted to see what Cobain's hometown looked like. The town can be described with one syllable: *bleak*. Everything appears belted by sea air; the buildings look like they're suffering from hangovers. Just being here makes me feel exhausted. It makes the saliva inside my mouth taste like Old Milwaukee.

In the early 1990s, demographic studies indicated that the suicide rate in Aberdeen was roughly twice as high as the national average. This does not surprise me. It's also a hard-drinking town, and that doesn't surprise me, either: There are actually road signs that inform drivers that the Washington DUI limit is .08 (although it would seem that seeing said sign *while you were actually driving your vehicle* would be akin to closing the barn door after the cows were already in the corn). I see these road signs as I drive around, looking for a bridge that does not exist.

What I am looking for is the bridge on the Wishkah River that Kurt Cobain never slept under. He liked to *claim* that he did (the last official track on *Nevermind*, "Something in the Way," is the supposed story of this nonexperience), and it's quite possible he hung out down there, since hanging out under bridges is something bored, stoned high school kids are wont to do. But Cobain didn't really live under any bridge; he just said he did to be cool—which is a totally acceptable thing to do, considering what Kurt did for a living. He was a rock star. Being cool was more or less his whole job.

There are a lot of bridges in Aberdeen; this would be a wonderful community for trolls. I walk under several of these bridges, and I come to a striking conclusion: They all pretty much look the same, at least from the bottom. And it doesn't matter if Kurt Cobain slept underneath any of them; what matters is that people *believe* he did and that this is something they want to believe. Maybe it's something they *need* to believe, because if they don't, they will be struck with the mildly depressing revelation that dead people are simply dead. Everything else is human construction; everything else has nothing to do with the individual who died and everything to do with the people who are left behind (and who maybe wish those roles were somehow reversed).

As I walk back to my car and prepare to drive back to the world of the living, I think back to the conversation I had with the unabashedly annoyed man who runs the Chelsea Hotel. And it occurs to me that I am not a serious person, and that I do not have any understanding of death, and that I am looking for nothing.

I drop off the Tauntaun at the rental-car return office, four hours before my flight back to New York. I'd like to say I'd grown attached to this vehicle over the past two and a half weeks, but I really didn't; I could never get over the fact that the cup holder was exactly where I liked to put my elbow, so I was never truly comfortable. Details are important. I still hate cars.

With so much time to kill, I decide to check my e-mail one last time. There are three new messages. Two are about my upcoming fantasy football draft. The last one is from Quincy.

I don't want to open it.

For the past seven days, I have been rechecking every e-mail I had sent to Quincy prior to my arrival in Minneapolis, looking for subtext I might have unintentionally inserted into each message. This is all you can do when a woman you think is going to respond says nothing in response; all you can do is open your "sent mail" folder and stare at missives you already mailed electronically, deconstructing every sentence and wondering if— somehow—you accidentally offended her. But now I'm going to find out why she never called me back. And I have a feeling it's either going to be something horrible or something irrelevant.

I am wrong on both counts.

"Oh, Chuck," it begins. "I am so, so sorry I missed you. I got all your phone messages, and I feel terrible. But something crazy happened the day before you got here."

And then I know what the next sentence is going to say. I don't even have to read it, but I do.

"I guess I'm getting married."

The day before I arrived in the Twin Cities, Q's live-in boyfriend—a likable architect who rides a motorcycle—finally proposed to her. She accepted. They immediately drove to North Dakota to inform their parents. They're going to buy a house. They don't know when the date of the wedding will be, but they suspect next summer. They're freaking out, but this is what they want. They are now officially "they."

Now, I know what you're thinking.

You're thinking that this is going to devastate me, because you think I'm still in love with Quincy. But I'm not devastated, and I'm not in love with her. I have not been in love with her for years. I want her to get married to this architect, and I want her to buy a house, and I want her to be happy.

But I still feel like I lost.

We all have the potential to fall in love a thousand times in our lifetime. It's easy. The first girl I ever loved was someone I knew in sixth grade. Her name was Missy; we talked about horses. The last girl I love will be someone I haven't even met yet, probably. They all count. But there are certain people you love who do something else; they define how you classify what love is supposed to feel like. These are the most important people in your life, and you'll meet maybe four or five of these people over the span of 80 years. But there's still one more tier to all this; there is always one person you love who *becomes* that definition. It usually happens retrospectively, but it always happens eventually. This is the person who unknowingly sets the template for what you will always love about other people, even if some of those lovable qualities are self-destructive and unreasonable. You will remember having conversations with this person that never actually happened. You will recall sexual trysts with this person that never technically occurred. This is because the individual who embodies your personal definition of love does not really exist. The person is real, and the feelings are real—but you create the context. And context is every-thing. The person who defines your understanding of love is not inherently different than anyone else, and they're often just the person you happen to meet the first time you really, really want to love someone. But that person still wins. They win, and you lose. Because for the rest of your life, they will control how you feel about everyone else.

If someone asked Quincy to rank the romantic relationships of her life, I think I would place third or fourth. I might even end up seventh, which is a difficult thing to admit. But she will always be No. 1 for me, no matter whom I meet, and that has far more to do with me than it does with her. And now she's offi-cially gone, just as Lenore is figuratively gone and Diane is potentially gone. I'm still alive, but I feel myself dying, person by person by person by person.

"Dr. Cotard. Paging Dr. Cotard. You have a phone call."

"This is Chuck," I say into my cell phone, as if I am inside an office instead of looking for food inside the SeaTac airport.

"Chuck!"

"This is Chuck."

"This is Lucy."

"I know. I knew it the very moment you exclaimed, 'Chuck!' What's going on, my friend?"

"Absolutely nothing," she says. "We are all at the bar, and the bar is wondering when you're going to come back to New York. The bar misses you."

"I miss the bar," I say. "I'm actually in the airport right now. I will be back in the office tomorrow afternoon."

"Excellent," she says. "How did the trip go? Are you going to be able to write a compelling story that will dissect the perverse yet undeniable relationship between celebrity and mortality? Will the narrative illustrate how society glamorizes dying in order to perpetuate the hope that death validates life? Will you be able to prove that living *is* dying, and that we're all slowly dying through every moment of life?"

"I'm not sure," I say.

"I think you should probably do that," Lucy Chance says flatly.

"Well, that's the idea," I say. "But you know what? After I write this story for *Spin*, I think I'm going to try and expand it into a book. Because I've obviously been thinking a lot about Diane, and I saw that woman Lenore when I was in Minnesota, and just before I saw Lenore I met this amazingly daring rock girl who climbed up a roof in Minneapolis, and I talked with this interesting waitress in North Carolina who reads Kafka but lacks awareness of the Allman Brothers, and this totally fucked-up thing just happened with Quincy. And it suddenly feels like I've been inside a car for 1,000 years, worrying about women and thinking about death and playing KISS and Radiohead and all this other shit, and—for some reason—I keep writing all this stuff down, and I don't exactly know why. But it all feels the same, you know? It seems like love and death and rock 'n' roll are the same experience."

"Chuck, please don't write a book about women you used to be in love with."

"Why not?"

"Because that's exploitive. And narcissistic. And a bit desperate, because it makes you seem like someone who can't let go of the past."

"But that's actually true," I say. "I can't let go of the past. I can't fall out of love with any of these women. I can only exist in the past and in the future."

"I know, I know. We've talked about this before. But who wants to read another book about some death-obsessed drug addict who listens to Fleetwood Mac and lionizes the women who used to drive him crazy? It strikes me as dubious. You're going to become the male Elizabeth Wurtzel."

"Jesus Christ, Lucy. You've really got it in for that bitch."

"I just want to go on record as saying that the idea of writing such a book is dubious."

"But if I don't write the book, there will be no record of this entire conversation. Your disdain can only be voiced if I do the opposite of what you suggest."

"Well, fine," she says. "Just don't complain to me when all those idiot bloggers write things like, 'Ultimately, the author should have listened to his friend Lucy Chance.' Because you *know* that will happen."

"True," I say.

ACKNOWLEDGMENTS

This book could not exist without the following people: Brant Rumble, Daniel Greenberg, and Sia Michel.

This book could still exist without the following people, but it would be substantially worse: Andrew Beaujon, Bob Ethington, David Giffels, Eric Nuzum, Michael Weinreb, Kristin Earhart, Rex Sorgatz, Melissa Maerz, T. Phoebe Reilly, and the totality of the Klosterman collective.

Chuck Klosterman would also like to thank Alex Pappademas, Jon Dolan, Dave Itzkoff, Greg Milner, Charles Aaron, Doug Brod, Jeanann Pannasch, Regan Solmo, Tracey Pepper, Caryn Ganz, Sarah Lewitinn, Marc Spitz, Jenny Williams, Ellen Carpenter, Lisa Corson, Maili Holiman, Alexander Chow, Amy Fritch, Cory Jacobs, Joe Mejia, Michael Miller, Kyle Anderson, Elaine Garza, Erin Cox, Erica Gelbard, Chris Ryan, Sean Howe, Andy Greenwald, James Montgomery, Rob Sheffield, Dave Hollingsworth and Rudy Sarzo, Paul Tough, Brendan Vaughn, Kimberly Donovan, Kate Perotti, Ross Raihala, Patrick Condon, Jon Blixt, Michael Schauer, Chad Hansen, Dave Beck, Mark J. Price, Denise Bower-Johnson, Robert Huschka, Luke Shockman, Amy Everhart, Mark Pfeifle, Jon Miller, Nick Chase, Sarah Jackson, Ellen Shafer, John Lamb, Greg Korte, Karen Schiely, Laura Davis, Erin Schulte, Lacy Garrison, T. Cole Rachel, Gillian Blake, Jack Sullivan, Michael Byzewski, Tammy Swift, Matt Von Pinnon, Mitch Hedberg, Spalding Gray, God, and Mr. Pancake.

Killing Yourself To Live is dedicated to Quincy, Lenore, and Diane.

INDEX

INDEX

INDEX

INDEX

INDEX

Read on for an excerpt from

Downtown Owl
A Novel

Available wherever books are sold

AUGUST 15, 1983

(Mitch)

When Mitch Hrlicka heard that his high school football coach had gotten another teenage girl pregnant, he was forty bushels beyond bamboozled. He could not understand what so many females saw in Mr. Laidlaw. He was inhumane, and also sarcastic. Whenever Mitch made the slightest mental error, Laidlaw would rhetorically scream, "Vanna? *Vanna?* Are you *drowsy,* Vanna? Wake up! You can sleep when you are dead, Vanna!" Mr. Laidlaw seemed unnaturally proud that he had nicknamed Mitch "Vanna White" last winter, solely based on one semifunny joke about how the surname "Hrlicka" needed more vowels. Mitch did not mind when other kids called him Vanna, because almost everyone he knew had a nickname; as far as he could tell, there was nothing remotely humiliating about being called "Vanna," assuming everyone understood that the name had been assigned arbitrarily. It symbolized nothing. But Mitch hated when John Laidlaw called him "Vanna," because Laidlaw *assumed* it was humiliating. And that, clearly, was his goal.

Christ, it was humid. When Mitch and his teenage associates had practiced that morning at 7:30 a.m., it was almost cool; the ground had been wet with dew and the clouds hovered fourteen feet off the ground. But now—eleven hours later—the sun was burning and falling like the Hindenburg. The air was damp wool. Mitch limped toward the practice field for the evening's upcoming death session; he could already feel sweat forming on his back and above his nose and under his crotch. His quadriceps stored enough lactic acid to turn a triceratops into limestone. "God damn," he thought. "Why do I want this?" In two days the team would begin practicing in full pads. It would feel like being wrapped in cellophane while hauling bricks in a backpack. "God damn," he thought again. "This must be what it's like to live in Africa." Football was not designed for the summer, even if Herschel Walker believed otherwise.

When Mitch made it to the field, the other two Owl quarterbacks were already there, facing each other twelve yards apart, each standing next to a freshman. They were playing catch, but not directly; one QB would rifle the ball to the opposite freshman, who would (in theory) catch it and immediately flip it over to the second QB who was waiting at his side. The other quarterback would then throw the ball back to the other freshman, and the process would continue. This was how NFL quarterbacks warmed up on NFL sidelines. The process would have looked impressive to most objective onlookers, except for the fact that both freshman receivers dropped 30 percent of the passes that struck them in the hands. This detracted from the fake professionalism.

Mitch had no one to throw to, so he served as the holder while the kickers practiced field goals. This duty required him to crouch on one knee and remain motionless, which (of course) is not an ideal way to get one's throwing arm loose and relaxed. Which (of course) did not really matter, since Coach Laidlaw did not view Mitch's attempts at quarterbacking with any degree of seriousness. Mitch was not clutch. Nobody said this, but everybody knew. It was the biggest problem in his life.

At 7:01, John Laidlaw blew into a steel whistle and instructed everyone to *bring it in*. They did so posthaste.

"Okay," Laidlaw began. "This is the situation. The situation is this: We will not waste any light tonight, because we have a beautiful evening with not many mosquitoes and a first-class opportunity to start implementing some of the offense. I realize this is only the fourth practice, but we're already way behind on everything. It's obvious that most of you didn't put five god-damn minutes into thinking about football all goddamn sum-mer, so now we're *all* behind. And I don't like being behind. I've never been a follower. I'm not that kind of person. Maybe you are, but I am not.

"Classes start in two weeks. Our first game is in three weeks. We need to have *the entire offense* ready by the day we begin classes, and we need to have all of the defensive sets memorized *before* we begin classes. And right now, I must be honest: I don't even know who the hell is going to play for us. So this is the situation. The situation is this: Right now, everybody here is equally useless. This is going to be an important, crucial, important, critical, important two weeks for everyone here, and it's going to be a real kick in the face to any of you who still want to be home watching *The Price Is Right.* And I know there's going to be a lot of people in this town talking about a lot of bull crap that doesn't have any-thing to do with football, and you're going to hear about certain things that happened or didn't happen or that supposedly hap-pened or that supposedly allegedly didn't happen to somebody that probably doesn't even exist. These are what we call *distractions.* These distractions will come from all the people who don't want you to think about Owl Lobo football. So if I hear anyone on this team perpetuating those kinds of bullshit stories, everyone is going to pay for those distractions. Everyone. *Because we are here to think about Owl Lobo football.* And if you are not thinking exclusively—*exclusively*—about Owl Lobo football, go home and turn on *The Price Is Right.* Try to win yourself a washing machine."

It remains unclear why John Laidlaw carried such a specific, all-encompassing hatred for viewers of *The Price Is Right.* No one will ever know why this was. Almost as confusing was the expla-nation as to why Owl High School was nicknamed the Lobos, particularly since they had been the Owl Owls up until 1964. During the summer of '64, the citizens of Owl suddenly concluded that being called the Owl Owls was somewhat embarrassing, urging the school board to change the nickname to something "less repetitive." This proposal was deeply polarizing to much of the community. The motion didn't pass until the third vote. And because most of the existing Owl High School athletic gear still featured its long-standing logo of a feathered wing, it was decided that the new nickname should remain ornithological. As such, the program was known as the Owl Eagles for all of the 1964–1965 school year. Contrary to community hopes, this change dramatically increased the degree to which its sports teams were mocked by opposing schools. During the especially oppressive summer of 1969, they decided to change the nickname again, this time becoming the Owl High Screaming Satans. (New uniforms were immediately purchased.) Two games into the '69 football season, the local Lutheran and Methodist churches jointly petitioned the school board, arguing that the nickname "Satan" glorified the occult and needed to be changed on religious grounds; oddly (or perhaps predictably), the local Catholic church responded by aggressively supporting the new moniker, thereby initiating a bitter feud among the various congregations. (This was punctuated by a now infamous street fight that involved the punching of a horse.) When the Lutheran minister ultimately decreed that all Protestant athletes would have to quit all extracurricular activities if the name "Satan" remained in place, the school was forced to change nicknames midseason. Nobody knew how to handle this unprecedented turn of events. Eventually, one of the cheerleaders noticed that the existing satanic logo actually resembled an angry humanoid wolf, a realization that seemed brilliant at the time. (The cheerleader, Janelle Fluto, is now a lesbian living in Thunder Bay, Ontario.) The Screaming Satans subsequently became the Screaming Lobos, a name that was edited down to Lobos upon the recognition that wolves do not scream. This nickname still causes mild confusion, as strangers sometimes assume the existence of a mythological creature called the "Owl Lobo," which would (indeed) be a terrifying (and potentially winged) carnivore hailing from western Mexico. But—nonetheless, and more importantly— there has not been any major community controversy since the late sixties. Things have been perfect ever since, if by "perfect" you mean "exactly the same."

Mitch and the rest of the Lobos clapped their hands simultaneously and started to jog one lap around the practice field, ostensibly preparing to perform a variety of calisthenics while thinking exclusively about Owl Lobo football and not fantasizing about *The Price Is Right.* But such a goal was always impossible. It was still summer. As Mitch loped along the sidelines, his mind drifted to other subjects, most notably a) Gordon Kahl, b) the Georgetown Hoyas, c) how John Laidlaw managed to seduce and impregnate Tina McAndrew, and d) how awful it must feel to be John Laidlaw's wife.

AUGUST 25, 1983

(Julia)

"You're going to like it here," said Walter Valentine. He said this from behind a nine-hundred-pound cherrywood desk, hands interlocked behind his head while his eyes looked toward the ceiling, focusing on nothing. "I have no doubt about that. I mean, it's not like this is some kind of wonderland. This isn't anyone's destination city. It's not Las Vegas. It's not Monaco. It's not like you'll be phoning your gal pals every night and saying, 'I'm living in Owl, North Dakota, and it's a dream come true.' *But you will like it here.* It's a good place to live. The kids are great, in their own way. The people are friendly, by and large. You will be popular. You will be very, very popular."

Julia did not know what most of those sentences meant.

"I will be popular," she said, almost as if she was posing a question (but not quite).

"Oh, absolutely," Valentine continued, now rifling through documents that did not appear particularly official. "I know that you are scheduled to teach seventh-grade history, eighth-grade geography, U.S. History, World History, and something else. Are you teaching Our State? I think you're scheduled to teach Our State. Yes. Yes, you are. 'Our State.' But that's just an unfancy name for North Dakota history, so that's simple enough: Teddy Roosevelt, Angie Dickinson, lignite coal, that sort of thing. The Gordon Kahl incident, I suppose. Of course, the fact that you're not *from* North Dakota might make that a tad trickier, but only during the first year. After that, history just repeats itself. But I suppose the first thing we should talk about is volleyball."

"Pardon?"

"What do you know about volleyball?"

Julia had been in downtown Owl for less than forty-eight hours. The land here was so relentlessly flat; it was the flattest place she'd ever seen. She had driven from Madison, Wisconsin, in nine hours, easily packing her entire existence into the hatchback of a Honda Civic. There was only one apartment building in the entire town and it was on the edge of the city limits; it was a two-story four-plex, and the top two apartments were empty. She took the bigger one, which rented for fifty-five dollars a month. When she looked out her bedroom window, she could see for ten miles to the north. Maybe for twenty miles. Maybe she was seeing Manitoba. It was like the earth had been pounded with a rolling pin. The landlord told her that Owl was supposedly getting cable television services next spring, but he admitted some skepticism about the rumor; he had heard such rumors before.

Julia was now sitting in the office of the Owl High principal. He resumed looking at the ceiling, appreciating its flatness.

"I've never played volleyball," Julia replied. "I don't know the rules. I don't even know how the players keep score of the volley balling."

"Oh. Oh. Well, that's unfortunate," Valentine said. "No worries, but that's too bad. I only ask because it looks like we're going to have to add volleyball to the extracurricular schedule in two years, or maybe even as soon as next year. It's one of those idiotic Title IX situations—apparently, we can't offer three boys' sports unless we offer three girls' sports. So now we have to figure out who in the hell is going to coach girls' volleyball, which is proving to be damn near impossible. Are you sure that isn't something you might *eventually* be interested in? Just as a thought? You would be paid an additional three hundred dollars per season. You'd have a full year to get familiar with the sport. We'd pay for any books on the subject you might need. I'm sure there are some wonderful books out there on the nature of volleyball."

"I really, really cannot coach volleyball," Julia said. "I'm not coordinated."

"Oh. Oh! Okay, no problem. I just thought I'd ask." Mr. Valentine looked at her for a few moments before his pupils returned to the ceiling. "Obviously, it would be appreciated if you thought about it, but—ultimately—volleyball doesn't matter. We just want you to do all the things that you do, whatever those things may be. I'm sure you bring a lot to the table. Do you have any questions for me?"

Julia had 140,000 questions. She asked only one.

"What's it like to live here?"

This was not supposed to sound flip, but that's how it came out. Julia always came across as cocky whenever she felt nervous.

"It's like living anywhere, I suppose." Valentine unlocked his fingers and crossed his arms, glancing momentarily at Julia's face. He then proceeded to stare at the mallard duck that was painted on his coffee cup, half filled with cherry Kool-Aid. "Owl's population used to be around twelve hundred during the height of the 1970s, but now it's more like eight hundred. Maybe eight fifty. I don't know where all the people went. It's a down town, Owl. We still have a decent grocery store, which is important, but—these days—it seems like a lot of folks will drive to Jamestown, or even all the way to Valley City, just to do their food shopping. Americans are crazy. There's a hardware store, but I wonder how much longer that will last. We have a first-rate Chevrolet dealership. We have two gas stations. We have seven bars, although you can hardly count the Oasis Wheel. You probably don't want to spend your nights at the Oasis Wheel, unless you're not the kind of woman I think you are. Heh! And you've probably heard that the movie theater is going to close, and I'm afraid that's true: It *is* closing. But the bowling alley is thriving. It's probably the best bowling alley in the region. I honestly believe that."

By chance, Julia did enjoy bowling. However, when the most positive detail about your new home is that the bowling alley is thriving, you have to like bowling *a lot* in order to stave off depression. And—right now, in the middle of this conversation—Julia was more depressed than she had ever been in her entire twenty-three-year existence. As she sat in Walter Valentine's office, she felt herself wanting to take a nap on the floor. But she (of course) did not do this; she just looked at him, nodding and half smiling. She could always sleep later, after she finished crying.

"The thing that you have to realize about a place like Owl is that everyone is aware of all the same things. There's a lot of shared knowledge," Valentine said. He was now leaning forward in his chair, looking at Julia and casually pointing at her chest with both his index fingers. "Take this year's senior class, for example. There are twenty-six kids in that class. Fifteen of them started kindergarten together. That means that a lot of those students have sat next to each other—in just about every single class—for thirteen straight years. They've shared every single experience. You said you grew up in Milwaukee, correct?"

"Yes."

"How big was your graduating class?"

"Oh, man. I have no idea," Julia said. "Around seven hundred, I think. It was a normal public school."

"Exactly. *Normal.* But your normal class was almost as big as our whole town. And the thing is, when those twenty-six seniors graduate, the majority will go to college, at least for two years. But almost all the farm kids—or at least all the farm *boys*—inevitably come back here when they're done with school, and they start farming with their fathers. In other words, the same kids who spent thirteen years in class with each other start going to the same bars and they bowl together and they go to the same church and pretty much live an adult version of their high school life. You know, people always say that nothing changes in a small town, but—whenever they say that—they usually mean that nothing changes *figuratively*. The truth is that nothing changes *literally*: It's always all the same people, doing all the same things."

Upon hearing this description, the one singular phrase that went through Julia's head was "Jesus fucking Christ." However, those were not the words that she spoke.

"Wow," she said. "That sounds kind of . . . unmodern."

"It is," Valentine said. Then he chuckled. Then he re-interlocked his fingers behind his skull and refocused his gaze on the ceiling. "Except that it's not. It's actually not abnormal at all. Look: I came here as a math teacher twenty years ago, and I thought I would be bored out of my trousers. I had grown up in Minot and I went to college in Grand Forks, so I considered myself urban. I always imagined I'd end up in Minneapolis, or even maybe Chicago; I have a friend from college who lives just outside of Chicago, so I've eaten in restaurants in that area and I have an understanding of that life. But once I really settled in Owl, I never tried to leave. I mean . . . sure, sometimes you think, 'Hey, maybe there's something else out there.' But there really isn't. This is what being alive feels like, you know? The place doesn't matter. You just live."

Julia could feel hydrochloric acid inside her tear ducts. There was an especially fuzzy tennis ball in her esophagus, and she wanted to be high.

But she remained cool.

Julia told Mr. Valentine she was extremely excited to be working at Owl High, and she thanked him for giving her the opportunity to start a career in teaching, which she claimed was her lifelong dream. "Everybody only has one first job," he said in response. "No matter what you do in life, you'll always remember your first job. So welcome aboard and good luck, although you won't need it. You'll be extremely popular here. And if you change your mind about that excellent volleyball opportunity, do not hesitate to call. Keep me in the loop. I'm always here, obviously."

Julia exited Valentine's office and walked toward the school's main entrance, faster and more violent with every step. She was virtually running when she got to the door and sprinted to her car, which was one of only three vehicles in the parking lot. Ten days from now, school would officially start. This building would be the totality of her life. She already hated it. The overtly idyllic nature of Owl seemed paradoxically menacing; it was like a Burmese tiger trap for apolitical strangers who needed uninteresting jobs. She didn't know anyone and had no idea how she ever would. Her apartment was on the far side of town, which meant it was a three-minute drive. She passed two cars and two pickup trucks; all four drivers waved hello as she passed. The waving scared her. She soon arrived in her apartment, where she had no furniture (and no idea how to acquire any, as there were apparently no furniture stores within a thirty-mile radius). She cut open the cardboard box that held her cassettes and found a dubbed copy of Foreigner's *4*, which she robotically placed into a boom box sitting on the floor. She fast-forwarded to "Juke Box Hero" and pushed play; the emptiness of the room produced a slight echo behind Lou Gramm's voice. Her apartment was like a bank vault with a refrigerator. Julia reached into the same cardboard box and found her copy of *The Random House Thesaurus (College Edition)*, which contained drugs. The day before leaving Madison, Julia and her college roommates meticulously rolled four perfect joints and hid them in the thesaurus, operating under the assumption that buying pot would be impossible in small-town North Dakota (which was, in fact, the case). The plan was that Julia could smoke one joint after the first day of class, one on Thanksgiving (which she would have to spend alone), and one after the last day of school in May. The fourth was a spare that could be consumed when (and if) she needed to offset any major unforeseen emergency that might occur over the course of the school year.

Julia sat on her sleeping bag and smoked three of them, all in a row. It was 2:45 p.m.

AUGUST 28, 1983

(Horace)

His life revolved around coffee.

It was central to his existence.

He was that kind of person.

It wasn't even so much the taste, although he did consider coffee to be delicious; he mostly loved the process of drinking it. Every day at 3:00 p.m. (except on Sundays), he drove three miles into town, sat on the third stool in Harley's Café, and drank three cups of coffee, each cup with three tablespoons of sugar. This was not because Horace Jones had OCD or a superstitious obsession with the number three; it was just a coincidence. If you were to ask Horace which stool he sat in (or how many spoonfuls of sugar he placed in his coffee), he would have no idea. These were merely things he did. They were not things he considered.

All of the men in Harley's played poker dice to see who would pay for each round of coffee; the winner paid for everybody, which (curiously) was the goal. There were usually six players, so an entire round of coffee cost $1.50, plus tip. Horace won 16.6 percent of the time. He considered himself extremely unlucky. But winning or losing at poker dice was only a secondary issue, since the conversation at Harley's was always worth the trip into town; stimulating conversation was something Horace could look forward to every single afternoon. These are the topics that were primarily discussed:

1) How current meteorological conditions compared to whatever were supposed to be the average meteorological conditions (i.e., temperatures that were higher or lower than usual, rainfall amounts that seemed out of the ordinary, et cetera).

2) The success (or lack thereof) of the local high school athletic teams, and particularly how contemporary teams would have fared against Owl teams from the late 1960s and early '70s (the conclusion being "not very well").

3) Walter Mondale's potential run for the presidency, an undeniably hopeless venture that only served to illustrate how the state of Minnesota had been destroyed by the same kind of naïve Democrats who crashed all those helicopters in the Iranian desert.

4) The North Dakota State University football team, particularly the number of local North Dakota high school players the school was recruiting in comparison to the number of black, out-of-state, potentially criminal athletes who were already on the traveling roster.

5) The implausibility of specific plotlines on the television show *Dallas*.

6) Acquaintances who had recently died (or were in the process of dying, usually from cancer). This topic was increasing in regularity.

7) Area events they all recalled from the 1950s, generally described as having happened in the relatively recent past.

8) How the market price of hard red spring wheat ($3.51 per bushel) was barely a dollar more than its price during the Dirty Thirties. This made no goddamn sense to anyone.

9) Gordon Kahl.

10) Other people's problems.

"So . . . more problems with the Dog Lover." This was Edgar Camaro speaking. Edgar was the youngest of the coffee drinkers; he was sixty-three. "That idiot kid is going to end up sleeping with Jesus. Did you hear what he said the other night?"

"His statement about the rain?" asked Horace.

"Yes," replied Edgar. "The rain. Just imagine the goddamn scenario: The Dog Lover is tending bar on Saturday night—this is early in the night, maybe seven o'clock—and the idiot is already tight."

"Somebody needs to inform that kid that a good bartender never drinks before midnight," interjected Bud Haugen, a man who had briefly owned a bar during the Korean conflict. "Christ. You'd think everybody would know that."

"Well, sure," said Edgar. "You'd *think* someone would have given that idiot some sense, but I guess he only listens to that hound of his. Heh. But here we go: It starts to drizzle Saturday night, and a few of the guys in the bar—this is like Edmund and Kuch and Woo-Chuck and that whole crew of outlaws—they get up and start looking out the windows, because Lord knows we need the rain. And that idiot—that idiot Dog Lover—he *turns down the jukebox* and says, 'Haven't you farmers ever seen rain before?' Can you believe that? In the middle of the worst drought in forty years, he tells a bunch of *paying customers* that they're stupid for looking at the rain."

"I'm surprised Woo-Chuck didn't snap his spine," said eighty-eight-year-old Ollie Pinkerton, his lazy eye drifting around the room like a child looking for the bathroom. "I mean, don't get me wrong—Woo-Chuck is a nice kid and a hard worker. But let's shoot straight: The man is a criminal." This was true. "Woo-Chuck" was an abbreviation of "Woodchuck." Bob (The Wood-chuck) Hodgeman had served in Vietnam, which was something he never talked about. But everyone assumed he must have done (or at least *seen*) some crazy shit over there, because he drank in this awkward, exceedingly antisocial manner, and he drank all the time, and sometimes he punched his own friends for no reason and couldn't explain why. People called him Wood-chuck (or, more often, Woo-Chuck) because he used to stash Quaaludes in the upholstery of his Monte Carlo. This seemed like something a woodchuck would do. On balance, he was a good person.

"Supposedly, that almost happened," Edgar continued. "They say Woo-Chuck walked up to the Dog Lover with a really queer look on his face. Remember that night last Christmas, when Woo-Chuck got loaded and threw a pitchfork at his son-in-law? I guess he had those same crazy eyes. But that idiot Dog Lover—probably because he was already seventeen sheets to the wind—he had no fear whatsoever. He just stood there like a concrete shithouse. Words were exchanged. And then the Dog Lover threw everybody out of the bar. Everybody. He emptied the whole place, and it wasn't even seven thirty. Locked all the doors. And then he just sat there, alone, swilling his own booze, listening to the Twins game on the radio. Have you ever heard of anything more asinine? If he's not careful, that bar is gonna end up worse than the Oasis Wheel. Some people just can't stand prosperity."

The Dog Lover's real name was Chet. He had lived a dubious life: Chet's father was (supposedly) one of the most successful bar owners in the Twin Cities; he (supposedly) co-owned five sports bars with Minnesota Vikings quarterback Tommy Kramer. Chet, however, was an irresponsible train wreck: DWIs, dope smoking, girl crazy, gun crazy, car crazy—all the usual interests of the prototypical meathead miscreant. Chet flunked out of St. Cloud State University, was readmitted a year later, and was bounced a second time for selling (fake) pot on campus. His father didn't know what to do with him, and he certainly didn't want Chet hanging around Minneapolis with no job and no prospects; if that happened, Chet was destined to get involved with cocaine or gambling or arson. Chet was a twenty-five-year-old dirtbag. Everybody knew this. As such, his father played the only card he could manufacture: He bought his son a life in a place where it was hard to find trouble. He bought his son a bar in a town where nothing happened, moved him into a four-plex apartment complex, and told him to stay away from Minneapolis until he "learned how the world worked."

That was almost a year ago. Over the subsequent eleven months, Chet had managed to alienate almost every citizen in town, seemingly on purpose. The first thing he did was change the name of the bar from Teddy's (after the name of the previous owner) to Yoda's (a reference completely lost on the overwhelming majority of his clientele). He had a dangerous propensity for hiring Owl High School students as waitresses, getting them drunk on the job, and openly chiding them for dressing too conservatively; this practice was finally stopped after he fed sixteen-year-old Ann Marie Pegseth so many clandestine wine coolers that she removed her blouse and worked an entire shift in her bra. Two days later, Ann Marie's father threatened to destroy Chet's Z28 Camaro with dynamite. Chet was a prick and a provocateur, constantly outdrinking his patrons and ridiculing the blandness of their conversation. He told Phil Anderson that his wife needed to eat more salad. He told Cindy Brewer that her voice reminded him of "a cuntier version of Joan Rivers." One of his running shticks was insisting that he recognized Randy Pemberton's girlfriend from *Hustler* magazine's "Beaver Hunt" section. He charged way too much for booze (sometimes $2.50 a beer, even for Schmidt). But the one quality that truly drove the citizens of Owl bonkers—and particularly the old men who had coffee at Harley's Café every day at 3:00 p.m.—was Chet's intimacy with his dog. Chet had a black Labrador retriever, and he kept it *inside his apartment.* He turned a hunting animal into a house pet. This was less reasonable than talking to a brick wall. He would bring his dog *inside the bar,* and the dog often sat *in the front seat of his Camaro,* a vehicle *which supposedly cost sixteen thousand dollars.*

Just thinking about that dog made Horace furious. What kind of man treats his dog like a wife? You'd have to be mentally retarded. There were inside animals and there were outside animals, and any dog the size of a Labrador was absolutely, irrevocably, indisputably an outside animal. Oh, you might let a dog inside the pantry during a blizzard or a tornado, but kitchens are for humans. It was almost cruel: Dogs need to run. Dogs need to herd sheep and chase jackrabbits and retain the few grains of nobility that canines are born with. Only a fool couldn't tell the difference between a man and a beast, and this made Chet a fool; it made him the Dog Lover, which was a deeper insult than that bartender could possibly realize.

Horace wondered how long it had been since he'd set foot inside a tavern. Ten years? Probably ten years. He didn't like them anymore. The bars had changed: These days, all the young men drank beer. When he was in his thirties, men drank OFC whiskey. Nobody knew what the letters "OFC" technically stood for, but they all assumed it meant Only For Cowboys. Norwegians and Polacks were beer drinkers, but no legitimate white man would go into a bar and slurp sixteen fluid ounces of wheat foam. Beer drinkers were embarrassing. Sometimes Horace felt embarrassed for the totality of culture, and for the role he had played in its creation. "That's why all these modern men are soft," he thought to himself as he looked into the brown-black remnants of his sugar-saturated coffee. "They're all beer-gorged and lazy. They have no grit. They're scared of whiskey. They're scared of the world."

It was time for everyone to roll the dice. Horace rolled a pair of fives. It was not enough to win. His luck was never going to change.

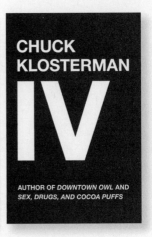
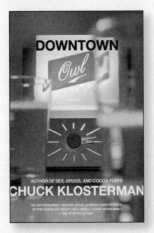